Computer Networks I

AF520173

R. Jaya

Dr.C. Rajan

Dr.K. Geetha

Published by

BONFRING®

Intellectual Integrity

Computer Networks I

9 789386 176585 >

ISBN 978-93-86176-58-5

Author

R. Jaya

Dr.C. Rajan

Dr.K. Geetha

Bonfring

309, 2nd Floor, 5th Street Extension, Gandhipuram,

Coimbatore-641 012.

Tamilnadu, India.

E-mail: info@bonfring.org

Website: www.bonfring.org

Phone: 0422 4213231

Preface

The importance of **Computer Networks I** is well known in various engineering fields. The book uses plain, lucid language to explain fundamental of this subject .This book provides logical method of explaining various complicated concepts and stepwise methods to explain the important topics.

Each chapter is well supported with necessary illustrations, practical examples and solved problems.

All care has been take care to make students comfortable in understanding the basic concepts of the subject.

We wish to express our thanks to all those who helped in making this book a reality.

We wish to thank the publisher and the entire team who have taken immense pain to get this book in time with quality printing.

R. Jaya

Dr.C. Rajan

Dr.K. Geetha

Acknowledgement

SYLLABUS COPY

COMPUTER NETWORKS I

Subject Code: 10CS55	I.A. Marks : 25
Hours/Week : 04	Exam Hours: 03
Total Hours : 52	Exam Marks:100

Part–A

UNIT - 1 **7 Hours**

Introduction: Data Communications, Networks, The Internet, Protocols & Standards, Layered Tasks, The OSI model, Layers in OSI model, TCP/IP Protocol suite, Addressing

UNIT- 2 **7 Hours**

Physical Layer-1: Analog & Digital Signals, Transmission Impairment, Data Rate limits, Performance, Digital-digital conversion (Only Line coding: Polar, Bipolar and Manchester coding), Analog-to-digital conversion (only PCM), Transmission Modes, Digital-to-analog conversion

UNIT- 3 **6 Hours**

Physical Layer-2 and Switching: Multiplexing, Spread Spectrum, Introduction to switching, Circuit Switched Networks, Datagram Networks, Virtual Circuit Networks

UNIT- 4 **6 Hours**

Data Link Layer-1: Error Detection & Correction: Introduction, Block coding, Linear block codes, Cyclic codes, Checksum.

Part-B

UNIT- 5 **6 Hours**

Data Link Layer-2: Framing, Flow and Error Control, Protocols, Noiseless Channels, Noisy channels, HDLC, PPP (Framing, Transition phases only)

UNIT- 6 **7 Hours**

Multiple Access & Ethernet: Random access, Controlled Access, Channelization, Ethernet: IEEE standards, Standard Ethernet, Changes in the standard, Fast Ethernet, Gigabit Ethernet

UNIT - 7 **6 Hours**

Wireless LANs and Cellular Networks: Introduction, IEEE 802.11, Bluetooth, Connecting devices, Cellular Telephony

UNIT - 8 **7 Hours**

Network Layer: Introduction, Logical addressing, IPv4 addresses, IPv6 addresses, Internetworking basics, IPv4, IPv6, Comparison of IPv4 and IPv6 Headers.

Text Books

1. Behrouz A. Forouzan,: Data Communication and Networking, 4th Edition Tata McGraw-Hill, 2006.
   (Chapters 1.1 to 1.4, 2.1 to 2.5, 3.1 To 3.6, 4.1 to 4.3, 5.1, 6.1, 6.2, 8.1 to 8.3, 10.1 to 10.5, 11.1 to 11.7, 12.1 to 12.3, 13.1 to 13.5, 14.1, 14.2,15.1, 16.1, 19.1, 19.2, 20.1 to 20.3)

Reference Books

1. Alberto Leon-Garcia and Indra Widjaja: Communication Networks-Fundamental Concepts and Key architectures, 2nd Edition Tata McGraw-Hill, 2004.
2. William Stallings: Data and Computer Communication, 8th Edition, Pearson Education, 2007.
3. Larry L. Peterson and Bruce S. Davie: Computer Networks–A Systems Approach, 4th Edition, Elsevier, 2007.
4. Nader F. Mir: Computer and Communication Networks, Pearson Education, 2007.

Unit	Contents	Page No

UNIT-1

Introduction: Data Communications, Networks, The Internet, Protocols & Standards, Layered Tasks, The OSI model, Layers in OSI model, TCP/IP Protocol suite, Addressing.

Introduction

1. Data Communications

Data communication is the exchange of data between two devices via some form of transmission medium such as a wire cable.

The effectiveness of a data communications system depends on four fundamental characteristics: delivery, accuracy, timeliness, and jitter.

1) **Delivery**: The system must deliver data to the correct destination. Data must be received by the intended device or user.
2) **Accuracy**: The system must deliver the data accurately. Data that have been altered in transmission and left uncorrected are unusable.
3) **Timeliness**: The system must deliver data in a timely manner. Data delivered late are useless. In the case of video and audio, timely delivery means delivering data in the same order that they are produced, and without significant delay. This kind of delivery is called real-time transmission.
4) **Jitter:** Jitter refers to the variation in the packet arrival time. Jitter is introduced in real-time data by the delay between packets. It is the uneven delay in the delivery of audio or video packets.

Example

Let us assume that video packets are sent every 30 ms.

If some of the packets arrive with 30-ms delay and others with 40-ms delay, an uneven quality in the video is the result.

Example

The video is digitized and packetized. There are only three packets, and each packet holds l0s of video information.

The first packet starts at 00:00:00, the second packet starts at 00:00: 10, and the third packet starts at 00:00:20.

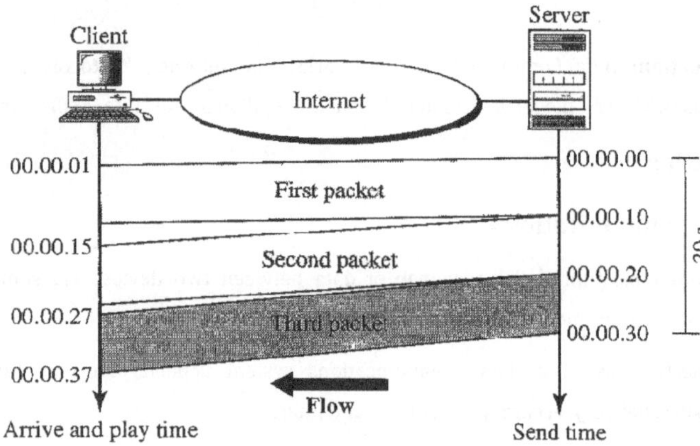

Assume that the first packet arrives at 00:00:01 (l-s delay), the second arrives at 00:00:15 (5-s delay), and the third arrives at 00:00:27 (7-s delay). If the receiver starts playing the first packet at 00:00:01, it will finish at 00:00: 11. However, the next packet has not yet arrived; it arrives 4 s later. There is a gap between the first and second packets and between the second and the third as the video is viewed at the remote site. This phenomenon is called **jitter**.

1.1. Components of Data Communication

A data communications system has five components

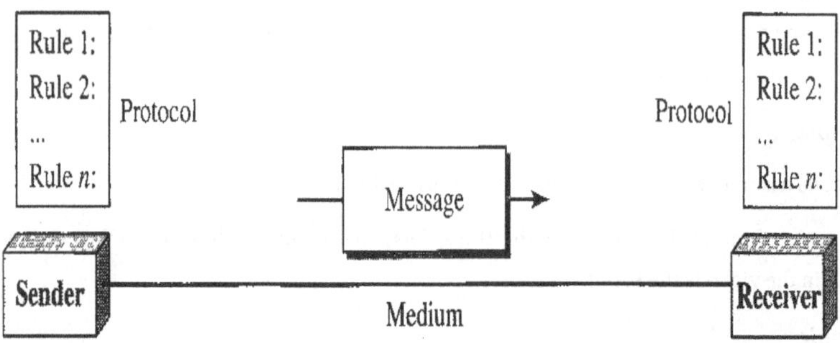

1) **Message**: The message is the information (data) to be communicated. EX: text, numbers, pictures, audio, and video.
2) **Sender**: The sender is the device that sends the data message. It can be a computer, workstation, telephone handset, video camera, and so on.

3) **Receiver**: The receiver is the device that receives the message. It can be a computer, workstation, telephone handset, television, and so on.
4) **Transmission Medium**: The transmission medium is the physical path by which a message travels from sender to receiver. Examples of transmission media include twisted-pair wire, coaxial cable, fibre-optic cable, and radio waves.
5) **Protocol**: A protocol is a set of rules that govern data communications. It represents an agreement between the communicating devices. Without a protocol, two devices may be connected but not communicating. EX: Internet Protocol(IP),Transmission control Protocol(TCP).

1.2. Data Representation

Information today comes in different forms such as text, numbers, images, audio, and video.

Text

1) In data communications, text is represented as a bit pattern, a sequence of bits (0s or 1s). Different sets of bit patterns have been designed to represent text symbols.
2) Each set is called a code, and the process of representing symbols is called coding.
3) Today, the prevalent coding system is called Unicode, which uses 32 bits to represent a symbol or character used in any language in the world.

Numbers

1) Numbers are also represented by bit patterns. However, a code such as ASCII is not used to represent numbers.
2) The number is directly converted to a binary number to simplify mathematical operations.

Images

1) Images are also represented by bit patterns. In its simplest form, an image is composed of a matrix of pixels (picture elements), where each pixel is a small dot. The size of the pixel depends on the resolution.
2) For example, an image can be divided into 1000 pixels or 10,000 pixels. In the second case, there is a better representation of the image (better resolution), but more memory is needed to store the image.
3) After an image is divided into pixels, each pixel is assigned a bit pattern. The size and the value of the pattern depend on the image. For an image made of only black- and-white dots (e.g., a chessboard), a 1-bit pattern is enough to represent a pixel. There are

several methods to represent color images. One method is called RGB, so called because each color is made of a combination of three primary colors: red, green, and blue.

Audio

1) Audio refers to the recording or broadcasting of sound or music. Audio is by nature different from text, numbers, or images.
2) It is continuous, not discrete. Even when we use a microphone to change voice or music to an electric signal, we create a continuous signal.

Video

1) Video refers to the recording or broadcasting of a picture or movie.
2) Video can either be produced as a continuous entity (e.g., by a TV camera), or it can be a combination of images, each a discrete entity, arranged to convey the idea of motion.

1.3. Data Flow

Communication between two devices can be simplex, half-duplex, or full-duplex **based on the direction of data flow**.

Simplex

1) In simplex mode, the communication is unidirectional, as on a one-way street. Only one of the two devices on a link can transmit; the other can only receive.
2) The simplex mode can use the entire capacity of the channel to send data in one direction.

Example

Keyboards and traditional monitors are examples of simplex devices. The keyboard can only introduce input; the monitor can only accept output.

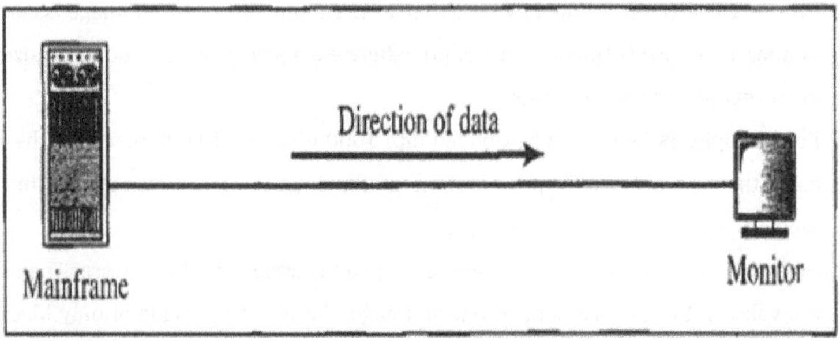

a. Simplex

Half-Duplex

1) In half-duplex mode, each station can both transmit and receive, but not at the same time. When one device is sending, the other can only receive, and vice versa.
2) In a half-duplex transmission, the entire capacity of a channel is taken over by whichever of the two devices is transmitting at the time.
3) The half-duplex mode is used in cases where there is no need for communication in both directions at the same time; the entire capacity of the channel can be utilized for each direction.

Example

Walkie-talkies and CB (citizens band) radios.

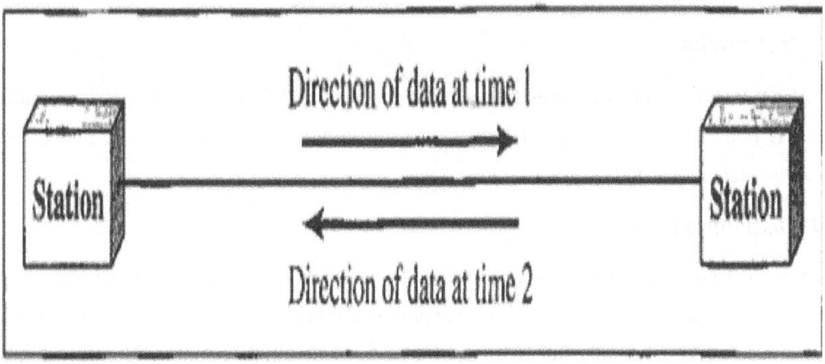

b. Half-duplex

Full-Duplex

1) In full-duplex mode (also, called duplex), both stations can transmit and receive simultaneously.
2) In full-duplex mode, signals going in one direction share the capacity of the link with signals going in the other direction.
3) This sharing can occur in two ways: Either the link must contain two physically separate transmission paths, one for sending and the other for receiving; or the capacity of the channel is divided between signals travelling in both directions.
4) The full-duplex mode is used when communication in both directions is required all the time.

Example

Telephone network.

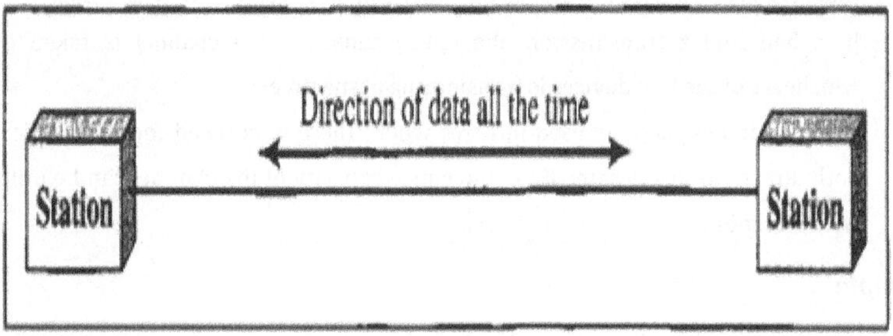

c. Full-duplex

2. Networks

A network is a set of devices (often referred to as nodes) connected by communication links. A node can be a computer, printer, or any other device capable of sending and/or receiving data generated by other nodes on the network.

2.1. Distributed Processing

Most networks use distributed processing, in which a task is divided among multiple computers. Instead of one single large machine being responsible for all aspects of process, separate computers (usually a personal computer or workstation) handle a subset.

2.2. Network Criteria

A network must be able to meet a certain number of criteria. The most important of these are performance, reliability, and security.

Performance

Performance can be measured in many ways, including transit time and response time.

Transit time is the amount of time required for a message to travel from one device to another. Response time is the elapsed time between an inquiry and a response.

The performance of a network depends on a number of factors, including the number of users, the type of transmission medium, the capabilities of the connected hardware, and the efficiency of the software. Performance is often evaluated by two networking metrics: throughput and delay. We often need **more throughputs and less delay.**

Reliability

Network reliability is measured by the accuracy of delivery, frequency of failure, the time it takes a link to recover from a failure, and the network's robustness in a catastrophe.

Security

Network security issues include protecting data from unauthorized access, protecting data from damage and development, and implementing policies and procedures for recovery from breaches and data losses.

2.3. Physical Structures

2.3.1. Type of Connection

A network is two or more devices connected through links. A link is a communications pathway that transfers data from one device to another.

For communication to occur, two devices must be connected in some way to the same link at the same time. There are two possible types of connections: point-to-point and multipoint.

Point-to-Point

1) A point-to-point connection provides a dedicated link between two devices.
2) The entire capacity of the link is reserved for transmission between those two devices.

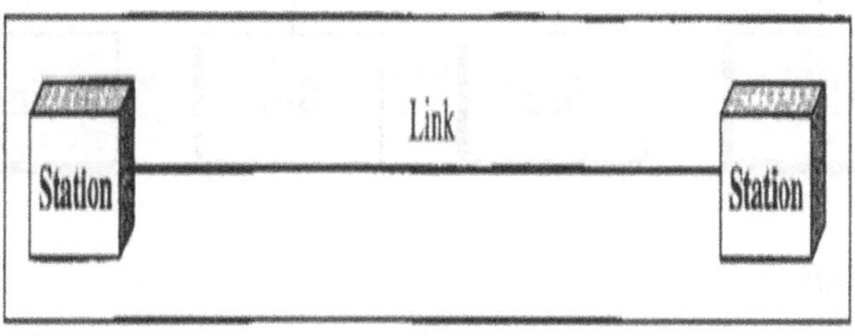

a. Point-to-point

Multipoint

1) A multipoint (also called multidrop) connection is one in which more than two specific devices share a single link.
2) In a multipoint environment, the capacity of the channel is shared, either spatially or temporally.

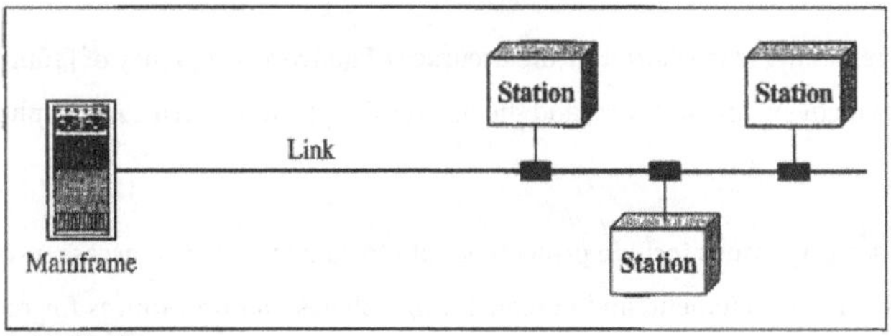

b. Multipoint

2.3.2. Physical Topology

The term physical topology refers to the way in which a network is laid out physically. The topology of a network is the geometric representation of the relationship of all the links and linking devices (usually called nodes) to one another.

There are four basic topologies possible: mesh, star, bus, and ring.

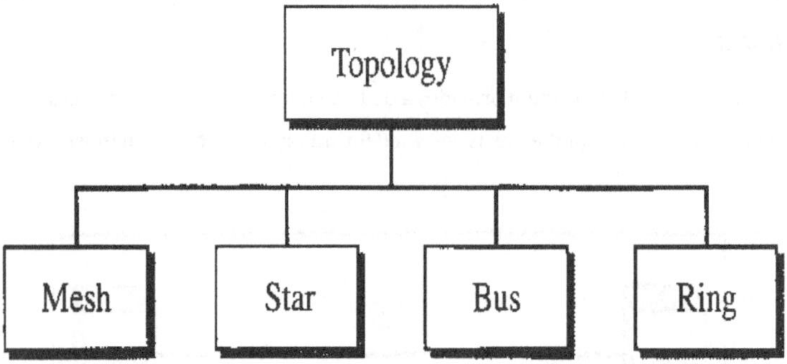

Mesh Topology

In a mesh topology, every device has a dedicated point-to-point link to every other device. The term dedicated means that the link carries traffic only between the two devices it connects.

A fully connected mesh can have **n(n-1)/2** physical channels to link **n devices**. It must have (n-1) I/O ports.

Example of a mesh topology is the connection of telephone regional offices in which each regional office needs to be connected to every other regional office.

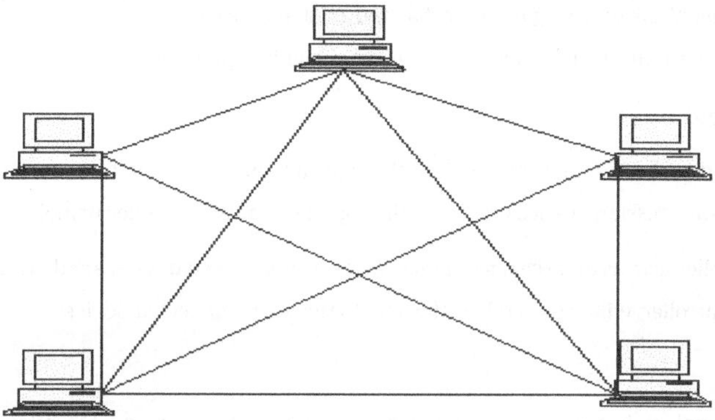

Mesh Topology

Example

A mesh network has 8 devices. Calculate total number of cable links and IO ports needed.

Solution

Number of devices = 8

Number of links = n (n-1)/2

= 8(8-1)/2

= 28

Number of port/device = n-1

= 8-1 = 7

Advantages

1) They use dedicated links so each link can only carry its own data load. So traffic problem can be avoided.
2) It is robust. If anyone link get damaged it cannot affect others.
3) It gives privacy and security to the messages.
4) Fault identification and fault isolation are easy.

Disadvantages

1) The amount of cabling and the number of IO ports required are very large. Since every device is connected to each other devices through dedicated links.
2) The amount of cabling and the number IO ports required are very large. Since every device is connected to each other devices through dedicated links.

3) The sheer bulk of wiring is larger than the available space.
4) Hardware required to connect each device is highly expensive.

Star Topology

Here each device has a dedicated link to the central hub. There is no direct traffic between devices. The transmission are occurred only through the central controller namely hub.

The controller acts as an exchange: If one device wants to send data to another, it sends the data to the controller, which then relays the data to the other connected device.

Example

The star topology is used in local-area networks (LANs). High-speed LANs often use a star topology with a central hub.

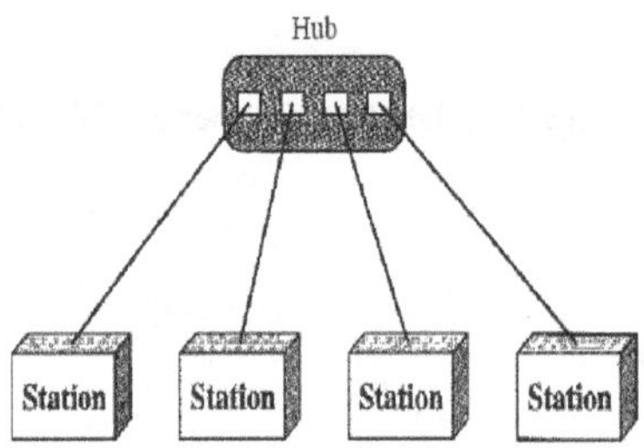

Star Topology

Advantages

1) Less expensive than mesh since each device is connected only to the hub.
2) Installation and configuration are easy.
3) Less cabling is need than mesh.
4) Robustness- If one link fails, only that link is affected. All other links remain active.
5) Easy to fault identification & isolation.
6) Additions, moves, and deletions involve only one connection: between that device and the hub.

Disadvantages

1) Dependency of the whole topology on one single point, the hub. If the hub goes down, the whole system is dead.
2) Even it requires less cabling than mesh when compared with other topologies it still large.

Tree Topology

Tree topology is a variation of star. Instead of all devices connected to a central hub here most of the devices are connected to a secondary hub that in turn connected with central hub.

The central hub is an active hub. An active hub contains a repeater, which regenerate the received bit pattern before sending.

The secondary hub may be active or passive. A passive hub means it just precedes a physical connection only.

Advantages

1) Can connect more than star.
2) The distance can be increased.
3) Can isolate and prioritize communication between different computers.

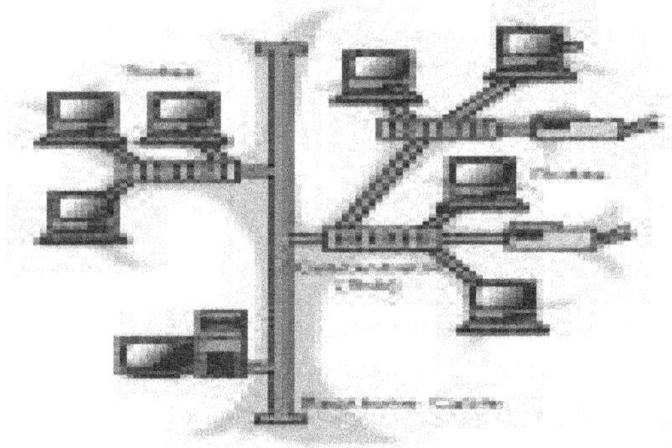

Tree Topology

Bus topology

1) A bus topology is multipoint. Here one long cable act as a backbone to link all the devices are connected to the backbone by drop lines and taps.
2) A drop line is a connection running between the device and the main cable. A tap is a connector that either splices into the main cable or punctures the sheathing of a cable to create a contact with the metallic core.
3) As a signal travels along the backbone, some of its energy is transformed into heat. Therefore, it becomes weaker and weaker as it travels farther and farther. For this reason there is a limit on the number of taps a bus can support and on the distance between those taps.

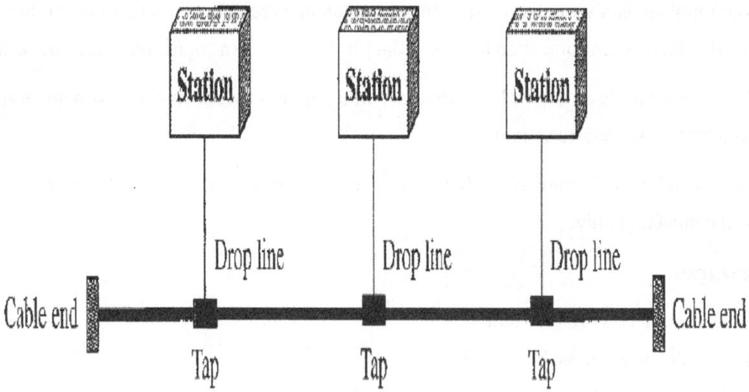

Bus Topology

Advantages

1) Ease of installation.
2) Less cabling.

Disadvantages

1) Difficult reconfiguration and fault isolation.
2) The bus is usually designed to be optimally efficient at installation. So difficult to add new devices.
3) Signal reflection at tap can cause degradation in quality which leads to limitation in no. of devices connected and the length of cables.
4) If any fault in backbone can stop all transmission because the damaged area reflects the signal in both the directions.

Ring Topology

In ring topology each device has a dedicated connection with two devices on either side of it.

The signal is passed in one direction from device to device until it reaches the destination and each device have repeater.

When a device receives a signal intended for another device, its repeater regenerates the bits and passes them along.

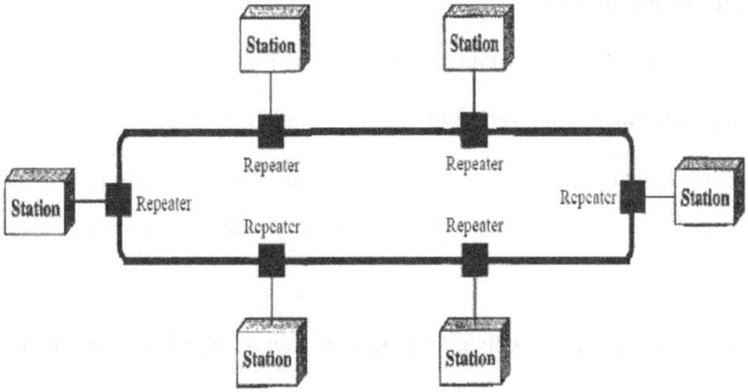

Ring Topology

Advantages

1) Easy to install and reconfigure.-To add or delete a device requires changing only two connections.
2) Fault identification is easy-in a ring, a signal is circulating at all times. If one device does not receive a signal within a specified period, it can issue an alarm. The alarm alerts the network operator to the problem and its location.

Disadvantages

1) Unidirectional traffic.
2) Break in a single ring can break entire network.

Hybrid Topology

A network can be hybrid. For example, we can have a main star topology with each branch connecting several stations in a bus topology as shown in Figure.

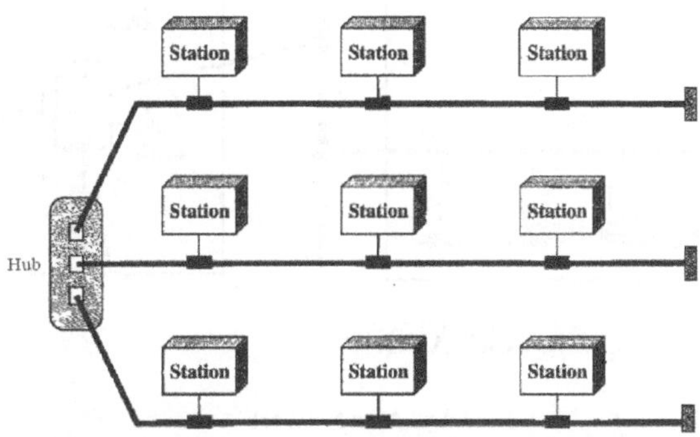

2.4. Categories of Networks

Two primary categories: local-area networks and wide-area networks.

The category into which a network falls is determined by its size.

A LAN normally covers an area less than 2m; a WAN can be worldwide. Networks of a size in between are normally referred to as metropolitan area networks and span tens of miles.

Local Area Network

A local area network (LAN) is usually privately owned and links the devices in a single office, building, or campus.

Depending on the needs of an organization and the type of technology used, a LAN can be as simple as two PCs and a printer in someone's home office; or it can extend throughout a company and include audio and video peripherals. Currently, LAN size is limited to a few kilometers.

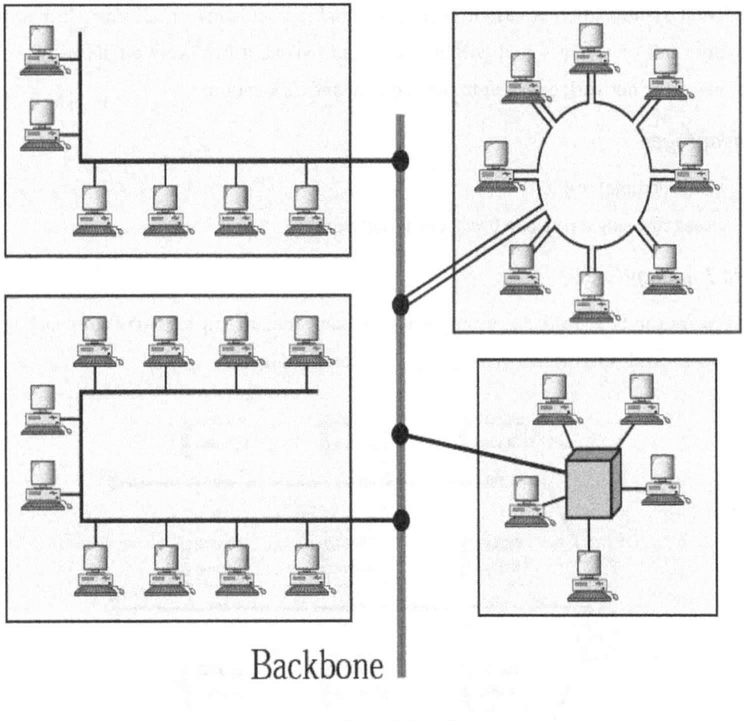

Local Area Network

1) LANs are designed to allow resources to be shared between personal computers or workstations.

2) LANs are designed to:

    a) Operate within a limited geographic area.

    b) Allow multi-access to high-bandwidth media.

    c) Control the network privately under local administration.

    d) Provide full-time connectivity to local services.

    e) Connect physically adjacent devices.

3) A common example of a LAN, found in many business environments, links a workgroup of task-related computers, for example, engineering workstations or accounting PCs.

4) One of the computers may be given a large capacity disk drive and may become a server to clients. Software can be stored on this central server and used as needed by the whole group. In this example, the size of the LAN may be determined by licensing restrictions on the number of users per copy of software, or by restrictions on the number of users licensed to access the operating system.

5) In addition to size, LANs are distinguished from other types of networks by their transmission media and topology.

6) The most common LAN topologies are bus, ring, and star.

7) Early LANs had data rates in the 4 to 16 megabits per second (Mbps) range. Today, however, speeds are normally 100 or 1000 Mbps.

Wide Area Network

1) A wide area network (WAN) provides long-distance transmission of data, image, audio, and video information over large geographic areas that may comprise a country, a continent, or even the whole world.

2) A WAN can be as complex as the backbones that connect the Internet or as simple as a dial-up line that connects a home computer to the Internet.

3) Two types os WAN: switched WAN and a point-to-point WAN.

4) The switched WAN connects the end systems, which usually comprise a router (internetworking connecting device) that connects to another LAN or WAN.

5) Example of a switched WAN is X.25, Asynchronous Transfer Mode(ATM) network.

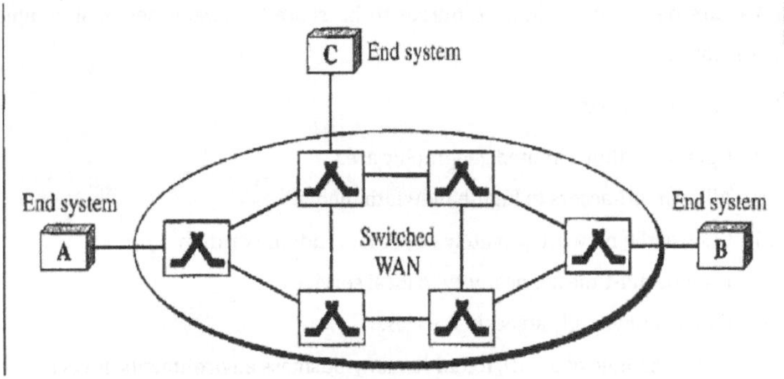

Switched WAN

6) The point-to-point WAN is normally a line leased from a telephone or cable TV provider that connects a home computer or a small LAN to an Internet service provider (ISP). This type of WAN is often used to provide Internet access. An early example of a switched WAN is X.25

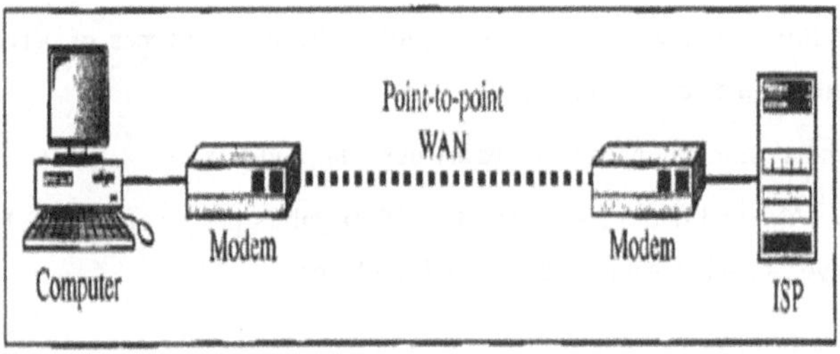

Point-to-Point WAN

Metropolitan Area Networks

A metropolitan area network (MAN) is a network with a size between a LAN and a WAN. It normally covers the area inside a town or a city.

It is designed for customers who need a high-speed connectivity, normally to the Internet, and have endpoints spread over a city or part of city.

A good example of a MAN is the part of the telephone company network that can provide a high-speed DSL line to the customer.

Another example is the cable TV network that originally was designed for cable TV, but today can also be used for high-speed data connection to the Internet.

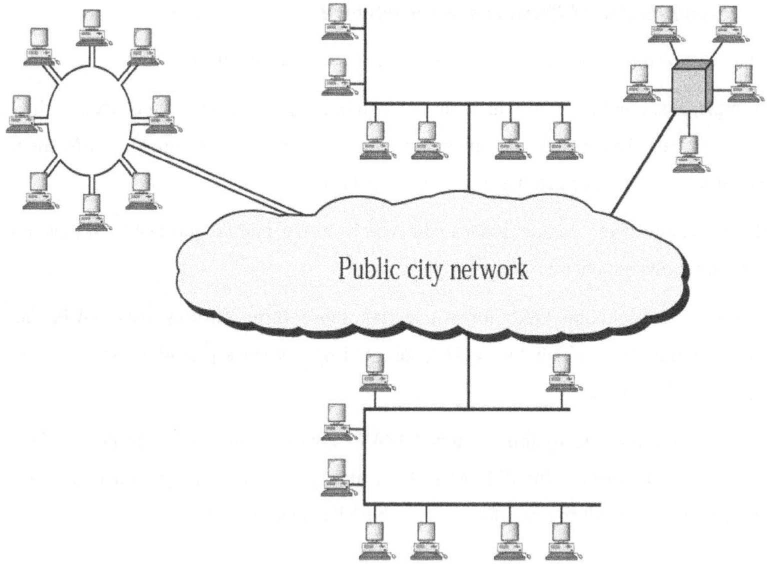

Compare and contrast LAN, WAN, MAN **(June/July 2013, Dec 2010)**

Local Area Network(LAN)	**Wide Area Network (WAN)**	**Metropolitan Area Network (MAN)**
All the devices that are part of LAN are within a building or multiple building.	WAN (Wide Area Network) is a group of computers and other network devices which are connected together which is not restricted to a geographical location.	MAN ((Metropolitan Area Network) is a larger network of computers and other network devices which are connected together usually spans several buildings or large geographical area.
LAN network has very high speed mainly due to proximity of computer and network devices.	WAN speed varies based on geographical location of the servers. WAN connects several LANs	MAN network has lower speed compared to LAN.
LAN connection speeds can be 10Mbps or 100Mbps or 1000Mpbs also.	WAN connection speeds can be 10Mbps or 100Mbps.	MAN connection speeds can be 10Mbps or 100Mbps
LAN uses Guided Media	WAN mainly uses Guided Media or Unguided media. Its long distance communications, which may or may not be provided by public packet network.	MAN uses Guided Media or Unguided media.
Ex: A common example of a LAN links a workgroup of task-related computers	Ex: Internet is WAN	Ex: Example of a MAN is the part of the telephone company network that can provide a high-speed DSL line to the customer.

2.5. Interconnection of Networks: Internetwork

When two or more networks are connected, they become an internetwork, or internet.

Example, assume that an organization has two offices, one on the east coast and the other on the west coast. The established office on the west coast has a bus topology LAN; the newly opened office on the east coast has a star topology LAN.

The president of the company lives somewhere in the middle and needs to have control over the company from her home.

To create a backbone WAN for connecting these three entities (two LANs and the president's computer), a switched WAN (operated by a service provider such as a telecom company) has been leased.

To connect the LANs to this switched WAN, however, three point-to-point WANs are required. These point-to-point WANs can be a high-speed DSL line offered by a telephone company or a cable modern line offered by a cable TV provider.

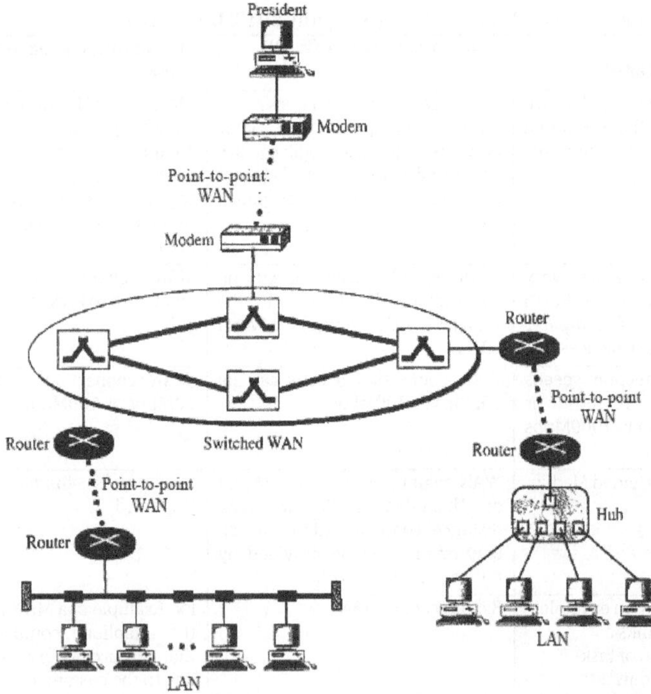

3. The Internet

An internet is two or more networks that can communicate with each other.

The Internet is a communication system that has brought a wealth of information to our fingertips and organized it for our use.

A brief History

Time Line

The following is a list of important Internet events in chronological order:

1969. Four-node ARPANET established.

1970. ARPA hosts implement NCP.

1973. Development of TCP/IP suite begins.

1977. An internet tested using TCP/IP.

1978. UNIX distributed to academic sites.

1981. CSNET established.

1983. TCP/IP becomes the official protocol

1983. MILNET was born.

1986. NSFNET established.

1990. ARPANET replaced by NSFNET.

1995. NSFNET became a research network.

1995. ISPs started.

The Internet Today

The Internet today is made up of many wide- and local-area networks joined by connecting devices and switching stations. The structure of internet is continually changing-new networks are being added, existing networks are adding addresses, and networks of defunct companies are being removed.

Today most end users who want Internet connection use the services of Internet service providers (ISPs). There are international service providers, national service providers, regional service providers, and local service providers.

Figure shows a conceptual(not geographic) view of the Internet.

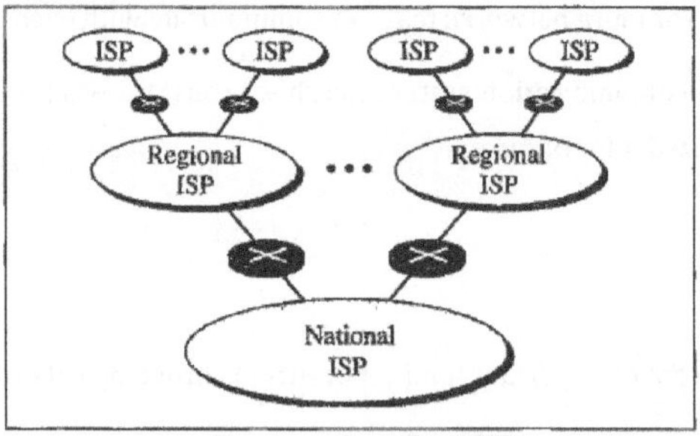

a. Structure of a national ISP

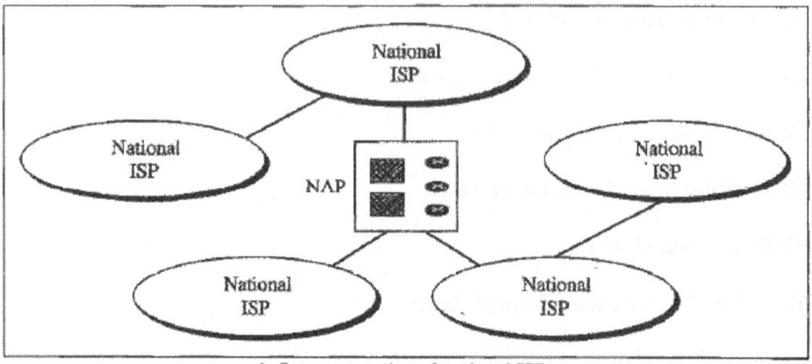

b. Interconnection of national ISPs

Hierarchical Organization of Internet

International Internet Service Providers

At the top of the hierarchy are the international service providers that connect nations together.

National Internet Service Providers

The national Internet service providers are backbone networks created and maintained by specialized companies. To provide connectivity between the end users, these backbone networks are connected by complex switching stations (normally run by a third party) called network access points (NAPs)

Regional Internet Service Providers

Regional internet service providers or regional ISPs are smaller ISPs that are connected to one or more national ISPs. They are at the third level of the hierarchy with a smaller data rate.

Local Internet Service Providers

Local Internet service providers provide direct service to the end users. The local ISPs can be connected to regional ISPs or directly to national ISPs. Most end users are connected to the local ISPs. A local ISP can be a company that just provides Internet services, a corporation with a network that supplies services to its own employees, or a nonprofit organization, such as a college or a university, which runs its own network.

4. Protocols and Standards

Protocols

A protocol is a set of rules that govern data communication. A protocol defines what is communicated how it is communicated, and when it is communicated. The key elements of a protocol are syntax, semantics and timing.

Syntax

Syntax refers to the structure or format of the data, means to the order how it is presented.

Example

A simple protocol might expect the first 8 bits of data to be the address of the sender, the second 8 bits to be the address of the receiver, and the rest of the stream to be the message itself.

Semantics

Semantics refers to the meaning of each section of bits. How is a particular pattern to be interpreted, and when action is to be taken based on the interpretation.

Example

Does an address identify the route to be taken or the final destination of the message?

Timing

Timing refers to two characteristics. They are,

1) When data should be sent
2) When data to be received.

Example

If a sender produces data at 100 Mbps but the receiver can process data at only 1 Mbps, the transmission will overload the receiver and some data will be lost.

Standards

A standard provides a model for development of a product, which is going to develop. Standards are essential to create and maintain a product. Data communication products are fall into two categories. They are:

1) De facto
2) De jure

1) De Facto

Standards that have not been approved by an organized body but have been adopted as standards through widespread use are de facto standards.

De facto standards are often established originally by manufacturers who seek to define the functionality of a new product or technology. They are further classified into:

A. Proprietary
B. Non proprietary

A. Proprietary

They are originally invented by a commercial organization as a basis for the operation of its product. They are wholly owned by the company, which invented them. They are closed standards.

B. Non-Proprietary

Groups or committees that have passed them into public domain develop them. They are open standards.

2) De Jure

They have been legislated by an officially recognized body.

Standards organization

Standards are developed by:

1) Standards creation committee
2) Forums
3) Regularity agencies

1) Standards Creation Committees

1) International Standards Organization (ISO).
2) International Telecommunications Union–Telecommunications Standards Section (ITU-T formally CCITT).

3) The American National Standards Institute (ANSI).
4) The Institute of Electrical and Electronics Engineers (IEEE).
5) The Electronic Industries Association (EIA).
6) Telcordia.

2) Forums

1) Frame Relay Forum.
2) ATM Forum & ATM consortium.
3) Internet Society (ISOC) & Internet Engineering Task Force (IETF).

3) Regularity Agencies

1) Federal Communication commission

Internet Standards

An **Internet standard** is a thoroughly tested specification that is useful to and adhered to by those who work with the Internet.

A specification begins as an Internet draft. An **Internet draft** is a working document (a work in progress) with no official status and a 6-month lifetime.

Upon recommendation from the Internet authorities, a draft may be published as a **Request for Comment** (RFC). Each RFC is edited, assigned a number, and made available to all interested parties.

5. Network Models

A computer network must provide general, cost effective, fair and robust communication among a large number of computers. It must evolve to accommodate changes in the underlying technologies.

To help to deal this network designers have developed general blueprints called network architecture on models that guide the design and implementation of networks.

6. The OSI (Open Systems Interconnection) Model

The OSI model is a layered framework for the design of network systems that allows communication between all types of computer systems regardless of their underlying architecture.

The OSI model is not a protocol; it is a model for understanding and designing a network architecture that is flexible, robust, and interoperable.

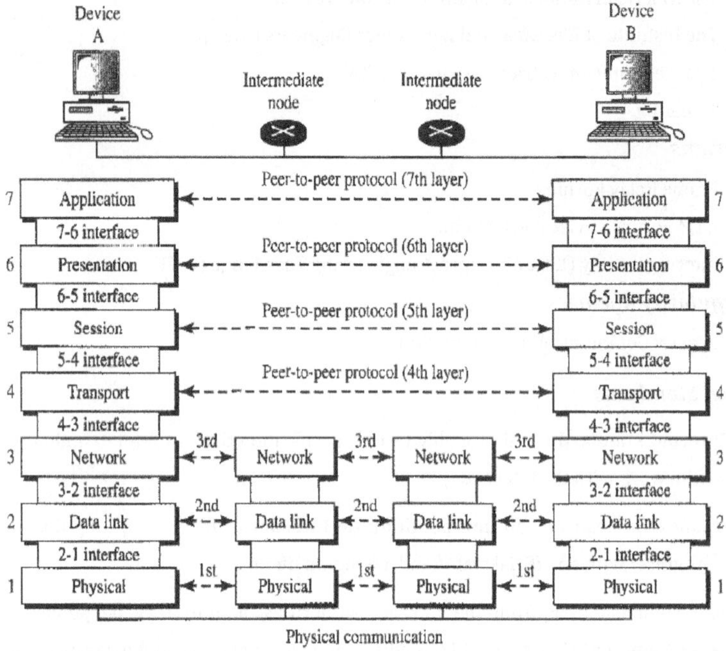

Seven Layers of OSI Model & Interaction between OSI Layers

6.1. Layered Architecture

The OSI model is composed of seven ordered layers:

1) Physical (layer 1).
2) Data link (layer 2).
3) Network (layer 3).
4) Transport (layer 4).
5) Session (layer 5).
6) Presentation (layer 6).
7) Application (layer 7).

Above Figure shows the layers involved when a message is sent from device A to device B. As the message travels from A to B, it may pass through many intermediate nodes. These intermediate nodes usually involve only the first three layers of the OSI model.

In developing the model, the designers distilled the process of transmitting data to its most fundamental elements. The networking functions that had related uses were identified and collected those functions into discrete groups that became the **layers**. Each **layer** defines a family of functions distinct from those of the other layers.

Within a single machine, each layer calls upon the services of the layer just below it. Layer 3, for example, uses the services provided by layer 2 and provides services for layer 4.

Between machines, layer *x* on one machine communicates with layer *x* on another machine. The processes on each machine that communicate at a given layer are called **peer-to-peer processes**. Communication between machines is therefore a peer-to-peer process using the protocols appropriate to a given layer.

6.2. Interaction Between OSI Layers

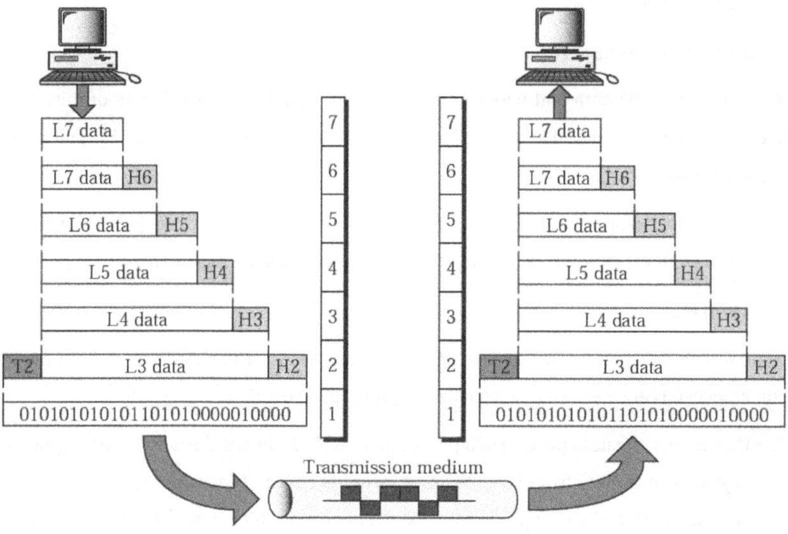

The above figure gives an overall view of the OSI layers, D7 means the data unit at layer 7, D6 means the data unit at layer 6, and so on. The process starts at layer 7 (the application layer), then moves from layer to layer in descending, sequential order.

Each layer in the sending device adds its own information called **header and trailer** (trailer added only at the Data Link Layer) to the message it receives from the layer just above it and passes the whole package to the layer just below it.

When the formatted data unit passes through the physical layer (layer 1), it is changed into an electromagnetic signal and transported along a physical link.

At the receiving machine, the message is unwrapped layer by layer, with each process receiving and removing the header at the corresponding layers.

Peer-to-Peer Processes

At the higher layers, communication must move down through the layers on device A, over to device B, and then back up through the layers. At the physical layer, communication is direct.

At layer 1 the entire package is converted to a form that can be transmitted to the receiving device. At the receiving machine, the message is unwrapped layer by layer, with each process receiving and removing the data meant for it. For example, layer 2 removes the data meant for it, and then passes the rest to layer 3. Layer 3 then removes the data meant for it and passes the rest to layer 4, and so on.

Interfaces between Layers

The passing of the data and network information down through the layers of the sending device and back up through the layers of the receiving device is made possible by an **interface** between each pair of adjacent layers.

Each interface defines the information and services a layer must provide for the layer above it. Well-defined interfaces and layer functions provide modularity to a network.

Encapsulation

A packet (header and data) at level 7 is encapsulated in a packet at level 6. The whole packet at level 6 is encapsulated in a packet at level 5, and so on.

In other words, the data portion of a packet at level N - 1 carries the whole packet (data and header and maybe trailer) from level N. The concept is called *encapsulation;* level N - 1 is not aware of which part of the encapsulated packet is data and which part is the header or trailer and treats the packet as a single integral unit.

6.3. Organization of the Layers

The seven layers can be thought of as belonging to three subgroups. Layers I, 2, and 3-physical, data link, and network-are the network support layers; they deal with the physical aspects of moving data from one device to another.

Layers 5, 6, and 7-session, presentation, and application-can be thought of as the user support layers.

Layer 4, the transport layer, links the two subgroups and ensures that what the lower layers have transmitted is in a form that the upper layers can use.

6.4. Functions of the Layers

6.4.1. Physical Layer

The physical layer coordinates the functions required to transmit a bit stream over a physical medium.

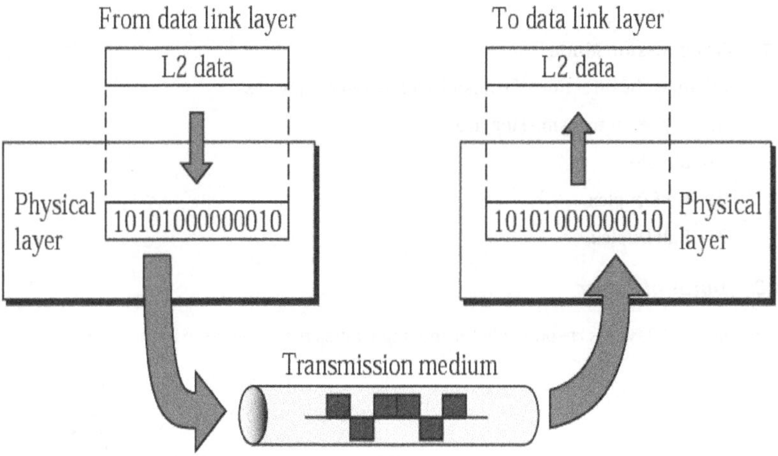

The functions are,

1) **Physical Characteristics of Interfaces and Media:**
   a) Physical Layer defines the electrical and mechanical characteristics of the interface and the media.
   b) It defines the types of transmission medium.
2) **Representation of Bits**

   To transmit the stream of bits they must be encoded into signal. It defines the type of encoding weather **electrical or optical**.
3) **Data Rate**

   It defines the transmission rate i.e. the number of bits sent per second.
4) **Synchronization of Bits**

   The sender and receiver must be synchronized at bit level.
5) **Line Configuration**

   It defines the type of connection between the devices. Two types of connection are:
   1) Point to point.
   2) Multipoint.

6) **Physical Topology**

It defines how devices are connected to make a network. Topologies are,

1) Mesh.
2) Star.
3) Bus.
4) Ring.

7) **Transmission Mode**

It defines the direction of transmission between devices.

Three types of transmission are:

1) Simplex.
2) Half Duplex.
3) Full Duplex.

6.4.2. Datalink Layer

The data link layer is responsible for moving frames from one node to the next.

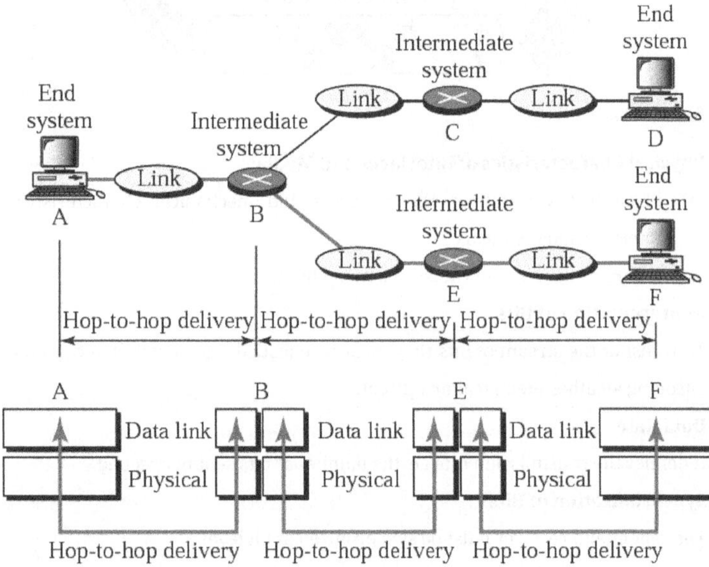

The responsibilities of Data link layer are:

1) **Framing:** It divides the stream of bits received from network layer into manageable data units called frames.

2) **Physical Addressing** It adds a header that defines the physical address of the sender and the receiver.

   If the sender and the receiver are in different networks, then the receiver address is the address of the device which connects the two networks.

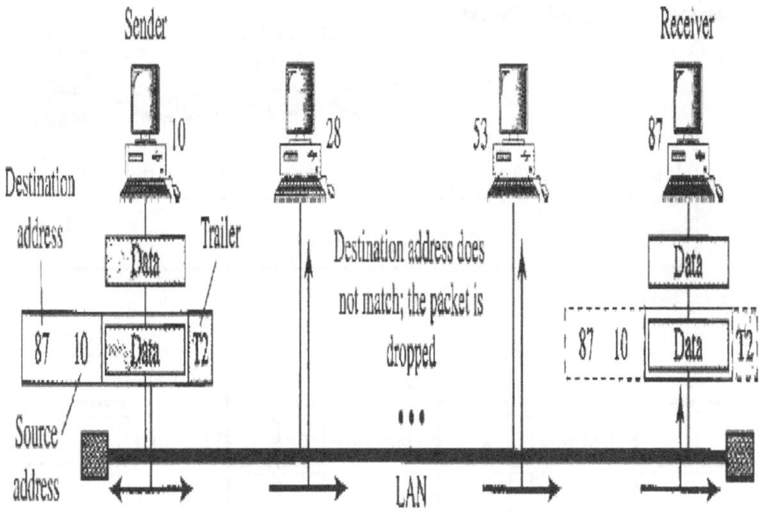

Physical Addressing

3) **Flow Control** If the rate at which the data are absorbed by the receiver is less than the rate at which data are produced in the sender, the data link layer imposes a flow control mechanism to avoid overwhelming the receiver.
4) **Error Control** To improve the reliability, the Data link layer adds a trailer which contains the error control mechanism like CRC, Checksum etc.
5) **Access Control** When two or more devices connected at the same link, then the Data link layer uses access control techniques to determine which device has control over the link at any given time.

6.4.3. Network Layer

When the sender is in one network and the receiver is in some other network then the network layer has the responsibility for the source to destination delivery (end to end delivery).

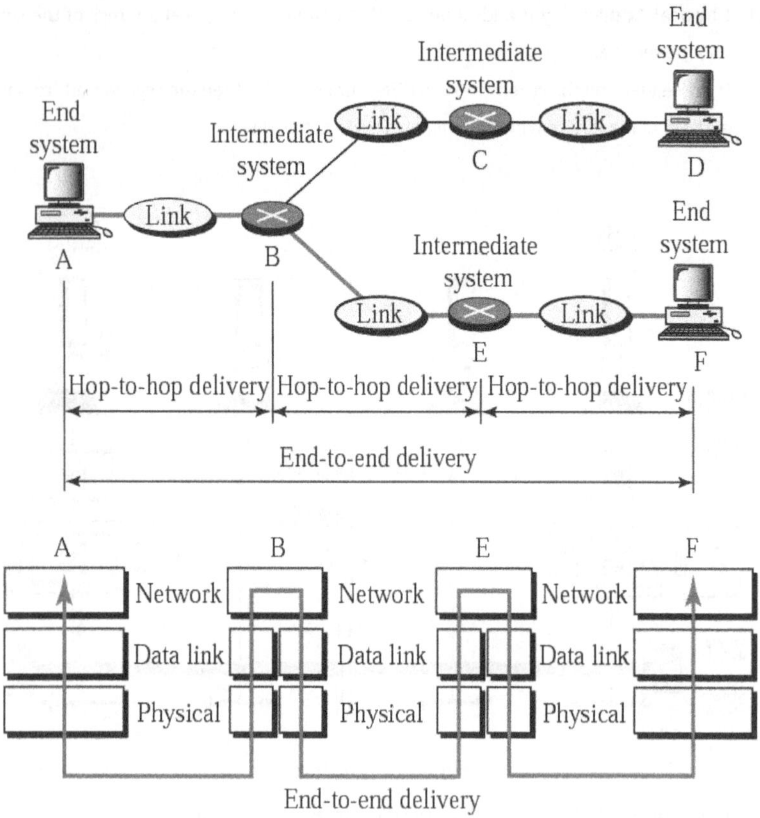

Source to Destination Delivery

The responsibilities are,

1) **Logical Addressing** when the sender and receiver are in different networks then the network layer adds a header that defines the logical address **(IP Address)** of the devices.
2) **Routing** When more than one networks connected to form an internetwork, the inter connecting devices (EX: router and switches) route the packet to its final destination based on the IP address.

6.4.4. Transport Layer

The transport layer is responsible for the delivery of a message from one process to another.

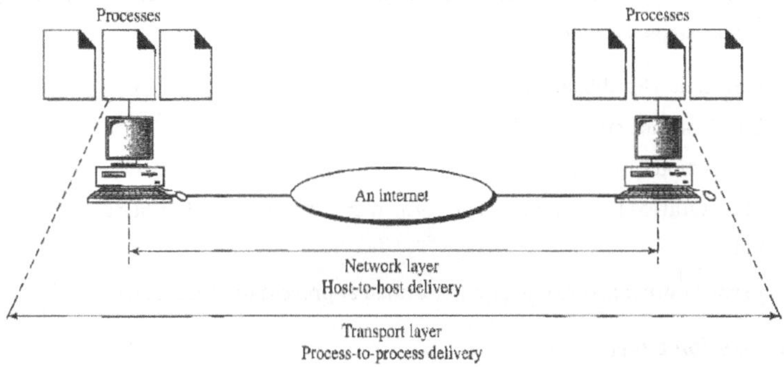

The responsibilities are,

1) **Service point Addressing** A single computer can often run several programs at the same time. The transport layer gets the entire message to the correct process on that computer.

   It adds a header that defines the **port address (Service Point addressing)** which used to identify the exact process on the receiver.

2) **Segmentation and Reassembly** A message is divided into manageable units called as segments. Each segment is given a **sequence number.** Each segment is reassembled after received that information at the receiver end based on their sequence numbers

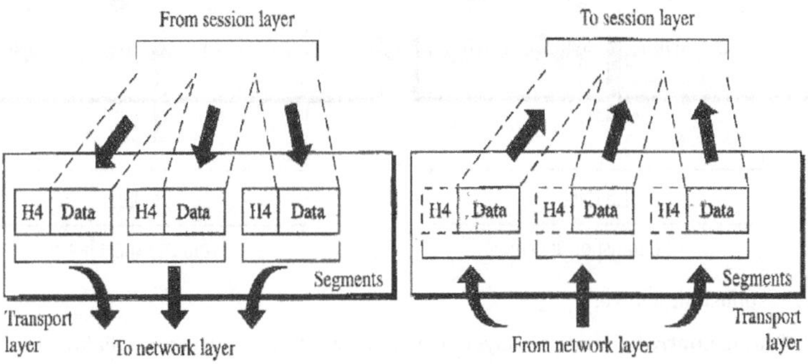

3) **Connection Control** The transport layer can be either connectionless or connection oriented.

   A connectionless transport layer treats each segment as an independent packet and delivers it to the transport layer at the destination machine.

A connection oriented transport layer creates a connection between the two end ports. It involves three steps. They are:

1) Connection Establishment.
2) Data Transmission.
3) Connection Discard.
4) **Flow Control** Flow control is performed at end to end level rather than across a single link.
5) **Error Control** Error control is performed at process to process level.

6.4.5. Session Layer

It acts as a dialog controller. It establishes, maintains and synchronizes the interaction between the communication devices.

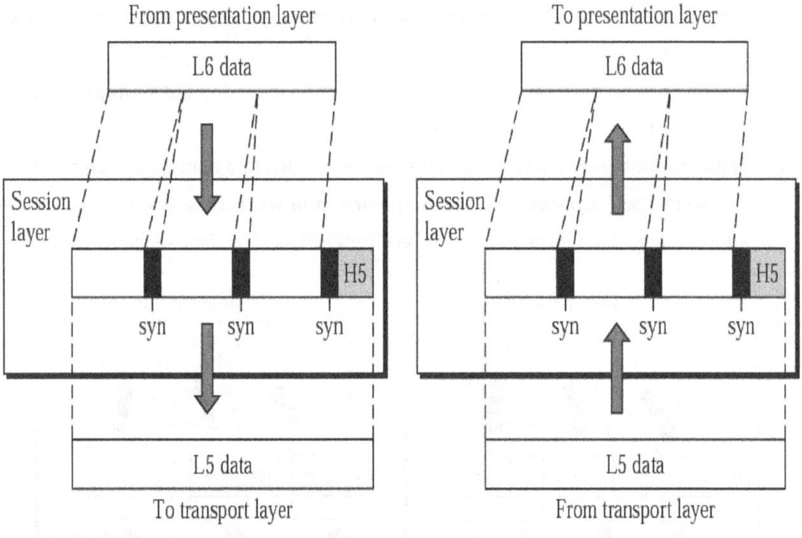

The responsibilities are:

1) **Dialog Control** The session layer allows two systems to enter into a dialog.
2) **Synchronization** This layer adds synchronization points into a stream of bits. For example, if a system is sending a file of 2000 pages, it is advisable to insert checkpoints after every 100 pages to ensure that each 100-page unit is received and acknowledged independently. In this case, if a crash happens during the transmission of page 523, the only pages that need to be resent after system recovery are pages 501 to 523.

6.4.6. *Presentation Layer*

The presentation layer is responsible for the semantics and the syntax of the information exchanged. The responsibilities are:

1) Translation

1) Different systems use different encoding systems.
2) The presentation layer is responsible for interoperability between different systems.
3) The presentation layer at the sender side translates the information from the sender dependent format to a common format. Likewise, at the receiver side presentation layer translate the information from common format to receiver dependent format.

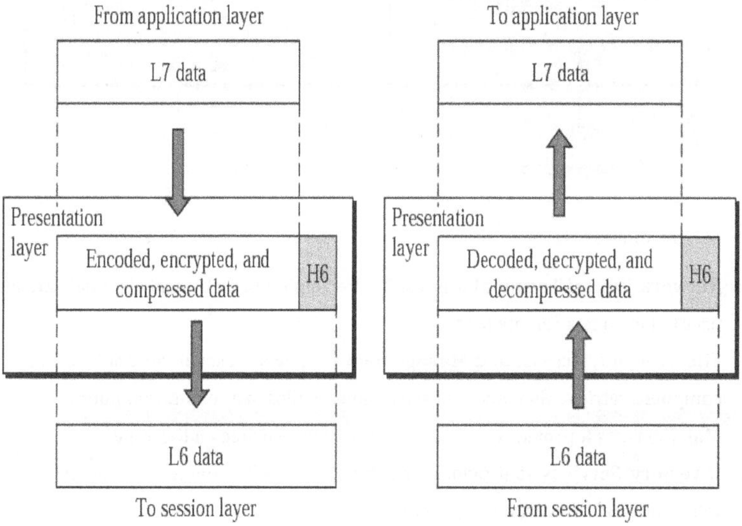

2) Encryption

1) To ensure security encryption/decryption is used.
2) Encryption means transforms the original information to another form. Decryption means retrieve the original information from the encrypted data.

3) Compression

1) It is used to reduce the number of bits to be transmitted.

6.4.7. *Application Layer*

The application layer enables the user to access the network. It provides interfaces between the users to the network.

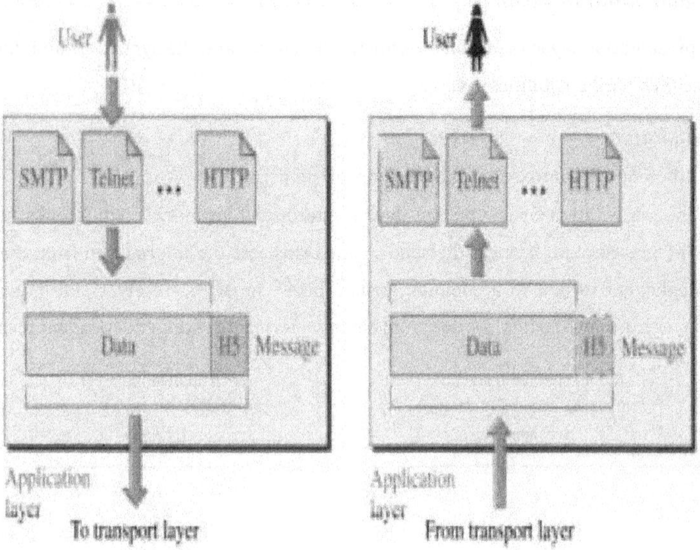

The responsibilities are:

1) **Network Virtual Terminal** It is a software version of a physical terminal and allows a user to log on to a remote host.
2) **File Transfer, Access, and Management** It allows a user to access files in a remote computer, retrieve files, and manage or control files in a remote computer.
3) **Mail Services** It provides the basis for e-mail forwarding and storage.
4) **Directory Services** It provides distributed database sources and access for global information about various objects and services.

7. TCP/IP Protocol Suite

The TCP/IP protocol suite is made of four layers: **Host-to-network Layer, Network Layer, Transport Layer, and Application Layer.**

Host-to-network layer is equivalent to the combination of the physical and data link layers. The internet layer is equivalent to the network layer and provides physical standards, network interfaces. The transport functions that correspond to the fourth layers of the OSI model.

The three topmost layers in the OSI model are represented in TCP/IP by a single layer called the application layer.

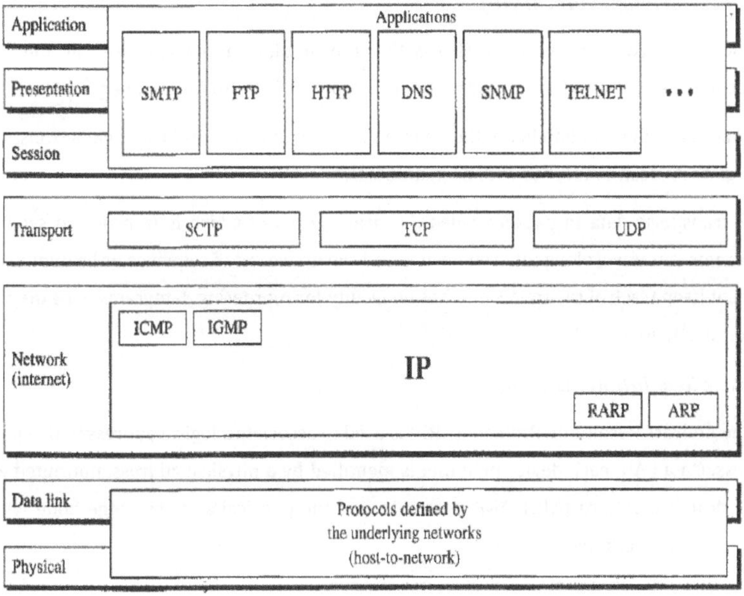

TCP/IP and OSI Model

TCP/IP is a hierarchical protocol made up of interactive modules, each of which provides a specific functionality. Whereas the OSI model specifies which functions belong to each of its layers, the layers of the TCP/IP protocol suite contain relatively independent protocols that can be mixed and matched depending on the needs of the system.

The term hierarchical protocol means that each upper-level protocol is supported by one or more lower-level protocols.

7.1. Layers in TCP/IP Protocol Suite

7.1.1. Physical and Data Link Layers

At the physical and data link layers, TCP/IP suite does not define any specific protocol. It supports all the standard and proprietary protocols. A network in a TCP/IP internetwork can be a local-area network or a wide-area network.

7.1.2. Internetwork Layer

At the network, TCP/IP supports the Internetworking Protocol. IP, in turn, uses four supporting protocols: ARP, RARP, ICMP, and IGMP.

Internetworking Protocol (IP)

The Internetworking Protocol (IP) is the transmission mechanism used by the TCP/IP protocols. It is an unreliable and connectionless protocol (a best-effort delivery service).

IP assumes the unreliability of the underlying layers and does its best to get a transmission through to its destination, but with no guarantees.

IP transports data in packets called datagrams, each of which is transported separately. Datagrams can travel along different routes and can arrive out of sequence or be duplicated. IP does not keep track of the routes and has no facility for reordering datagrams once they arrive at their destination.

Address Resolution Protocol

The Address Resolution Protocol (ARP) is used to associate a logical address with a physical address. On a LAN, each device on a link is identified by a physical address, imprinted on the network interface card (NIC). ARP is used to find the physical address of the node when its Internet address is known.

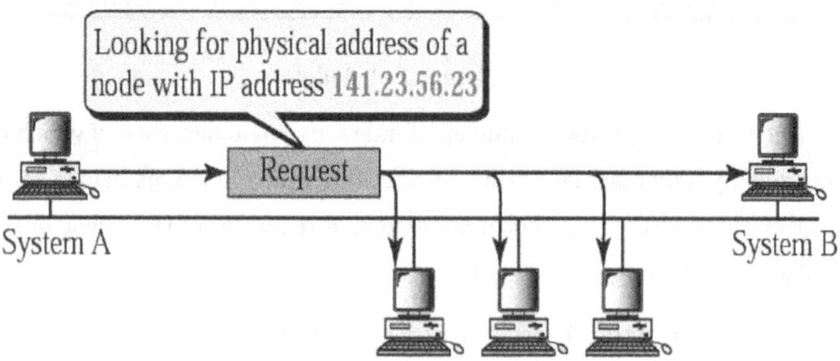

a. ARP request is broadcast

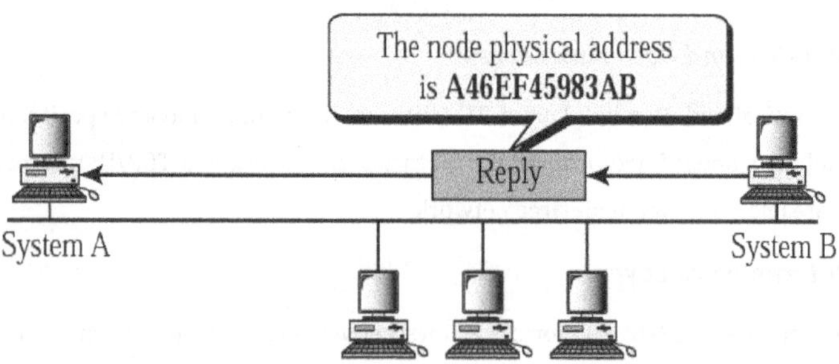

b. ARP reply is unicast

Reverse Address Resolution Protocol

The Reverse Address Resolution Protocol (RARP) allows a host to discover its Internet address when it knows only its physical address. It is used when a computer is connected to a network for the first time or when a diskless computer is booted.

a. RARP request is broadcast

b. RARP reply is unicast

Internet Control Message Protocol

The Internet Control Message Protocol (ICMP) is a mechanism used by hosts and gateways to send notification of datagram problems back to the sender. ICMP sends query and error reporting messages.

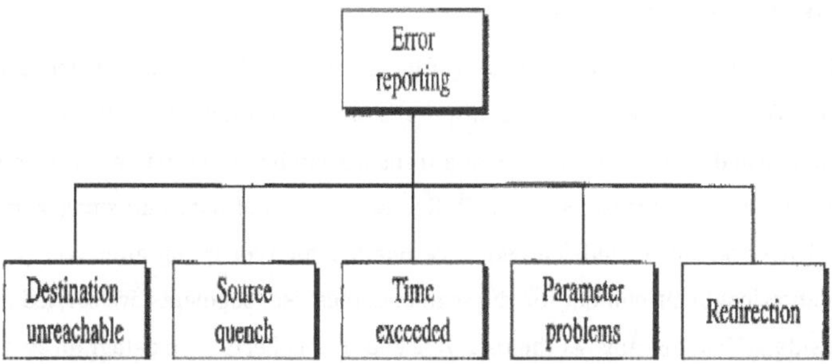

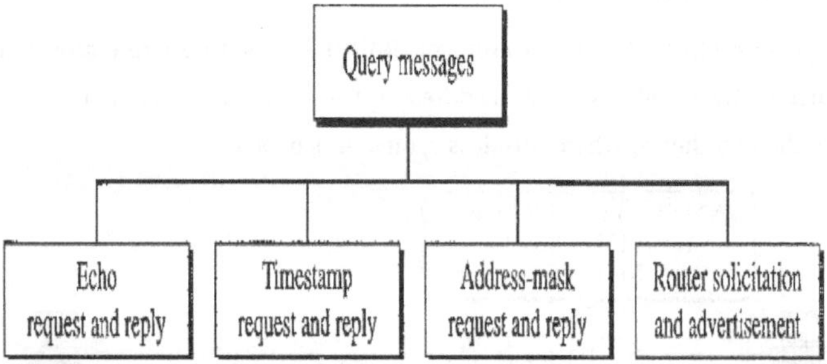

Internet Group Message Protocol

The Internet Group Message Protocol (IGMP) is used to facilitate the simultaneous transmission of a message to a group of recipients. IGMP has three types of messages: the query, the membership report, and the leave report.

7.1.3. Transport Layer

The transport layer was represented in TCP/IP by two protocols: TCP and UDP. UDP and TCP are transport level protocols responsible for delivery of a message from a process (running program) to another process. A new transport layer protocol, SCTP, has been devised to meet the needs of some newer applications.

User Datagram Protocol

The User Datagram Protocol (UDP) is called a connectionless, unreliable transport protocol. It is a process-to-process protocol that adds only port addresses, checksum error control, and length information to the data from the upper layer. UDP is a very simple protocol using a minimum of overhead. If a process wants to send a small message and does not care much about reliability, it can use UDP.

Transmission Control Protocol

The Transmission Control Protocol (TCP) provides full transport-layer services to applications. TCP is a reliable stream transport (connection oriented) protocol. A connection must be established between both ends of a transmission before either can transmit data. At the sending end of each transmission, TCP divides a stream of data into smaller units called segments. Each segment includes a sequence number for reordering after receipt, together with an acknowledgment number for the segments received. Segments are carried across the internet inside of IP datagrams. At the receiving end, TCP collects each datagram as it comes in and reorders the transmission based on sequence numbers.

Stream Control Transmission Protocol

The Stream Control Transmission Protocol (SCTP) provides support for newer applications such as voice over the Internet. It is a transport layer protocol that combines the best features of UDP and TCP.

7.1.4. Application Layer

The application layer in TCP/IP is equivalent to the combined session, presentation, and application layers in the OSI model.

Simple Mail Transfer Protocol (SMTP)

The formal protocol that defines the MTA(Message Transfer Agent) client and server in the Internet is called the Simple Mail Transfer Protocol (SMTP). MTA does the following tasks : Composing messages, Reading messages, Replying to messages Forwarding messages Handling mailboxes

Domain Name System(DNS)

DNS client/server program that is used to map specific address(Email id, URL) into IP addresses.

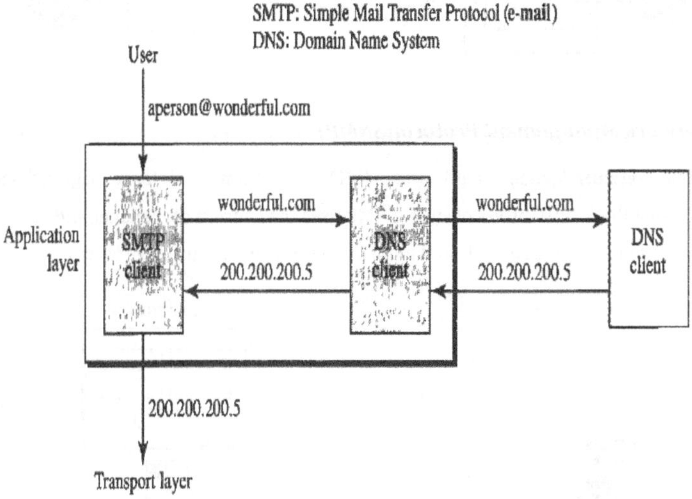

A user of an e-mail program may know the e-mail address of the recipient; however, the IP protocol needs the IP address. The DNS client program sends a request to a DNS server to map the e-mail address to the corresponding IP address. It uses services of TCP on port 53.

TELNET(TErminaL NETwork)

TELNET enables the establishment of a connection to a remote system in such a way that the local terminal appears to be a terminal at the remote system. TELNET is a general-purpose client/server application program.

File Transfer Protocol(FTP)

File Transfer Protocol (FTP) is the standard mechanism provided by *TCP/IP* for copying a file from one host to another. It needs two TCP connections. The well-known port 21 is used for the control connection and the well-known port 20 for the data connection.

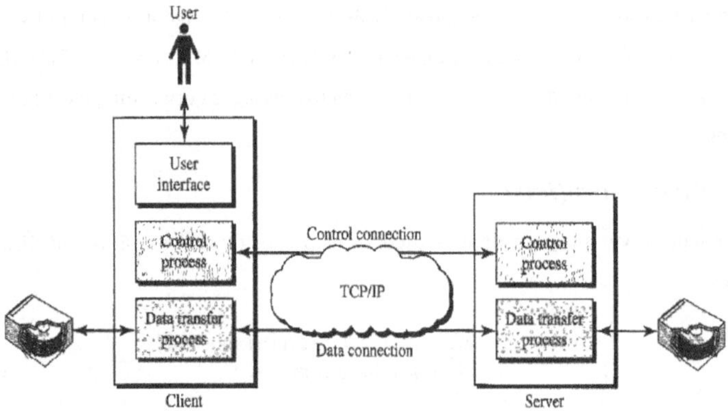

Simple Network Management Protocol(SNMP)

The Simple Network Management Protocol (SNMP) is a framework for managing devices in an internet using the TCPIIP protocol suite. SNMP uses the concept of manager and agent. That is, a manager, usually a host, controls and monitors a set of agents, usually routers

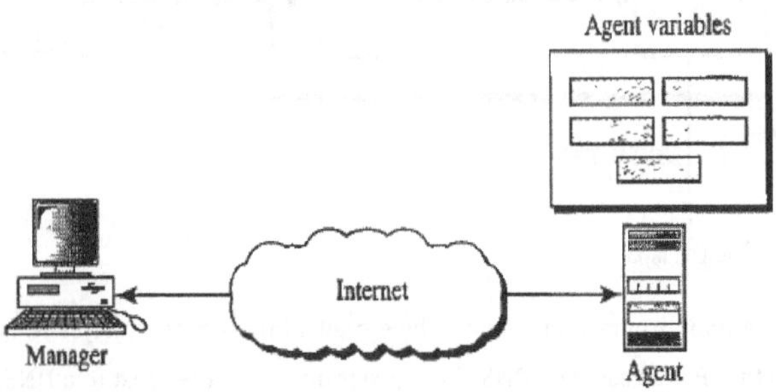

Hyper Text Transfer Protocol (HTTP)

The Hypertext Transfer Protocol (HTTP) is a protocol used mainly to access data on the World Wide Web. HTTP uses the services of TCP on well-known port 80. The HTTP messages are not destined to be read by humans; they are read and interpreted by the HTTP server and HTTP client (browser).

Differentiate Between

1) TCP and UDP (2marks).
2) ARP and RARP(2marks) DEC2013/Jan 2014,DEC 09/Jan 2010.

Transmission Control Protocol(TCP)	User Datagram Protocol(UDP)
Connection oriented protocol	Connection less protocol
Reliable Protocol 1. TCP supports flow control 2. Congestion control 3. Error Control	Unreliable Protocol 1. No flow control 2. No congestion control 3. No error control except checksum in the header
Data is divided into segments and numbered and all the segments will take same connection (route)established to reach the destination	Data is divided into datagrams and these datagrams can take different routes to reach the destination

Address resolution Protocol (ARP)	Reverse Address Resolution Protocol(RARP)
ARP is used to find the Physical Address of the node when its IP address in not known	RARP allows a host to discover its internet address when its IP address is not known
The sender uses this protocol to get the physical address of the receiver.	Any host who has their physical address may use this protocol to get their IP address which is needed to create an IP datagram
A host or router who needs to know the physical address of the receiver broadcasts an ARP request message contain the IP address of the receiver. Only the intended recipient recognizes its IP address and send back an ARP reply containing its IP and Physical address	A RARP request containing the host's physical address is created and broadcasted on the local network. Another machine that knows the IP address for the physical address will send a reply containing the host's IP address.

Internet Control Message Protocol(ICMP)	Internet Group Message Protocol(IGMP)
ICMP is a mechanism used by hosts and gateways to send notification of datagram problems back to the sender.	IGMP is used to facilitate the simultaneous transmission of a message to a group of recipients.
ICMP uses unicast	IGMP uses multi cast
Ex : A PING message is used to with an IP address to check if there is connectivity or not.	Example : It is used for group packet transfer like DTS service where customers watch television through satellite connection.

8. Addressing

Four levels of addressing are used in an internet:

1) Physical (link) addresses.
2) Logical (IP) addresses.
3) Port addresses(Service Point Address).
4) Specific addresses.

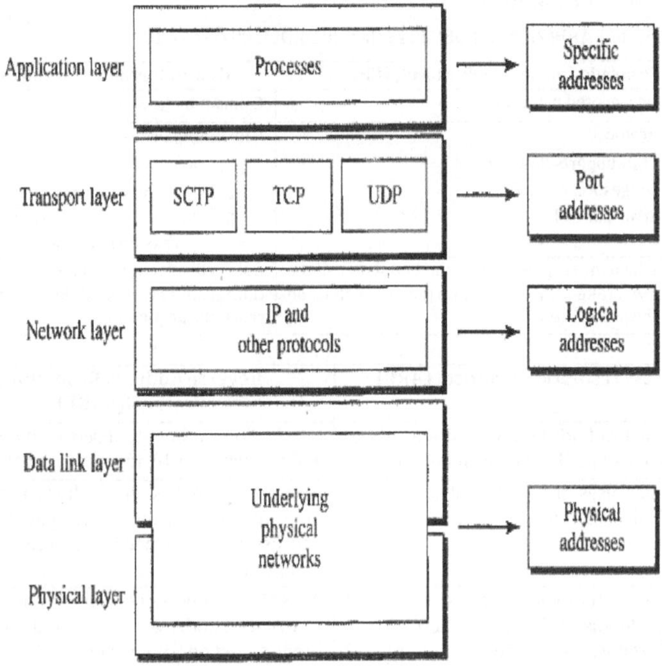

Relationship of Layers and addresses of TCP/IP

8.1. Physical Address

The physical address, also known as the link address, is the address of a node as defined by its LAN or WAN. It is included in the frame at the data link layer. It is the lowest-level address.

Example

Ethernet uses a 48 bit size, represented in hexadecimal. It is a permanent address printed on the NIC.

07:01:02:01:2C:4B
A 6-byte (12 hexadecimal digits) physical address.

A node with physical address 10 sends a frame to a node with physical address 87. The two nodes are connected by a link (bus topology LAN). As the figure shows, the computer with physical address 10 is the sender, and the computer with physical address 87 is the receiver.

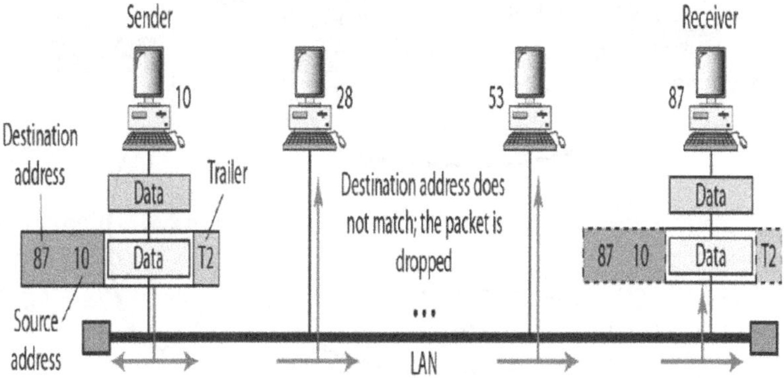

In a bus topology as shown in figure, the frame is propagated in both directions (left and right). The frame propagated to the left dies when it reaches the end of the cable if the cable end is terminated appropriately. The frame propagated to the right is sent to every station on the network. Each station with a physical addresses other than 87 drops the frame because the destination address in the frame does not match its own physical address.

The intended destination computer finds a match between the destination address in the frame and its own physical address. The frame is checked, the header and trailer are dropped, and the data part is decapsulated and delivered to the upper layer.

If the frame is intended for a system outside the sender's network, the receiver address is the address of the device that connects the network to the next one.

8.2. Logical Address

Physical addresses are not adequate in an internetwork environment where different networks can have different address formats. A universal addressing system is needed in which each host can be identified uniquely, regardless of the underlying physical network. It is also called as IP address or Network address. It is a 32 bits size. It is represented in 4 decimal dots.

Example

190. 25. 26.45

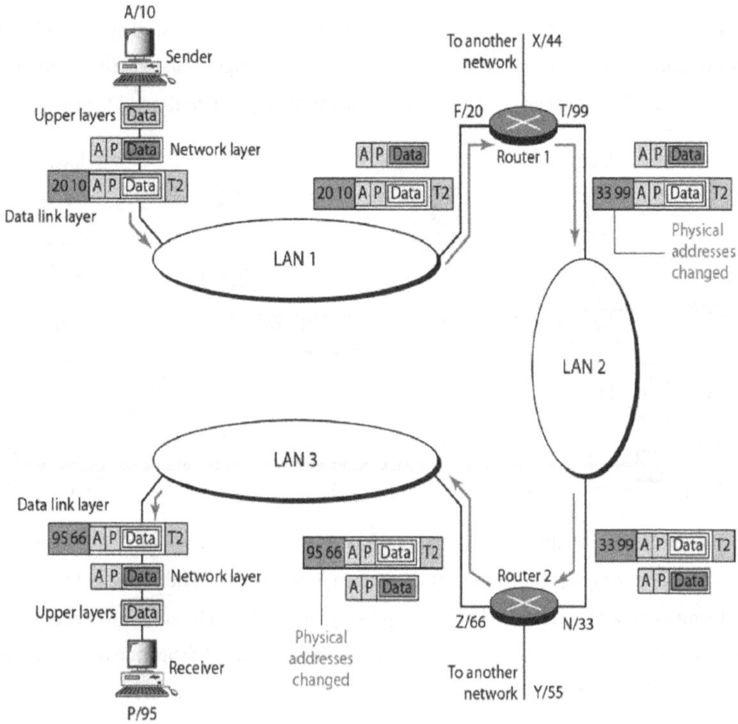

The computer with logical address A and physical address 10 needs to send a packet to the computer with logical address P and physical address 95. The sender encapsulates its data in a packet at the network layer and adds two logical addresses (A and P). The network layer passes this address to the data link layer, which in turn, encapsulates the packet with physical address 20 of router 1 and physical address of source address 10 for the first hop.

The frame is received by router 1, which finds that the destination physical address in the frame matches with its own physical address. The router decapsulates the packet from the frame to read the logical destination address P. Since the logical destination address does not match the router's logical address, the router knows that the packet needs to be forwarded. The router consults its routing table and ARP to find the physical destination address of the next hop (router 2), creates a new frame, encapsulates the packet, and sends it to router 2.

At router 2 again the physical addresses are changed, and a new frame is sent to the destination computer. When the frame reaches the destination, the packet is decapsulated. The destination logical address P matches the logical address of the computer. The data are decapsulated from the packet and delivered to the upper layer. Note that although physical addresses will change from hop to hop, logical addresses remain the same from the source to destination.

8.3. Port Address

Computers can run multiple processes at the same time. The end objective of Internet communication is a process communicating with another process. Port address defines a process running on a host. It is a 16 bits decimal representation.

The physical addresses change from hop to hop, but the logical and port addresses usually remain the same.

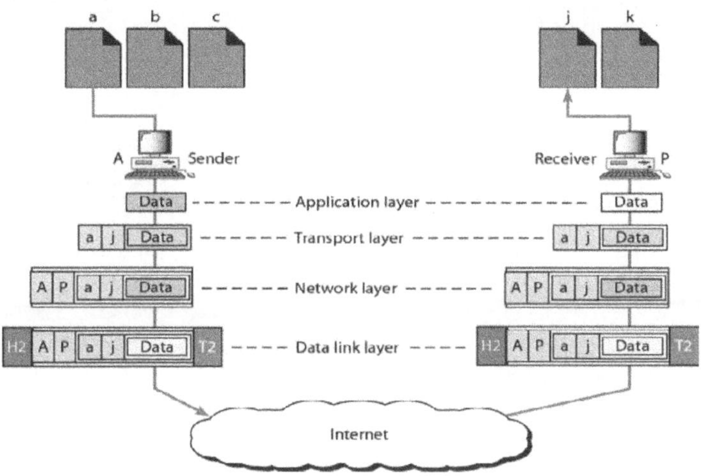

Example

TELNET-23, FTP-21, SMTP-25, DNS–53.

The sending computer is running three processes at this time with port addresses a, b, and c. The receiving computer is running two processes at this time with port addresses j and k. Process a in the sending computer needs to communicate with process j in the receiving computer. To show this the transport layer encapsulates data from the application layer in a packet and adds two port addresses (a and j), source and destination.

Specific Address

User friendly address are known as specific addresses Examples include the e-mail address (for example, forouzan@fhda.edu) and the Universal Resource Locator (URL) (for example, www.mhhe.com). Example–www.hotmail.com. The email id defines the recipient of an e-mail; the site address is used to find a document on the World Wide Web.

UNIT-2

Physical Layer-1: Analog and digital signal, Transmission Impairment, Data Rate Limits, Performance, Digital-Digital conversion (Only Line coding: Polar, Bipolar and Manchester coding), Analog-to-digital conversion (only PCM), transmission modes, digital-Analog conversion

Physical Layer-1

1. Analog & Digital Data

Data can be in analog or digital.

1) Analog Data: Refers to information that is continuous and takes continuous values. Example: Human voice.
2) Digital Data: Refers to information that has discrete states and takes discrete values. Example: Data stored in a computer memory.

Analog & Digital Signals

Signals can be Analog or Digital. Before transmitting the data over a medium, the data must be converted in to electromagnetic signals.

Analog Signal

An analog signal is a continuous signal. It has an infinite number of values in a range.

Example

Human Voice.

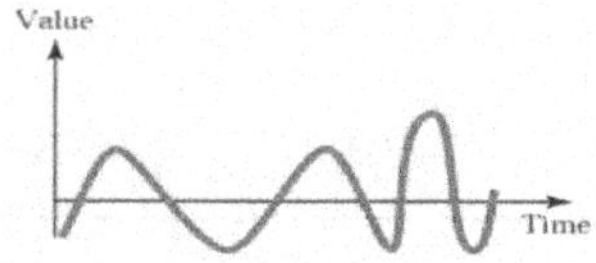

Analog signal

Digital Signal

A digital signal is a discrete signal. It has a limited number of values.

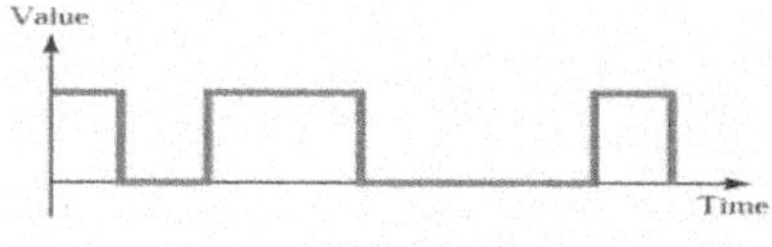

Digital signal

Periodic and Non-Periodic Signals

1) Both analog and digital signals can take one of two forms:
   - Periodic.
   - Non periodic.

A Periodic signal completes a pattern within a measurable time frame, called a period and repeats that pattern over subsequent identical periods.

The completion of one full cycle is **period.**

A Nonperiodic signal changes without exhibiting a pattern or cycle that repeats over a time.

In data communication we use both periodic analog signal (because they need less bandwidth) and nonperiodic digital signals(because they can represent variation in data.

Periodic Analog Signal

1) Periodic analog signals can be classified as simple or composite.
2) A simple periodic analog signal, a sine wave, cannot be decomposed into simpler signals.
3) A composite periodic analog signal is composed of multiple sine waves.

Sine Wave

1) The sine wave is the most fundamental form of a periodic analog signal.
2) A sine wave can be represented by three parameters: the peak amplitude, the frequency, and the phase.

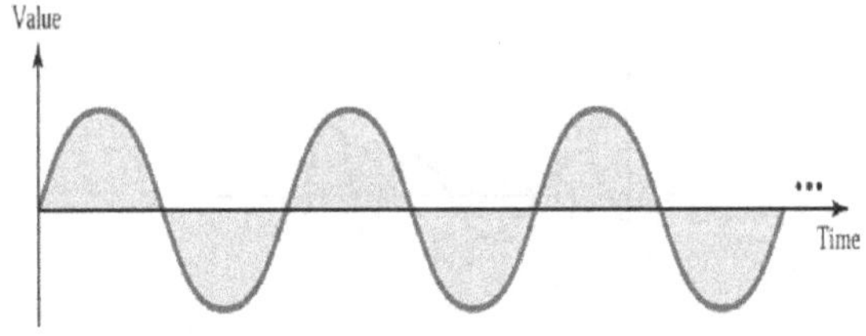

Amplitude

1) Highest intensity of a signal represents the peak amplitude of the signal. The intensity is proportional to the energy it carries.
2) Amplitude is measured in volts.

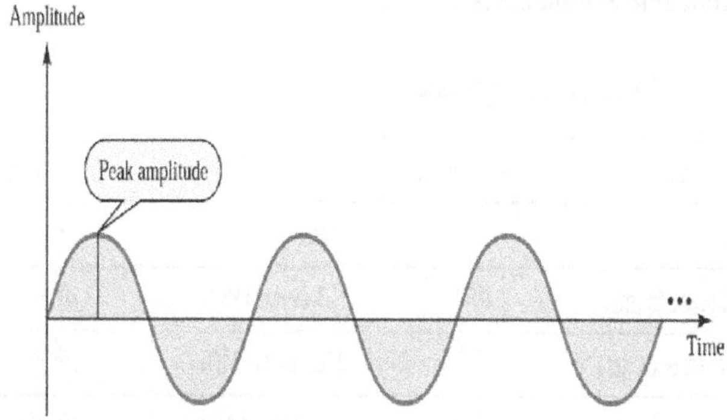

Period & Frequency

Period refers to the time taken by a signal to complete one cycle & expressed in seconds. It is denoted by T. Frequency refers to numbers of cycles produced in one second & and expressed in hertz (Hz). It is denoted by ' f '.

The relation between period and frequency is given by

$$T \times f = 1.$$

$$f = 1/T \qquad T = 1/f$$

Frequency and period are inverses of each other.

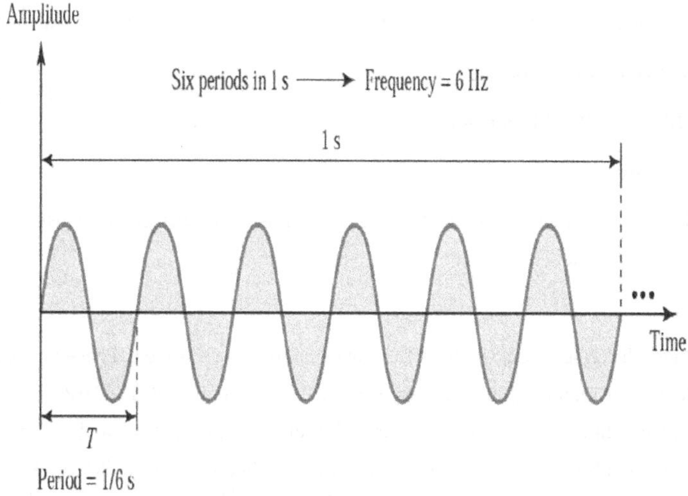

Period is formally expressed in seconds. Frequency is formally expressed in Hertz (Hz)

Units of Periods and Frequencies

Units of period and frequency

Unit	*Equivalent*	*Unit*	*Equivalent*
Seconds (s)	1 s	Hertz (Hz)	1 Hz
Milliseconds (ms)	10^{-3} s	Kilohertz (kHz)	10^{3} Hz
Microseconds (μs)	10^{-6} s	Megahertz (MHz)	10^{6} Hz
Nanoseconds (ns)	10^{-9} s	Gigahertz (GHz)	10^{9} Hz
Picoseconds (ps)	10^{-12} s	Terahertz (THz)	10^{12} Hz

Example

Express a period of 100 ms in microseconds, and express the corresponding frequency in kilohertz.

We Know that, 1 ms = **10^{3} μs.**

100 ms = 100 × 10^{3} μs = 10^{5} ms.

Now we use the inverse relationship to find the frequency, changing hertz to kilohertz

100ms = 100 × 10^{-3} s = 10^{-1} s = T.

f = 1/10^{-1} Hz = 10 × 10^{-3} KHz = 10^{-2} KHz.

Two Extremes

If a signal does not change at all, its frequency is zero. If a signal changes instantaneously, its frequency is infinite.

Phase

1) Phase describes the position of the waveform relative to time 0. Phase is measured in degrees or radians [360° is 2n rad; 1° is 2n/360 rad, and 1 rad is 360/(2n)].
2) A phase shift of 360° corresponds to a shift of a complete period; a phase shift of 180° corresponds to a shift of one-half of a period; and a phase shift of 90° corresponds to a shift of one-quarter of a period.

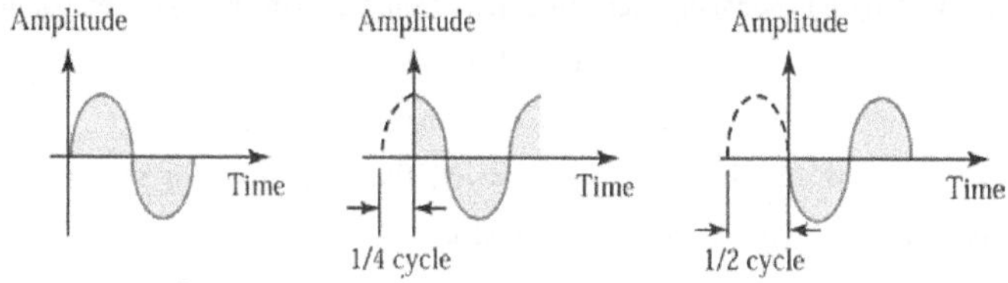

a. 0°   b. 90°   c. 180°

3) A sine wave with a phase of 0° starts at time 0 with a zero amplitude. The amplitude is increasing.
4) A sine wave with a phase of 90° is shifted to the left by 1/4 cycle. However, note that the signal does not really exist before time 0.A sine wave with a phase of 90° starts at time 0 with a peak amplitude. The amplitude is decreasing.
5) A sine wave with a phase of 180° is shifted to the left by 1/2 cycle. However, note that the signal does not really exist before time 0. A sine wave with a phase of 180° starts at time 0 with a zero amplitude. The amplitude is decreasing.

Example

A sine wave is offset one-sixth of a cycle with respect to time zero. What is its phase in degrees and radians?

Solution

We know that one complete cycle is 360 degrees. Therefore, 1/6 cycle is.

$$(1/6)\ 360 = 60 \text{ degrees} = 60 \times 2p\ /360 \text{ rad} = 1.046 \text{ rad}$$

Wavelength

Wavelength binds the period or the frequency of a simple sine wave to the propagation speed of the medium.

1) The wavelength is the distance a simple signal can travel in one period.
2) Wavelength =propagation speed x period=propagation speed/frequency.

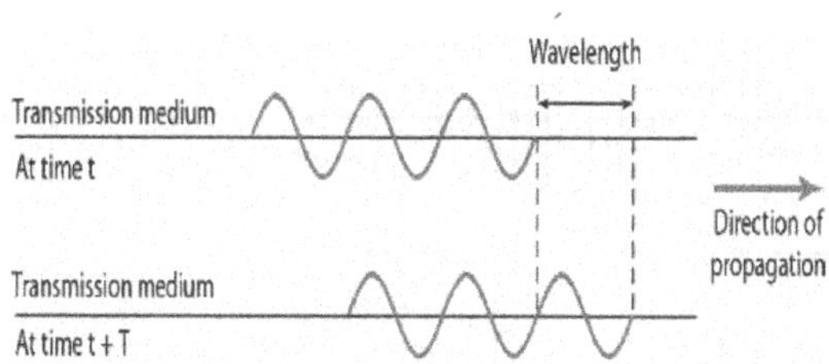

1) The wavelength is normally measured in micrometers (microns) instead of meters.

2) For example, the wavelength of red light (frequency =4 x 1014) in air is

$$c = 3x10^8 / 4x10^{14} = 0.75 \times 10^{-6} m = 0.75 \text{ micro metres}$$

3) In a coaxial or fiber-optic cable, however, the wavelength is shorter because the propagation speed in the cable is decreased.

Time and Frequency Domains

1) Time-domain plot shows changes in signal amplitude with respect to time.

2) Frequency-domain plot show a relations between amplitude and frequency.

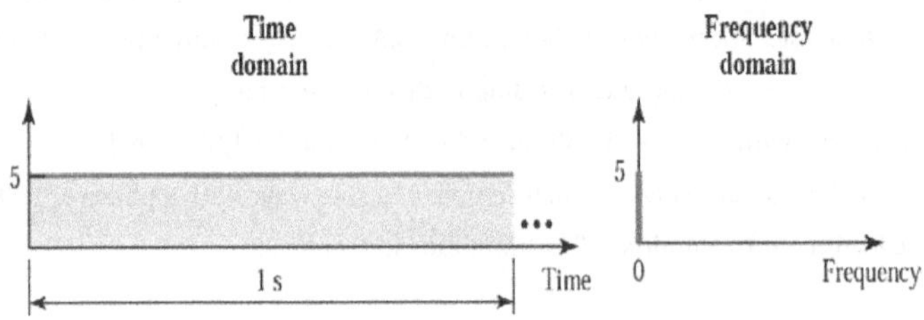

a. A signal with frequency 0

A Signal with Peak Amplitude= 5 volts, and Frequency =0

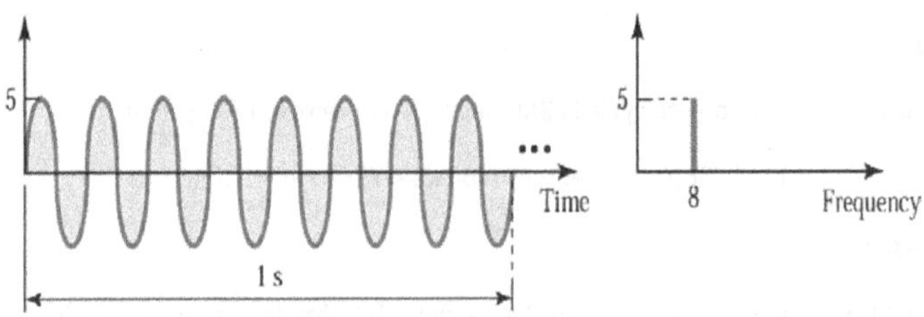

b. A signal with frequency 8

A Signal with Peak amplitude= 5 volts, and Frequency = 8

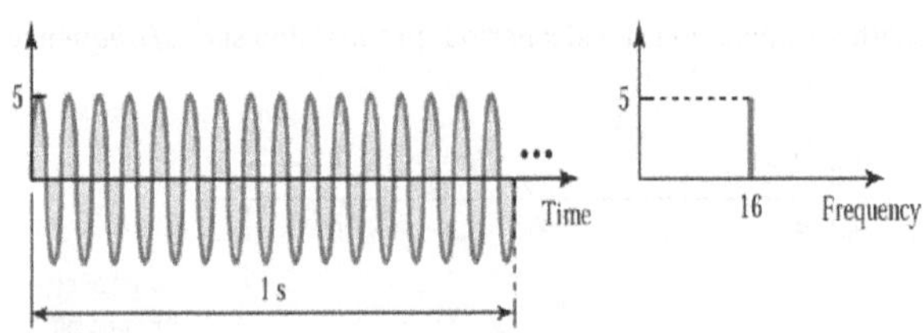

c. A signal with frequency 16

A Signal with Peak Amplitude= 5 Volts, and Frequency = 16

Composite Signals

1) A composite signal can be periodic or nonperiodic.
2) A periodic composite signal can be decomposed into a series of simple sine waves with discrete frequencies, frequencies that have integer values (1, 2, 3, and so on).
3) A nonperiodic composite signal can be decomposed into a combination of an infinite number of simple sine waves with continuous frequencies, frequencies that have real values.

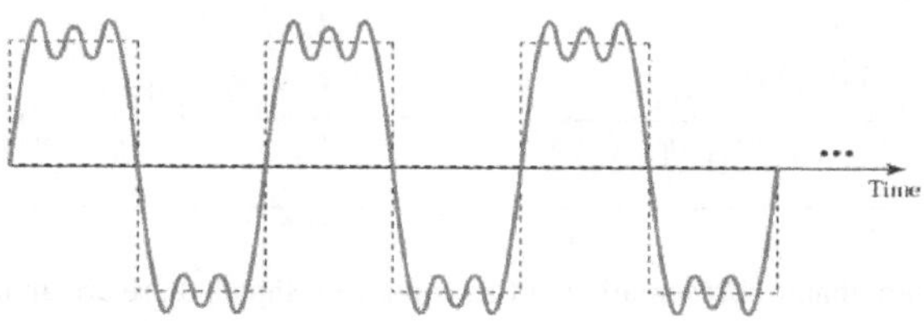

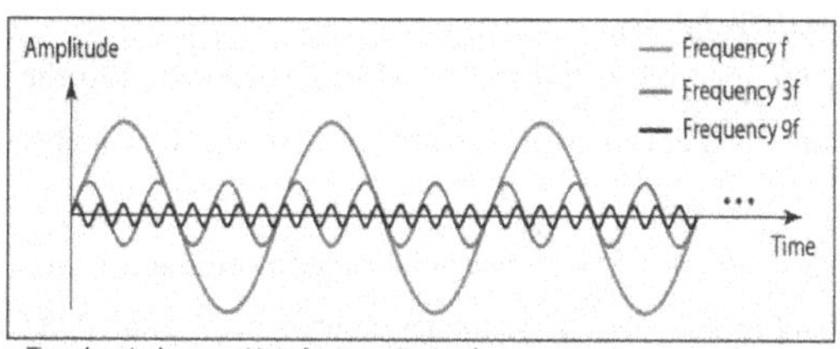

a. Time-domain decomposition of a composite signal

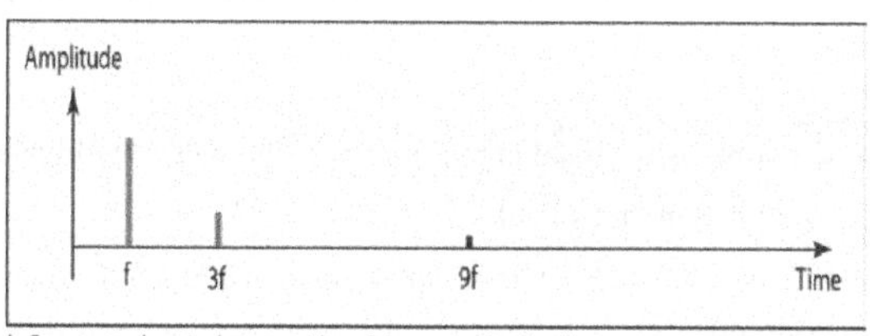

b. Frequency-domain decomposition of the composite signal

1) The amplitude of the sine wave with frequency f is almost the same as the peak amplitude of the composite signal.
2) The amplitude of the sine wave with frequency 3f is one-third of that of the first, and the amplitude of the sine wave with frequency 9f is one-ninth of the first.
3) The frequency of the sine wave with frequency f is the same as the frequency of the composite signal; it is called the fundamental frequency, or first harmonic.
4) The sine wave with frequency 3f has a frequency of 3 times the fundamental frequency; it is called the third harmonic. The third sine wave with frequency.

5) 9f has a frequency of 9 times the fundamental frequency; it is called the ninth harmonic.

Decomposition of Non Periodic Signal

EX: signal created by a microphone or a telephone set when a word or two is pronounced.

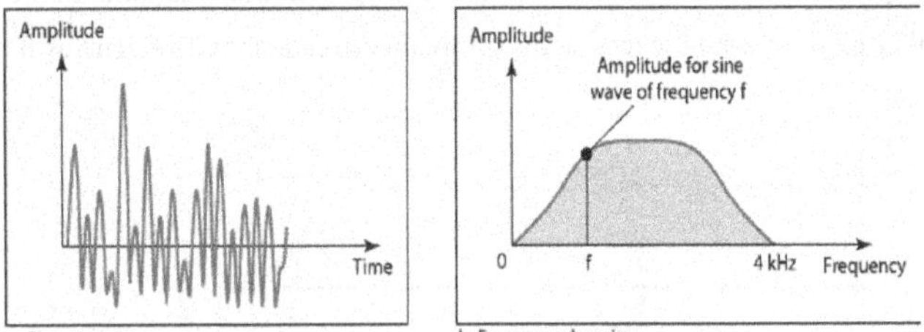

a. Time domain
b. Frequency domain

1) In a time-domain representation of this composite signal, there are an infinite number of simple sine frequencies.
2) Although the number of frequencies in a human voice is infinite, the range is limited.
3) A normal human being can create a continuous range of frequencies between 0 and 4 kHz.
4) The frequency decomposition of the signal yields a continuous curve.
5) There are an infinite number of frequencies between 0.0 and 4000.0 (real values).
6) The height of the vertical line is the amplitude of the corresponding frequency.

Bandwidth

1) Bandwidth of a composite signal is the difference between the highest and the lowest frequencies contained in that signal.
2) For example, Voice normally has a spectrum of 300–3300 Hz. Thus, requires a bandwidth of 3000 Hz.

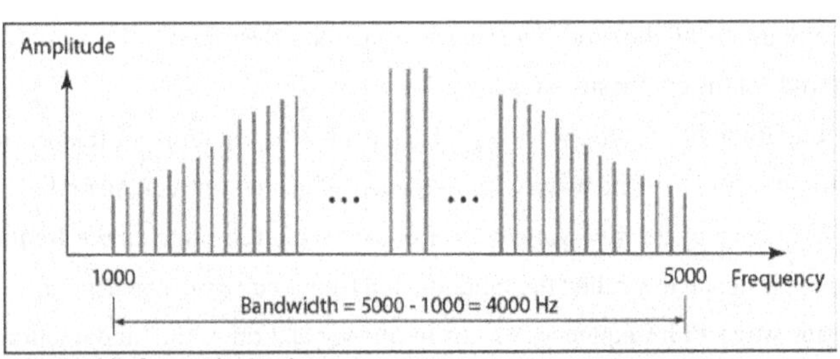

a. Bandwidth of a periodic signal

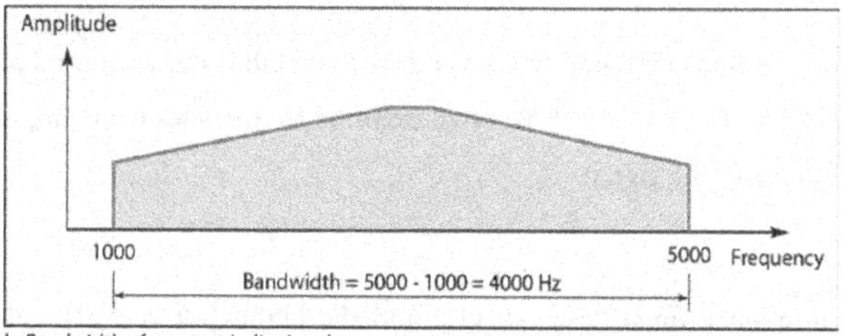

b. Bandwidth of a nonperiodic signal

Example

If a periodic signal is decomposed into five sine waves with frequencies of 100, 300, 500, 700, and 900 Hz, what is the bandwidth? Draw the spectrum, assuming all components have maximum amplitude of 10 V.

Solution

$$B = f_{high} - f_{low} = 900 - 100 = 800 \text{ Hz}$$

The spectrum has only five spikes, at 100, 300, 500, 700, and 900

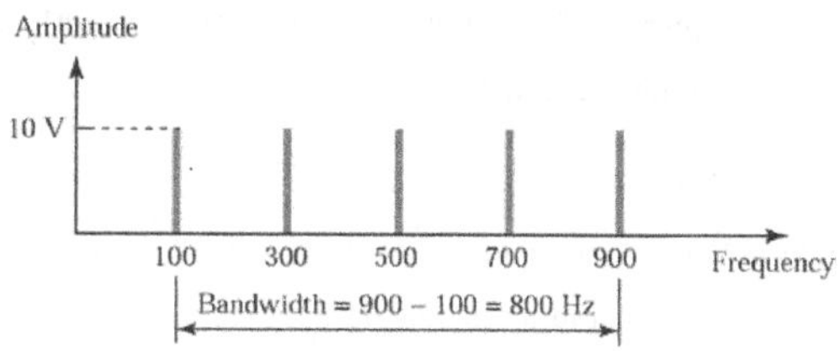

Example

A signal has a bandwidth of 20 Hz. The highest frequency is 60 Hz. What is the lowest frequency? Draw the spectrum if the signal contains all integral frequencies of the same amplitude.

Solution

$$B = f_{high} - f_{low} \rightarrow 20 = 60 - f_{low} \rightarrow f_l = 60 - 20 = 40 \text{ Hz}$$

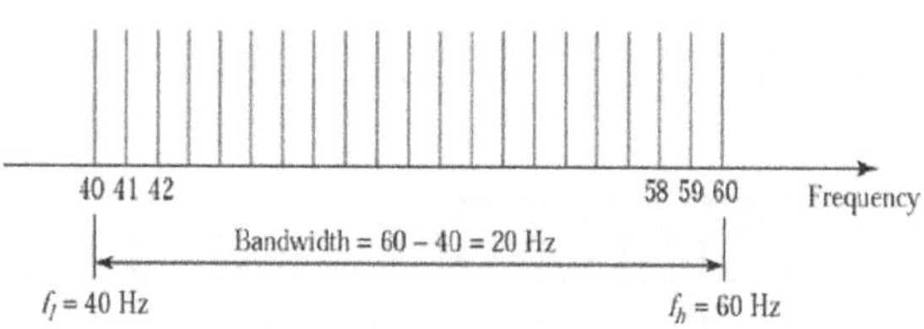

Example

A non periodic composite signal has a bandwidth of 200 kHz, with a middle frequency of 140 kHz and peak amplitude of 20 V. The two extreme frequencies have amplitude of 0. Draw the frequency domain of the signal.

Solution

The lowest frequency must be at 40 kHz and the highest at 240 kHz. Figure shows the frequency domain and the bandwidth.

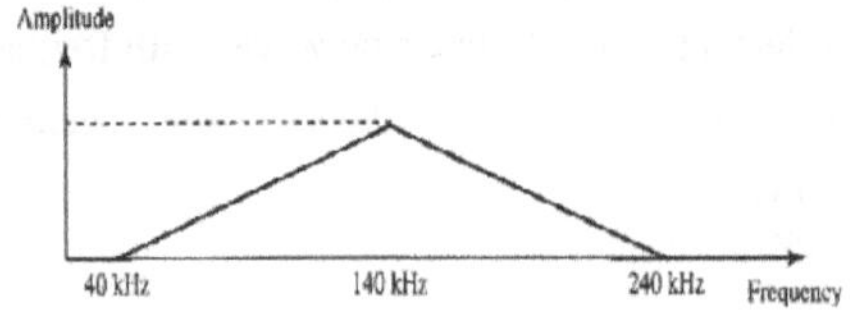

Example

A signal has a spectrum with frequencies between 1000 and 2000 Hz (bandwidth of 1000 Hz). A medium can pass frequencies from 3000 to 4000 Hz (a bandwidth of 1000 Hz). Can this signal faithfully pass through this medium?

Solution

The answer is definitely no. Although the signal can have the same bandwidth (1000 Hz), the range does not overlap. The medium can only pass the frequencies between 3000 and 4000 Hz. The signal with frequency 1000 & 2000 Hz is totally lost.

Digital Signals

1) Data can be represented by a digital signal.
2) For example Bit 1 can be encoded by positive voltage and bit 0 can be encoded by zero voltage.
3) A digital signal can have more than two levels. In this case, we can send more than 1 bit for each level.

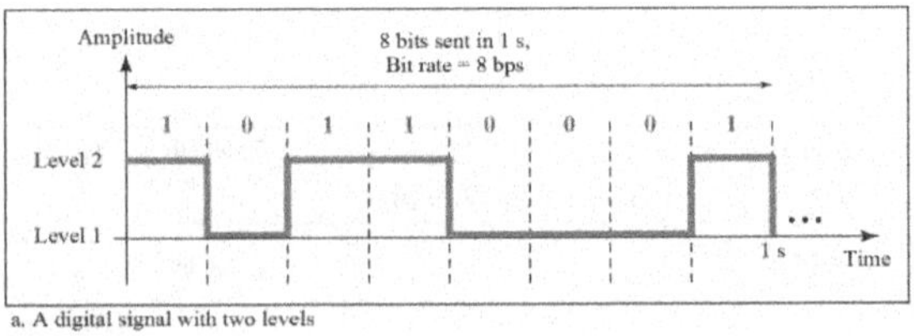

a. A digital signal with two levels

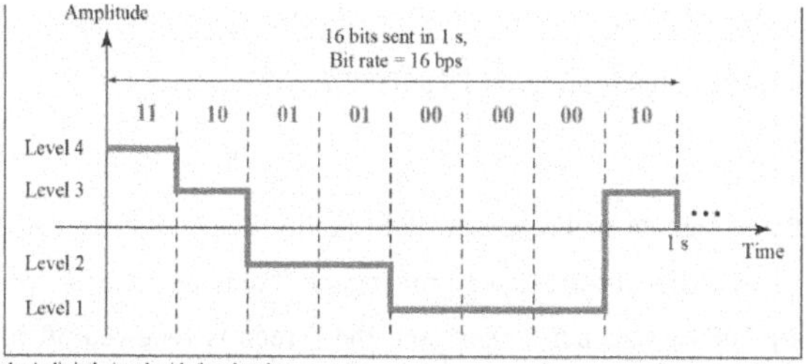

b. A digital signal with four levels

Example

A digital signal has eight levels. How many bits are needed per level? We calculate the number of bits from the formula.

Number of bits per level $= \log_2 8 = 3$.

Each signal level is represented by 3 bits.

Bit Rate

The bit rate is the number of bits sent in Is, expressed in bits per second (bps).

Example

Assume we need to download text documents at the rate of 100 pages per minute. What is the required bit rate of the channel?

Solution

A page is an average of 24 lines with 80 characters in each line. If we assume that one character requires 8 bits, the bit rate is

$100 \times 24 \times 80 \times 8 = 1{,}636{,}000$ bps $= 1.636$ Mbps

Example

A digitized voice channel, as we will see in Chapter 4, is made by digitizing a 4-kHz bandwidth analog voice signal. We need to sample the signal at twice the highest frequency (two samples per hertz). We assume that each sample requires 8 bits. What is the required bit rate?

Solution

The bit rate can be calculated as

$$2 \times 4000 \times 8 = 64{,}000 \text{ bps} = 64 \text{ kbps}$$

Example

What is the bit rate for high-definition TV (HDTV)?

Solution

HDTV uses digital signals to broadcast high quality video signals. The HDTV Screen is normally a ratio of 16:9 (in contrast to 4 : 3 for regular TV), which means the screen is wider. There are 1920 by 1080 pixels per screen, and the screen is renewed 30 times per second. Twenty-four bits represents one color pixel. We can calculate the bit rate as

$$1920 \times 1080 \times 30 \times 24 = 1{,}492{,}992{,}000 \text{ or } 1.5 \text{ Gbps}$$

The TV stations reduce this rate to 20 to 40 Mbps through compression.

Bit Length

The bit length is the distance one bit occupies on the transmission medium.

Bit length =propagation speed x bit duration

2. Transmission Impairment

Signals travel through transmission media, which are not perfect. This means that the signal at the beginning of the medium is not the same as the signal at the end of the medium. Three causes of impairment are attenuation, distortion, and noise.

Causes of impairment

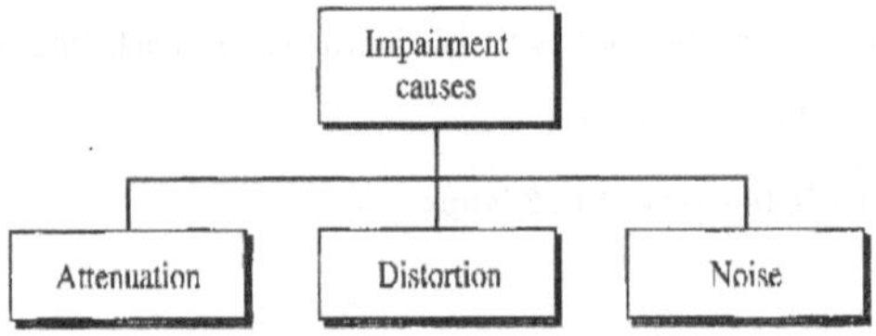

1) Attenuation

Attenuation means a loss of energy. When a signal, simple or composite, travels through a medium, it loses some of its energy in overcoming the resistance of the medium. So some of the electrical energy in the signal is converted to heat. That is why a wire carrying electric signals gets warm after a while.

To compensate for this loss, amplifiers are used to amplify the signal. Figure shows the effect of attenuation and amplification.

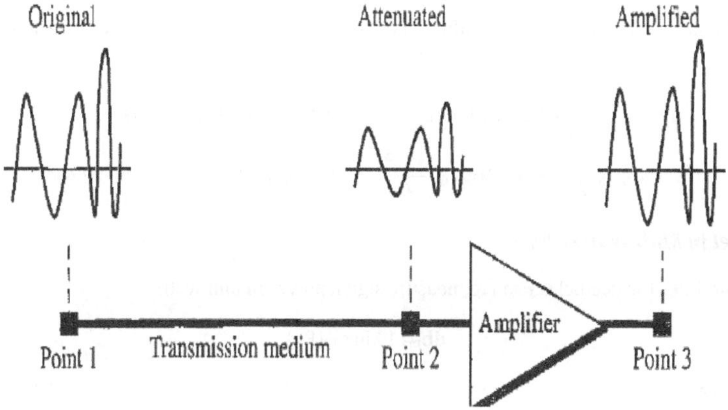

Effect of Attenuation and Amplification

Decibel

To show that a signal has lost or gained strength, the unit decibel is used.

The decibel (dB) measures the relative strengths of two signals or one signal at two different points.

The decibel is negative if a signal is attenuated and positive if a signal is amplified.

$$\mathbf{dB = 10 \log_{10} \frac{P_2}{P_1}}$$

Variables *P1* and *P2* are the powers of a signal at points 1 and 2, respectively.

Defining the Decibel in Terms of Voltage Instead of Power

dB =20 $\log_{10}$ *(V2 / V1).* (Because power is proportional to the square of the voltage)

Example

Suppose a signal travels through a transmission medium and its power is reduced to one-half. This means that *P2* =P1 / 2 In this case, the attenuation (loss of power) can be calculated as

$$10 \log_{10}(P2 / P1) = 10 \log_{10}(0.5\, P1/P1) = 10 \log_{10}(0.5) = 10(-0.3) = -3 \text{ dB}$$

A loss of 3 dB (-3 dB) is equivalent to losing one-half the power.

Example

A signal travels through an amplifier, and its power is increased 10 times. This means that

P2=10 P1

1*OP*I' In this case, the amplification (gain of power) can be calculated **as**

$$10 \log_{10} \frac{P_2}{P_1} = 10 \log_{10} \frac{10P_1}{P_1} = 10 \log_{10} 10 = 10(1) = 10 \text{ dB}$$

Decibel in Milli Wattz(db$_m$)

Sometimes the decibel is used to measure signal power in milliwatts.

$$\mathbf{db_m} = 10 \log_{10}(P_m)$$

Example

The loss in a cable is usually defined in decibels per kilometer (dB/km). If the signal at the beginning of a cable with -0.3 dB / km has a power of 2 mW, what is the power of the signal at 5 km?

Solution

The loss in the cable in decibels is 5 x (-0.3)= -1.5 dB. We can calculate the power as

$$\text{dB} = 10 \log_{10} \frac{P_2}{P_1} = -1.5$$

$$\frac{P_2}{P_1} = 10^{-0.15} = 0.71$$

$$P_2 = 0.71 P_1 = 0.7 \times 2 = 1.4 \text{ mW}$$

2) Distortion

Distortion means that the signal changes its form or shape.

Distortion can occur in a composite signal made of different frequencies.

Each signal component has its own propagation speed through a medium and, therefore, its own delay in arriving at the final destination.

Differences in delay may create a difference in phase if the delay is not exactly the same as the period duration.

The shape of the composite signal is therefore not the same. Figure shows the effect of distortion on a composite signal.

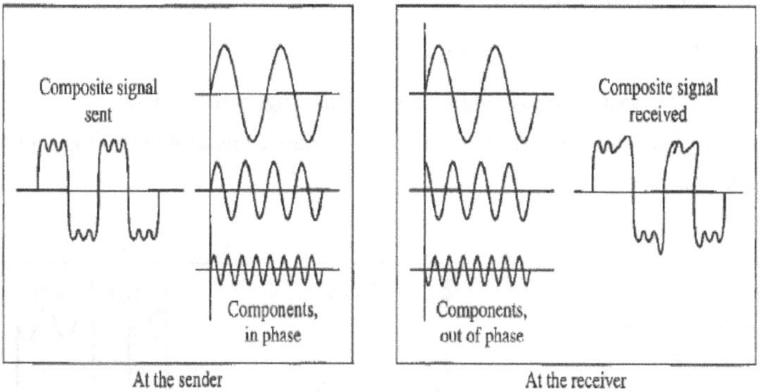

3) *Noise*

Noise is another cause of impairment.

Types of noise: thermal noise, induced noise, crosstalk, and impulse noise.

Thermal noise is the random motion of electrons in a wire which creates an extra signal not originally sent by the transmitter.

Induced noise comes from sources such as motors and appliances. These devices act as a sending antenna, and the transmission medium acts as the receiving antenna.

Crosstalk is the effect of one wire on the other. One wire acts as a sending antenna and the other as the receiving antenna.

Impulse noise is a spike (a signal with high energy in a very short time) that comes from power lines, lightning, and so on.

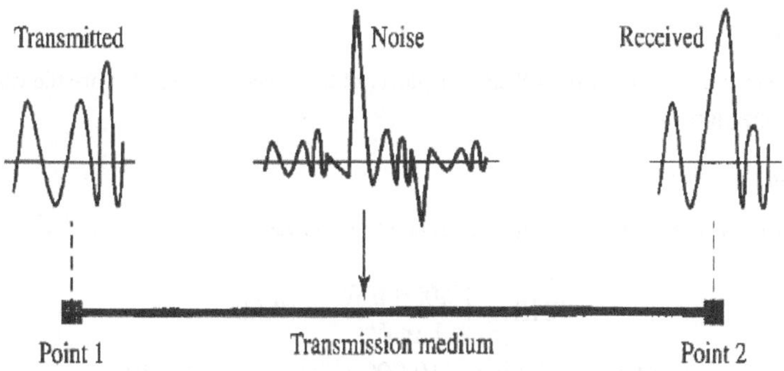

Signal-to-Noise Ratio (SNR)

The signal-to-noise ratio is defined as

SNR = average signal power / average noise power

A high SNR means the signal is less corrupted by noise; a low SNR means the signal is more corrupted by noise.

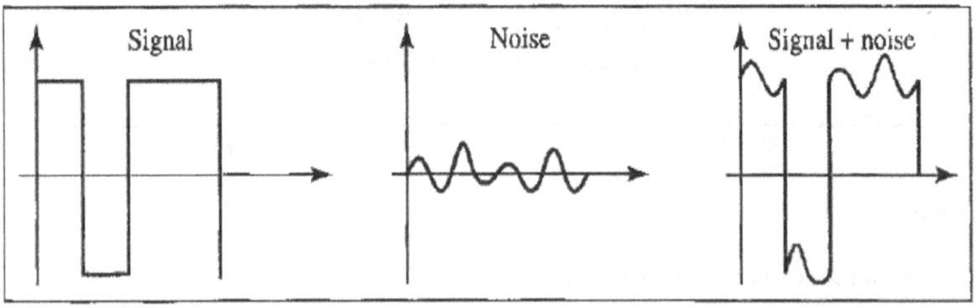

a. Large SNR

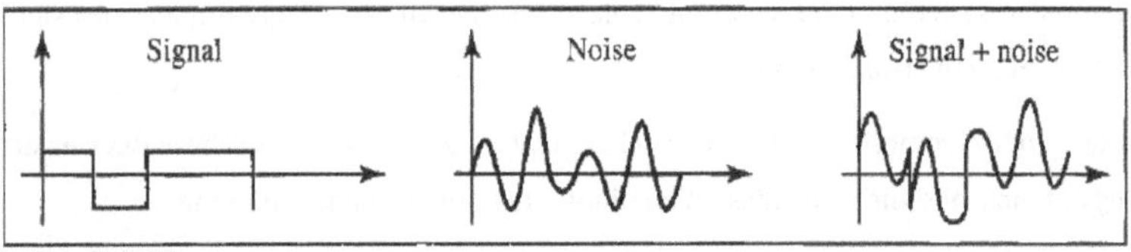

b. Small SNR

Two cases of SNR: a) high SNR b)Low SNR

It is often described in decibel units, SNRdB, defined as

$$\mathbf{SNR_{dB} = 10 \log_{10} SNR}$$

Example

The power of a signal is 10 mW and the power of the noise is 1 μW; what are the values of SNR and SNRdB?

Solution

The values of SNR and SN~B can be calculated as follows:

$$SNR = \frac{10{,}000\ \mu W}{1\ mW} = 10{,}000$$

$$SNR_{dB} = 10 \log_{10} 10{,}000 = 10 \log_{10} 10^4 = 40$$

Example

The values of SNR and SNRdB for a noiseless channel are

The values of SNR and SNR_{dB} for a noiseless channel are

$$SNR = \frac{\text{signal power}}{0} = \infty$$

$$SNR_{dB} = 10 \log_{10} \infty = \infty$$

3. Data Rate Limits

Data rate depends on three factors:

1) The bandwidth available.
2) The level of the signals we use.
3) The quality of the channel (the level of noise).

Two theoretical formulas were developed to calculate the data rate:

1) by Nyquist for a noiseless channel.
2) by Shannon for a noisy channel.

Noiseless Channel: Nyquist Bit Rate

For a noiseless channel, the Nyquist bit rate formula defines the theoretical maximum bit rate

$$\textbf{BitRate} = 2 \times \textbf{bandwidth} \times \log_2 L$$

Where bandwidth is the bandwidth of the channel, L is the number of signal levels used to represent data, and BitRate is the bit rate in bits per second.

1) According to the formula given a specific bandwidth, we can have any bit rate we want by increasing the number of signal levels. But when the number of signallevels is increased, a burden on the receiver is imposed.
2) If the number of levels in a signal is just 2, the receiver can easily distinguish between a 0 and a 1.
3) If the level of a signal is 64, the receiver must be very sophisticated to distinguish between 64 different levels. So, increasing the levels of a signal reduces the reliability of the system.

Example

Consider a noiseless channel with a bandwidth of 3000 Hz transmitting a signal with two signal levels. The maximum bit rate can be calculated as

$$\textbf{BitRate} = 2 \times 3000 \times \log_2 2 = 6000 \text{ bps}$$

Example

Consider the same noiseless channel transmitting a signal with four signal levels (for each level, we send 2 bits). The maximum bit rate can be calculated as:

$$\text{BitRate} = 2 \times 3000 \times \log_2 4 = 12{,}000 \text{ bps}$$

Example

We need to send 265 kbps over a noiseless channel with a bandwidth of 20 kHz. How many signal levels do we need?

Solution

We can use the Nyquist formula as shown:

$$265{,}000 = 2 \times 20{,}000 \times \log_2 L$$

$$\log_2 L = 6.625 \qquad L = 2^{6.625} = 98.7 \text{ levels}$$

Since this result is not a power of 2, we need to either increase the number of levels or reduce the bit rate. If we have 128 levels, the bit rate is 280 kbps. If we have 64 levels, the bit rate is 240 kbps.

Noisy Channel: Shannon Capacity

In reality, the channel is always noisy. Claude Shannon introduced a formula, called the Shannon capacity, to determine the theoretical highest data rate for a noisy channel:

$$\textbf{Capacity} = \textbf{bandwidth} \times \log_2 (1 + \textbf{SNR})$$

Where bandwidth- bandwidth of the channel,

SNR - signal-to noise ratio,

capacity - capacity of the channel in bits per second.

In the Shannon formula there is no indication of the signal level, which means that no matter how many levels we have, we cannot achieve a data rate higher than the capacity of the channel.

Example

Consider an extremely noisy channel in which the value of the signal-to-noise ratio is almost zero. For this channel the capacity C is calculated as

$$C = B \log_2 (1 + \text{SNR}) = B \log_2 (1 + 0) = B \log_2 1 = B \times 0 = 0$$

The capacity of this channel is zero regardless of the bandwidth.

Example

A telephone line normally has a bandwidth of 3000 Hz (300 to 3300 Hz) assigned for data communications. The signal- to-noise ratio is usually 3162. For this channel the capacity is calculated as

$$C = B \log_2 (1 + \text{SNR}) = 3000 \log_2 (1 + 3162) = 3000 \log_2 3163$$
$$= 3000 \times 11.62 = 34{,}860 \text{ bps}$$

Example

The signal-to-noise ratio is often given in decibels. Assume that $\text{SNR}_{\text{dB}} = 36$ and the channel bandwidth is 2 MHz. The theoretical channel capacity can be calculated as

$$\text{SNR}_{\text{dB}} = 10 \log_{10} \text{SNR} \quad \Rightarrow \quad \text{SNR} = 10^{\text{SNR}_{\text{dB}}/10} \quad \Rightarrow \quad \text{SNR} = 10^{3.6} = 3981$$
$$C = B \log_2 (1 + \text{SNR}) = 2 \times 10^6 \times \log_2 3982 = 24 \text{ Mbps}$$

Using **Both** Limits. Shannon capacity gives the upper limit; Nyquist formula tells us how many signal levels needed.

Example

We have a channel with a I-MHz bandwidth. The SNR for this channel is 63. What are the appropriate bit rate and signal level?

Solution

First, we use the Shannon formula to find the upper limit.

$$C = B \log_2 (1 + \text{SNR}) = 10^6 \log_2 (1 + 63) = 10^6 \log_2 64 = 6 \text{ Mbps}$$

The Shannon formula gives us 6 Mbps, the upper limit. For better performance we choose something lower, 4 Mbps, for example. Then we use the Nyquist formula to find the number of signal levels.

$$4 \text{ Mbps} = 2 \times 1 \text{ MHz} \times \log_2 L \quad \Rightarrow \quad L = 4$$

4. Performance

Performance Measures

1) Bandwidth
2) Throughput
3) Latency
4) Bandwidth – delay Product
5) Jitter

1) Bandwidth

Bandwidth can be used in two different contexts with two different measuring values:

Bandwidth in hertz : Bandwidth in hertz is the range of frequencies contained in a composite signal or the range of frequencies a channel can pass. For example, we can say the bandwidth of a subscriber telephone line is 4 kHz.

Bandwidth in bits per second: Bandwidth in bps is the number of bits per second that a channel, a link, or even a network can transmit. For example, one can say the bandwidth of a Fast Ethernet network (or the links in this network) is a maximum of 100 Mbps.

2) Throughput

The throughput is a measure of how fast we can actually send data through a network.

The bandwidth is a potential measurement of a link; the throughput is an actual measurement of how fast we can send data.

For example, we may have a link with a bandwidth of 1 Mbps, but the devices connected to the end of the link may handle only 200 kbps. This means that we cannot send more than 200 kbps through this link.

Example

A network with bandwidth of 10 Mbps can pass only an average of 12,000 frames per minute with each frame carrying an average of 10,000 bits. What is the throughput of this network?

Solution

We can calculate the throughput as

Throughput= 12,000 x 10,000/60 =2 Mbps

The throughput is almost one-fifth of the bandwidth.

3) *Latency (Delay)*

The latency or delay defines how long it takes for an entire message to completely arrive at the destination from the time the first bit is sent out from the source.

Latency =propagation time +transmission time +queuing time + processing delay

a) Propagation Time

Propagation time measures the time required for a bit to travel from the source to the destination. The propagation time is calculated by dividing the distance by the propagation speed.

Propagation time = Distance / Propagation speed

The propagation speed of electromagnetic signals depends on the medium and on the frequency of the Signal. For example, in a vacuum, light is propagated with a speed of 3×10^8 m/s.

Example

What is the propagation time if the distance between the two points is 12,000 km? Assume the propagation speed to be 2.4×10^8 m/s in cable.

Solution

We can calculate the propagation time as Propagation time = $12000 \times 1000/2.4 \times 10^8$=50 ms

b) Transmission Time

The time required for transmission of a message depends on the size of the message and the bandwidth of the channel.

Transmission time =Message size / Bandwidth

Example

What are the propagation time and the transmission time for a 2.5-kbyte message (an e-mail) if the bandwidth of the network is 1 Gbps? Assume that the distance between the sender and the receiver is 12,000 km and that light travels at 2.4×10^8 *m/s.*

Solution

We can calculate the propagation and transmission time as

$$\text{Propagation time} = \frac{12{,}000 \times 1000}{2.4 \times 10^8} = 50 \text{ ms}$$

$$\text{Transmission time} = \frac{2500 \times 8}{10^9} = 0.020 \text{ ms}$$

c) *Queuing Time*

The third component in latency is the queuing time, the time needed for each intermediate or end device to hold the message before it can be processed. An intermediate device, such as a router, queues they arrived messages and processes them one by one. When there is heavy traffic on the network, the queuing time increases.

4) *Bandwidth-Delay Product*

The **Bandwidth-Delay** product defines the number of bits that can fill the link.

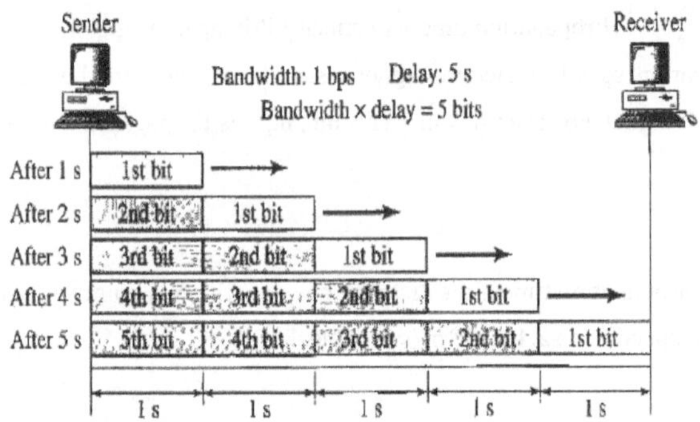

We can think about the link between two points as a pipe. The cross section of the pipe represents the bandwidth, and the length of the pipe represents the delay. We can say the volume of the pipe defines the bandwidth-delay product,

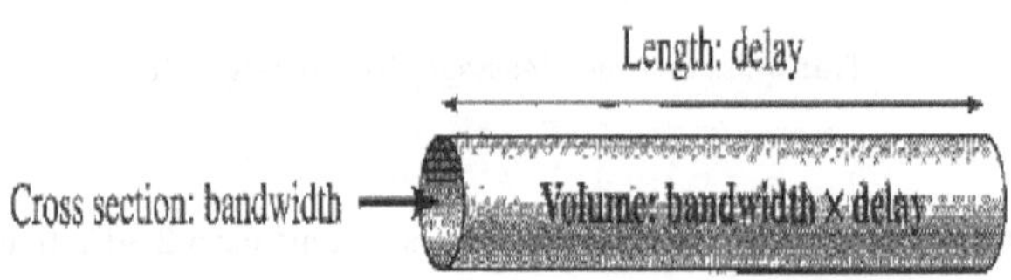

Concept of Bandwidth-Delay product

5) *Jitter*

Jitter is a problem if different packets of data encounter different delays and the application using the data at the receiver site is time-sensitive (audio and video data, for example).

If the delay for the first packet is 20 ms, for the second is 45 ms, and for the third is 40 ms, then the real-time application that uses the packets endures jitter.

5. Analog-to-Digital Conversion

Pulse Code Modulation (PCM)

The most common technique to change an analog signal to digital data (digitization) is called pulse code modulation (PCM). A PCM encoder has three processes, as shown in the figure.

1) **Sampling**: The analog signal is sampled.
2) **Quantization**: The sampled signal is quantized.
3) **Encoding:** The quantized values are encoded as streams of bits.

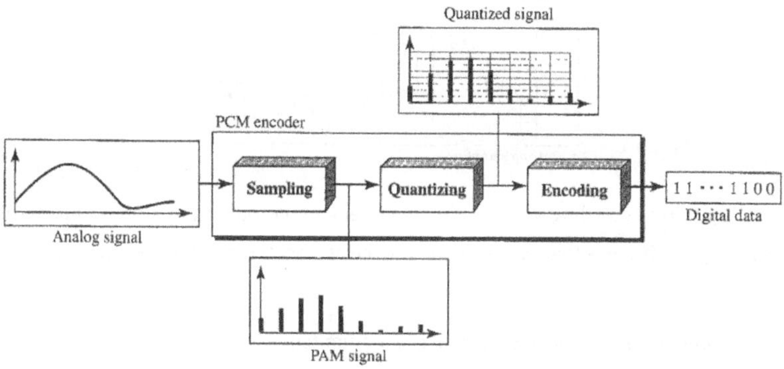

1. Sampling

1) The analog signal is sampled every Ts s, where Ts is the sample interval or period.
2) The inverse of the sampling interval is called the sampling rate or sampling frequency and denoted by fs, where fs = 1/Ts.
3) The sampling process is sometimes referred to as pulse amplitude modulation (PAM).
4) There are three sampling methods- ideal, natural, and flat-top -as shown below.

Ideal Sampling

1) Pulses from the analog signal are sampled. I
2) Ideal sampling method and cannot be easily implemented.

Natural Sampling

A high-speed switch is turned on for only the small period of time when the sampling occurs. The result is a sequence of samples that retains the shape of the analog signal.

Flat-Top Samples

The most common sampling method, called sample and hold, however, creates flat-top samples by using a circuit.

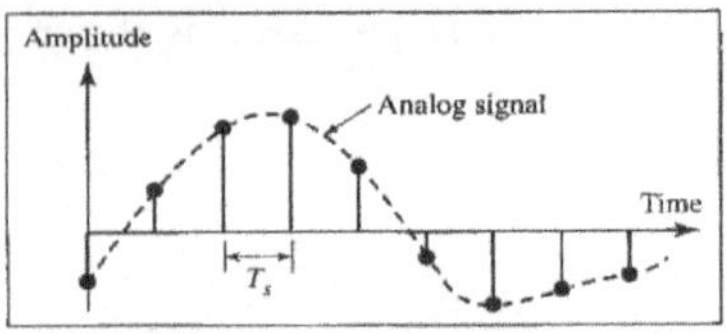

a. Ideal sampling

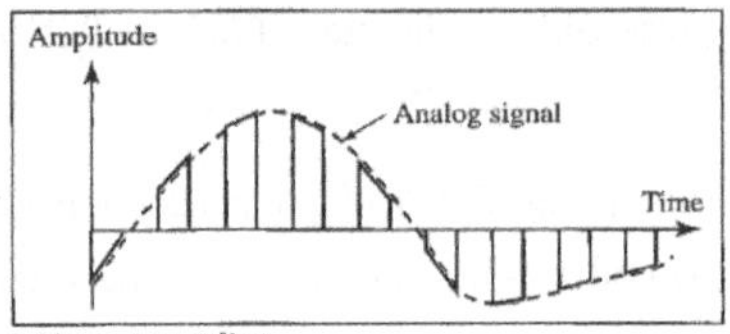

b. Natural sampling

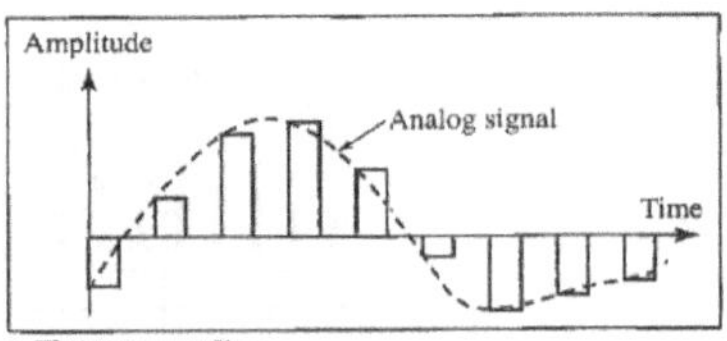

c. Flat-top sampling

Sampling Rate: According to the Nyquist theorem, to reproduce the original analog signal, one necessary condition is that the sampling rate be at least twice the highest frequency in the original signal.

We can sample a signal only if the signal is band-limited.

If the analog signal is low-pass, the bandwidth and the highest frequency are the same value.

If the analog signal is bandpass, the bandwidth value is lower than the value of the maximum frequency. The figure shows the value of the sampling rate for two types of signals.

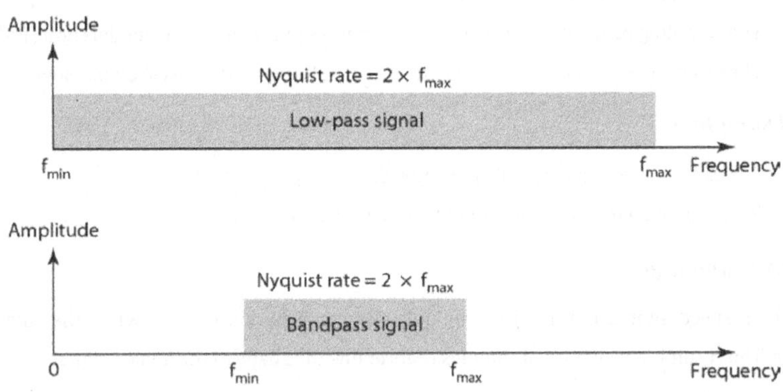

Example

Telephone companies digitize voice by assuming a maximum frequency of 4000 Hz. The sampling rate therefore is 8000 samples per second.

Example

A complex low-pass signal has a bandwidth of 200 kHz. What is the minimum sampling rate for this signal?

Solution

The bandwidth of a low-pass signal is between 0 and f, where *f* is the maximum frequency in the signal.

Sampling rate = 2 X highest frequency (200 kHz).

The sampling rate = 400,000 samples per second.

Example

A complex bandpass signal has a bandwidth of 200 kHz. What is the minimum sampling rate for this signal?

Solution

We cannot find the minimum sampling rate in this case because we do not know where the bandwidth starts or ends. We do not know the maximum frequency in the signal.

2. *Quantization*

The result of sampling is a series of pulses with amplitude values between the maximum and minimum amplitudes of the signal.

The set of amplitudes can be infinite with non integral values between the two limits that cannot be used in the encoding process.

The following are the steps in quantization:

1) Assume that the original analog signal has instantaneous amplitudes between Vmin and Vmax.
2) Divide the range into L zones, each of height Δ(delta).

$$\Delta = \frac{V_{max} - V_{min}}{L}$$

3) Assign quantized values of 0 to L - 1 to the midpoint of each zone.

4) Approximate the value of the sample amplitude to the quantized values.

Assume that we have a sampled signal and the sample amplitudes are between -20 and +20V and eight levels (L = 8). This means that Δ = 5 V. The figure shows this example.

The value at the top of each sample in the graph shows the actual amplitude. In the normalized value for each sample can be calculated as (actual amplitude / Δ).

The quantization process selects the quantization value from the middle of each zone. This means that the normalized quantized values are different from the normalized amplitudes.

The difference is called the normalized error. The quantization code for each sample based on the quantization levels at the left of the graph. The encoded words are the final products of the conversion.

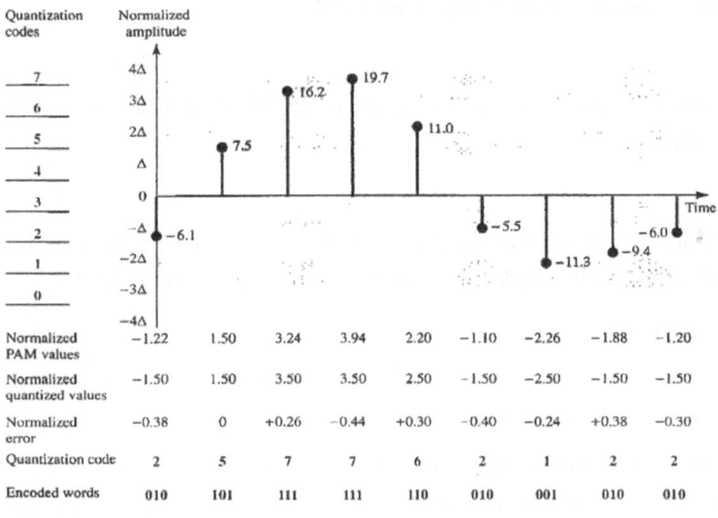

Normalized PAM values	−1.22	1.50	3.24	3.94	2.20	−1.10	−2.26	−1.88	−1.20
Normalized quantized values	−1.50	1.50	3.50	3.50	2.50	−1.50	−2.50	−1.50	−1.50
Normalized error	−0.38	0	+0.26	−0.44	+0.30	−0.40	−0.24	+0.38	−0.30
Quantization code	2	5	7	7	6	2	1	2	2
Encoded words	010	101	111	111	110	010	001	010	010

Quantization Levels

The choice of L, the number of levels, depends on the range of the amplitudes of the analog signal and how accurately the signal needs to be recovered. Choosing lower values of L increases the quantization error if there is a lot of fluctuation in the signal.

Quantization Error

Quantization is an approximation process. The input values to the quantizer are the real values; the output values are the approximated values.

The output values are chosen to be the middle value in the zone. The value of the error for any sample is $-\Delta/2 \leq$ error $\leq \Delta/2$.

The quantization error changes the signal-to-noise ratio of the signal. The contribution of the quantization error to the SNRdB of the signal depends on the number of quantization levels L, or the bits per sample nb, as shown in the following formula:

$$\mathbf{SNR_{dB} = 6.02}n_b \mathbf{+ 1.76 \quad dB}$$

3. *Encoding*

After each sample is quantized and the number of bits per sample is decided, each sample can be changed to an n_b-bit code word. A quantization code of 2 is encoded as 010; 5 is encoded as 101; and so on. The bit rate can be found from the formula:

Bit rate = sampling rate x number of bits per sample = $f_s \times n_b$

Original Signal Recovery

The recovery of the original signal requires the PCM decoder. The decoder first uses circuitry to convert the code words into quantized amplitude and connect the amplitudes.

After the staircase signal is completed, it is passed through a low-pass filter to smooth the staircase signal into an analog signal. The filter has the same cut-off frequency as the original signal at the sender.

If the signal has been sampled at (or greater than) the Nyquist sampling rate and if there are enough quantization levels, the original signal will be recreated.

The maximum and minimum values of the original signal can be achieved by using amplification. The figure shows the simplified process.

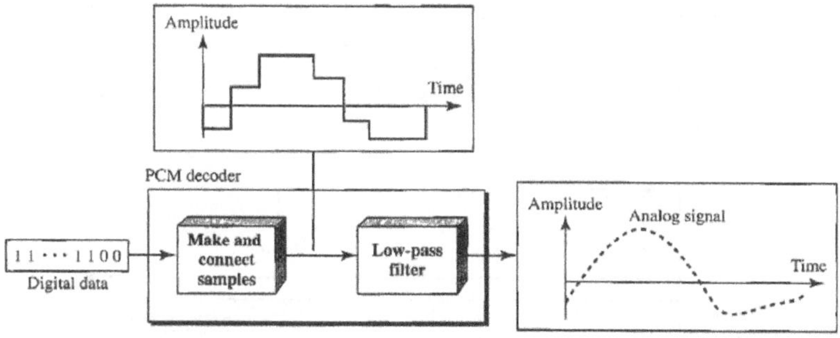

PCM Bandwidth

The minimum bandwidth of a line-encoded signal is Bmin = c x N x (l/r). We substitute the value of N in this formula:

$$B_{min} = c \times N \times \frac{1}{r} = c \times n_b \times f_s \times \frac{1}{r} = c \times n_b \times 2 \times B_{analog} \times \frac{1}{r}$$

When 1/r = 1 (for a NRZ or bipolar signal) and c = (1/2) (the average situation), the minimum bandwidth is

$$B_{min} = n_b \times B_{analog}$$

This means the minimum bandwidth of the digital signal is n_b times greater than the bandwidth of the analog signal.

Maximum Data Rate of a Channel : Assuming a low pass channel with bandwidth B, and L no. of levels used, f_s is the nyquist sampling rate, the data rate N =fs x nb = 2 x B x log2L. This is the maximum bandwidth.

$$N_{max} = 2 \times B \times \log_2 L \quad \text{bps}$$

Minimum Required Bandwidth. The minimum bandwidth if the data rate and the number of signal levels are fixed is

$$B_{min} = \frac{N}{2 \times \log_2 L} \quad \text{Hz}$$

Delta Modulation (DM)

PCM finds the value of the signal amplitude for each sample; DM finds the change from the previous sample. The figure shows the process. Note that there are no code words here; bits are sent one after another.

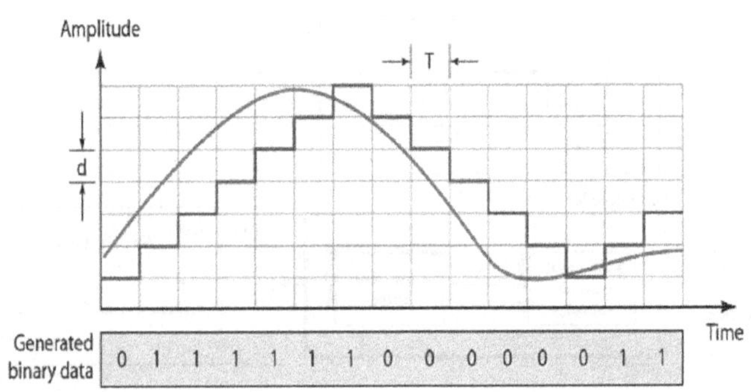

Modulator

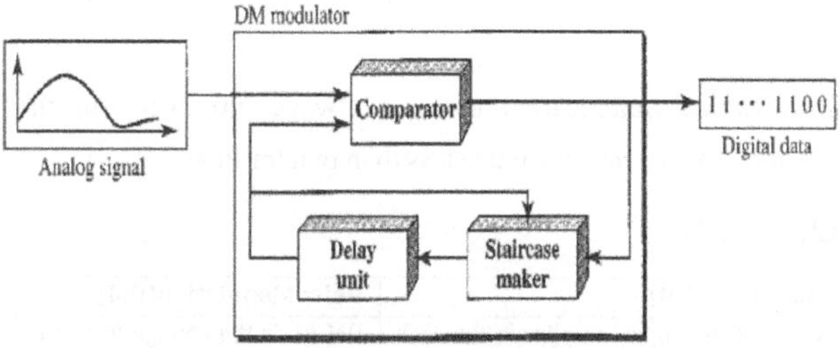

The modulator is used at the sender site to create a stream of bits from an analog signal. The process records the small positive or negative changes, called delta δ.

If the delta is positive, the process records a 1; if it is negative, the process records a 0. However, the process needs a base against which the analog signal is compared.

The modulator builds a second signal that resembles a staircase. Finding the change is then reduced to comparing the input signal with the gradually made staircase signal. The figure shows a diagram of the process.

The modulator, at each sampling interval, compares the value of the analog signal with the last value of the staircase signal.

If the amplitude of the analog signal is larger, the next bit in the digital data is 1; otherwise, it is 0. The output of the comparator, however, also makes the staircase itself. If the next bit is 1, the staircase maker moves the last point of the staircase signal δ up; it the next bit is 0, it moves it δ down.

Demodulator: The demodulator takes the digital data and, using the staircase maker and the delay unit, creates the analog signal. The created analog signal needs to pass through a low-pass filter for smoothing. The figure shows the schematic diagram.

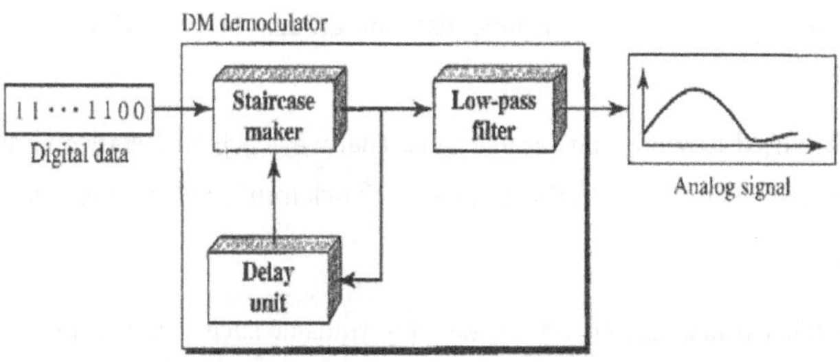

Adaptive DM: A better performance can be achieved if the value of δ is not fixed. In adaptive delta modulation, the value of δ changes according to the amplitude of the analog signal.

Quantization Error: Quantization error is always introduced in the process. The quantization error of DM, however, is much less than that for PCM.

Compare PCM and DM

Pulse Code Modulation(PCM)	Delta Modulation(DM)
PCM finds the value of the signal amplitude for each sample.	DM finds the change from the previous sample. Finding the change is done by comparing the input.
The analog speech waveform is sampled and converted directly into a multibit digital code by an A/D converter.	Signal with the gradually made staircase signal. There are no code words here. Only a single bit is stored for each sample.

6. Transmission Modes

The transmission of binary data across a link can be accomplished in either parallel or serial mode. In parallel mode, multiple bits are sent with each clock tick. In serial mode, 1 bit is sent with each clock tick.

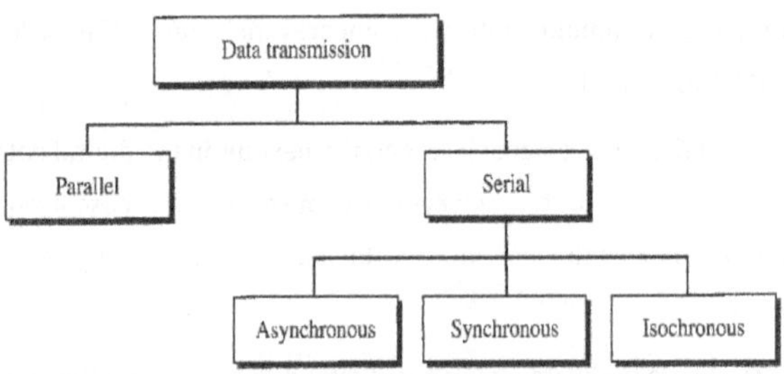

Parallel Transmission

Binary data, consisting of ls and Os, may be organized into groups of n bits and sent at a time. Computers produce and consume data in groups of bits. This is called **parallel transmission.**

n wires are used to send n bits at one time. That way each bit has its own wire, and all n bits of one group can be transmitted with each clock tick from one device to another.

Advantage

Speed: parallel transmission can increase the transfer speed by a factor of n over serial transmission.

Disadvantage

Cost. Parallel transmission requires n communication lines just to transmit the data stream. Because this is expensive, parallel transmission is usually limited to short distances.

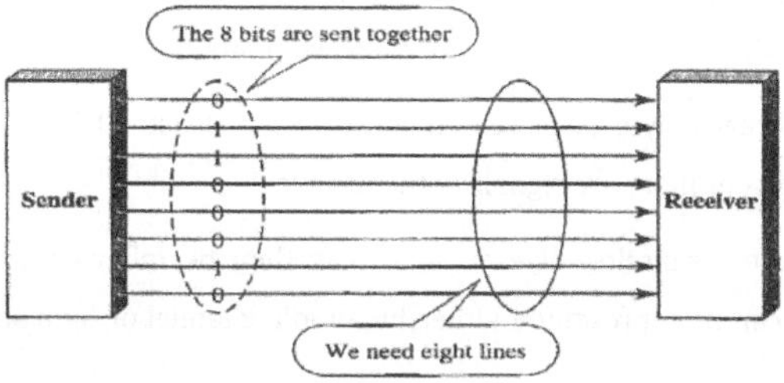

Serial Transmission

In **serial transmission** one bit follows another, so only one communication channel is needed rather than n to transmit data between two communicating devices.

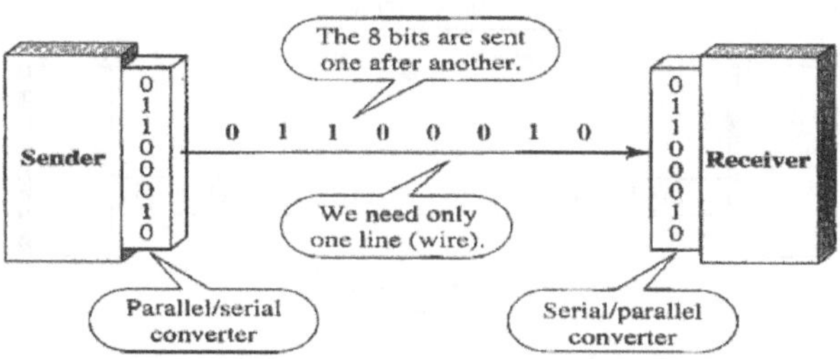

Advantage

Only one communication channel, serial transmission reduces the cost of transmission over parallel by roughly a factor of n.

Disadvantage

Since communication within devices is parallel, conversion devices are required at the interface between the sender and the line (parallel-to-serial) and between the line and the receiver (serial-to-parallel).

a) Asynchronous Transmission

Asynchronous transmission is so named because the timing of a signal is unimportant. Information is received and translated by agreed upon patterns. Patterns are based on grouping the bit stream into bytes. Each group, usually 8 bits, is sent along the link as a unit.

Without synchronization, the receiver cannot use timing to predict when the next group will arrive. To alert the receiver to the arrival of a new group, an extra bit is added to the beginning of each byte. This bit, usually a 0, is called the start bit.

To let the receiver know that the byte is finished, 1 or more additional bits are appended to the end of the byte. These bits, usually 1 s, are called stop bits.

By this method, each byte is increased in size to at least 10 bits, of which 8 bits is information and 2 bits or more are signals to the receiver.

In addition, the transmission of each byte may then be followed by a gap of varying duration. This gap can be represented either by an idle channel or by a stream of additional stop bits.

The start and stop bits and the gap alert the receiver to the beginning and end of each byte and allow it to synchronize with the data stream. This mechanism is called asynchronous because, at the byte level, the sender and receiver do not have to be synchronized.

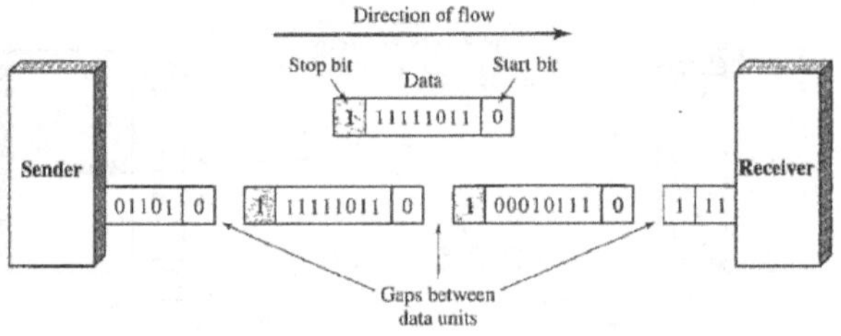

Advantages

It is cheap and effective.

Drawbacks

The addition of stop and start bits and the insertion of gaps into the bit stream make asynchronous transmission slower.

b) Synchronous Transmission

In synchronous transmission, the bit stream is combined into longer "frames," which may contain multiple bytes. Each byte, however, is introduced onto the transmission link without a gap between it and the next one.

The receiver separates that string into the bytes, or characters, it needs to reconstruct the information.

The figure gives a schematic illustration of synchronous transmission. The sender puts its data onto the line as one long string. The receiver counts the bits as they arrive and groups them in 8-bit units. **Example**: high-speed applications such as the transmission of data from one computer to another

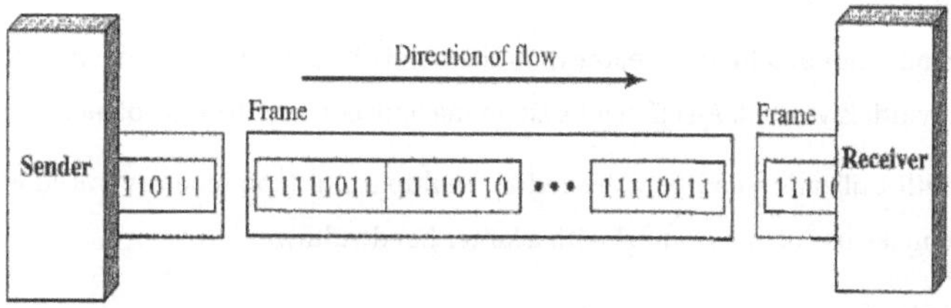

Advantages

Speed. With no extra bits or gaps to introduce at the sending end and remove at the receiving end, and with fewer bits to move across the link, synchronous transmission is faster than asynchronous transmission.

Disadvantage

Without gaps and start and stop bits, there is no built-in mechanism to help the receiving device adjust its bit synchronization midstream.

In real-time audio and video, in which uneven delays between frames are not acceptable, synchronous transmission fails.

c) Isochronous

The isochronous transmission guarantees that the data arrive at a fixed rate.

For example, TV images are broadcast at the rate of 30 images per second; they must be viewed at the same rate.

If each image is sent by using one or more flames, there should be no delays between frames. For this type of application, synchronization between characters is not enough; the entire stream of bits must be synchronized.

UNIT-3

Physical Layer-2 and Switching: Multiplexing, Spread Spectrum, Introduction to switching, Circuit Switched Networks, Datagram Networks, Virtual Circuit Networks

Bandwidth Utilization

If the bandwidth of a link is greater than the bandwidth needs of the devices connected to it, the bandwidth is wasted. An efficient system maximizes the utilization of all resources.

Bandwidth utilization can be achieved by multiplexing (combine several low-bandwidth channels to make use of one channel with a larger bandwidth);

1. Multiplexing

Multiplexing is the set of techniques that allows the simultaneous transmission of multiple signals across a single data link. Whenever the bandwidth of a medium linking two devices is greater than the bandwidth needs of the devices, the link can be shared

In a multiplexed system, *n* lines share the bandwidth of one link. Figure 1 shows the basic format of a multiplexed system. The lines on the left direct their transmission streams to a multiplexer (MUX), which combines them into a single stream (many-to-one).

At the receiving end, that stream is fed into a demultiplexer (DEMUX), which separates the stream back into its component transmissions (one-to-many) and directs them to their corresponding lines.

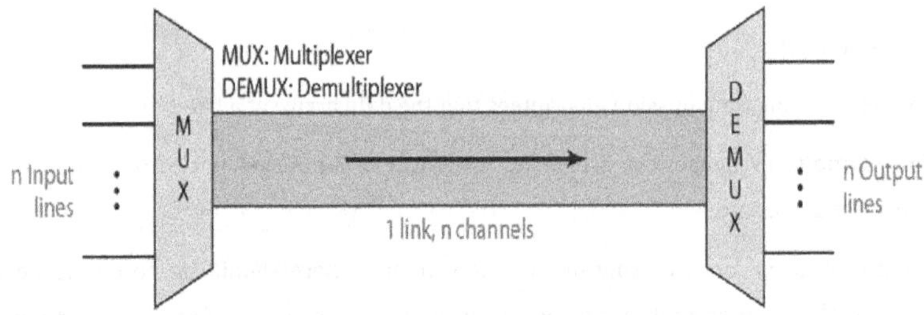

Dividing a Link into Channels

There are three basic multiplexing techniques

1) Frequency-Division Multiplexing(FDM)
2) Wavelength-Division Multiplexing(WDM)
3) Time-Division Multiplexing.(TDM)

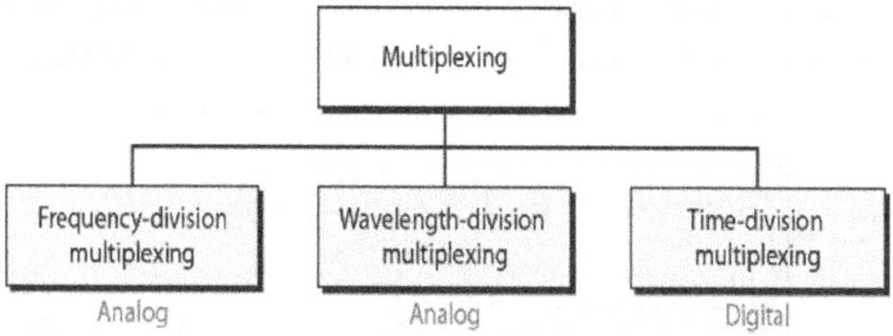

Frequency-Division Multiplexing (FDM)

Frequency-division multiplexing (FDM) is an analog technique that can be applied when the bandwidth of a link (in hertz) is greater than the combined bandwidths of the signals to be transmitted.

In FDM, signals generated by each sending device modulate different carrier frequencies. These modulated signals are then combined into a single composite signal that can be transported by the link.

Carrier frequencies are separated by sufficient bandwidth to accommodate the modulated signal.

Channels can be separated by strips of unused bands called **guard bands** to prevent signals from overlapping. In addition, carrier frequencies must not interfere with the original data frequencies.

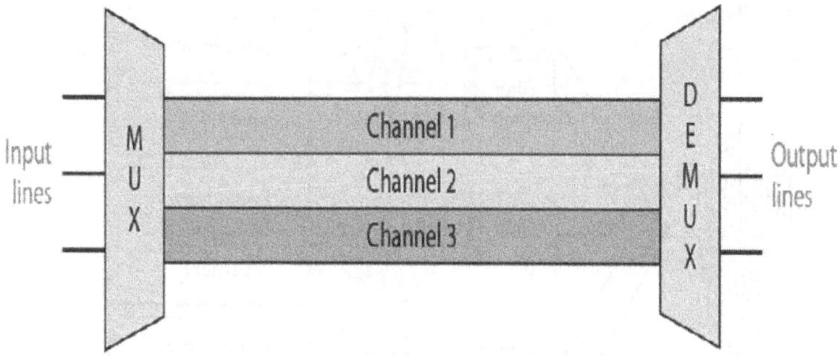

Frequency-Division Multiplexing

Frequency Multiplexing Process

Each source generates a signal of a similar frequency range. (EX: Users having telephonic conversation generates signals of frequency 0-4khz).

Inside the multiplexer, these similar signals **modulate** different carrier frequencies *(f1, f2* and f3*)*. The resulting modulated signals are then **combined** into a single composite signal that is sent out over a media link that has enough bandwidth to accommodate it.

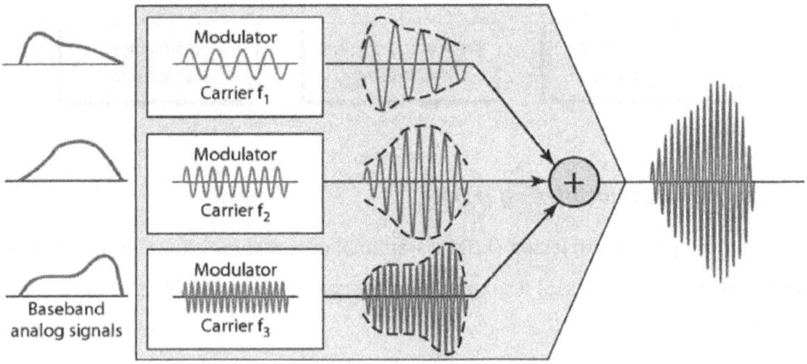

FDM Multiplexing Example

Demultiplexing Process

The demultiplexer uses a series of filters to **decompose** the multiplexed signal into its constituent component signals.

The individual signals are then passed to a **demodulator** that separates them from their carriers and passes them to the output lines.

Figure is a conceptual illustration of demultiplexing process.

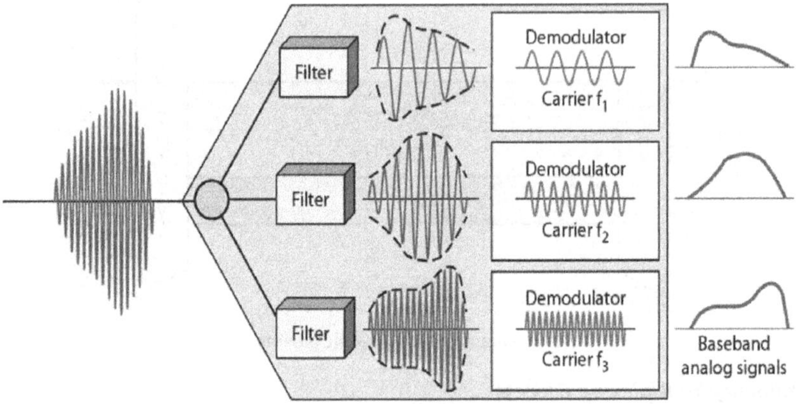

FDM Demultiplexing Example

Example

Assume that a voice channel occupies a bandwidth of 4 kHz. We need to combine three voice channels into a link with a bandwidth of 12 kHz, from 20 to 32 kHz. Show the configuration, using the frequency domain. Assume there are no guard bands.

Solution

We shift (modulate) each of the three voice channels to a different bandwidth, as shown in Figure 6. We use the 20- to 24-kHz bandwidth for the first channel, the 24- to 28-kHz bandwidth for the second channel, and the 28- to 32-kHz bandwidth for the third one. Then we combine them as shown in Figure. At the receiver, each channel receives the entire signal, using a filter to separate out its own signal. The first channel uses a filter that passes frequencies between 20 and 24 kHz and filters out (discards) any other frequencies. The second channel uses a filter that passes frequencies between 24 and 28 kHz, and the third channel uses a filter that passes frequencies between 28 and 32 kHz. Each channel then shifts the frequency to start from zero.

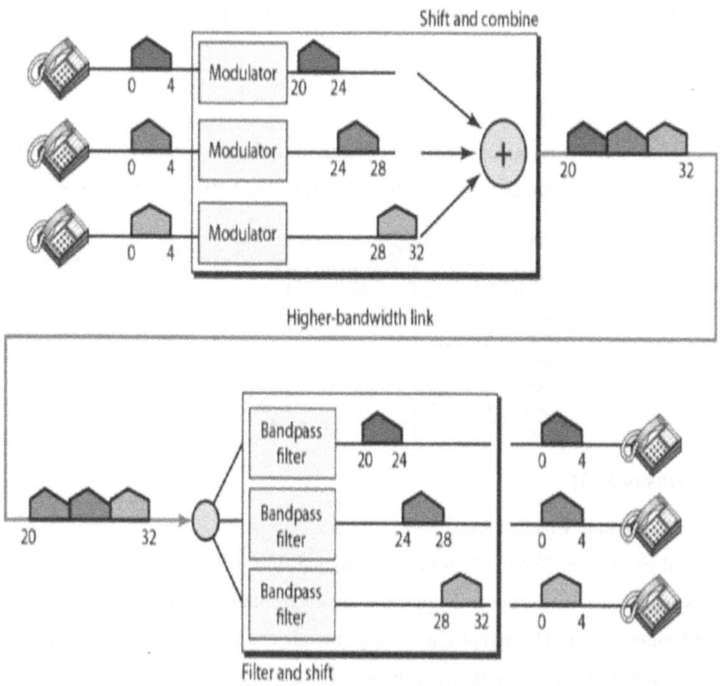

Example

Five channels, each with a 100-kHz bandwidth, are to be multiplexed together. What is the minimum bandwidth of the link if there is a need for a guard band of 10kHz between the channels to prevent interference?

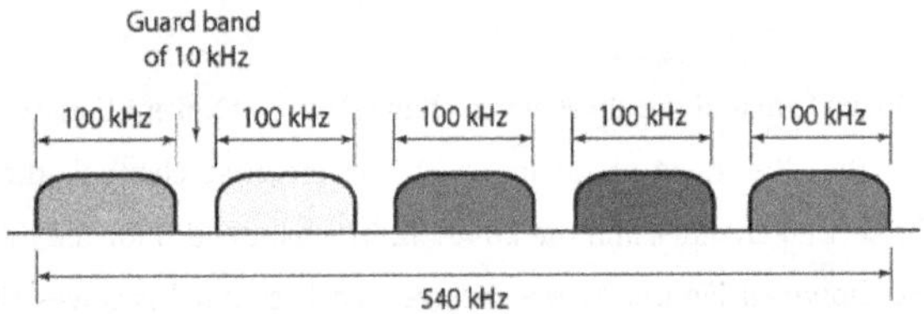

Solution

For five channels, we need at least four guard bands. This means that the required bandwidth is at least 5 x 100 + 4 x 10 =540 kHz

Example

Four data channels (digital), each transmitting at I Mbps, use a satellite channel of 1 MHz. Design an appropriate configuration, using FDM.

Solution

The satellite channel is analog. We divide it into four channels, each channel having a 250-kHz bandwidth. Each digital channel of I Mbps is modulated such that each 4 bits is modulated to 1 Hz.

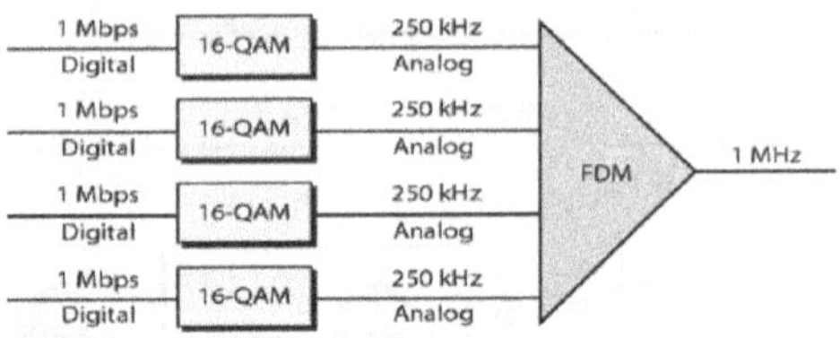

Applications of FDM

1) AM and FM Radio Broadcasting

A special band from 530 to 1700 kHz is assigned to AM Radio. All radio stations need to share this band. Each station uses a different carrier frequency, which means it is shifting its signal and multiplexing. The signal that goes to the air is a combination of signals. A receiver receives all these signals, but filters (by tuning) only the one which is desired. Without multiplexing, only one AM station could broadcast to the common link, the air.

FM has a wider band of 88 to 108 MHz because each station needs and width of 2000 kHz.

2) Television broadcasting: Each TV channel has its own bandwidth of 6 MHz
3) The first generation of cellular telephones (still in operation) also uses FDM.

Implementation

FDM can be implemented very easily. In many cases, such as radio and television broadcasting, there is no need for a physical multiplexer or demultiplexer. As long as the stations agree to send their broadcasts to the air using different carrier frequencies, multiplexing is achieved.

Wavelength-Division Multiplexing

1) WDM is an analog multiplexing technique to combine optical signals.
2) Wavelength-division multiplexing (WDM) is designed to use the high-data-rate capability of fiber-optic cable.
3) The optical fiber data rate is higher than the data rate of metallic transmission cable. Using a fiber-optic cable for one single line wastes the available bandwidth. Multiplexing allows us to combine several lines into one.
4) The idea of WDM is two different signals of different frequencies are combined.

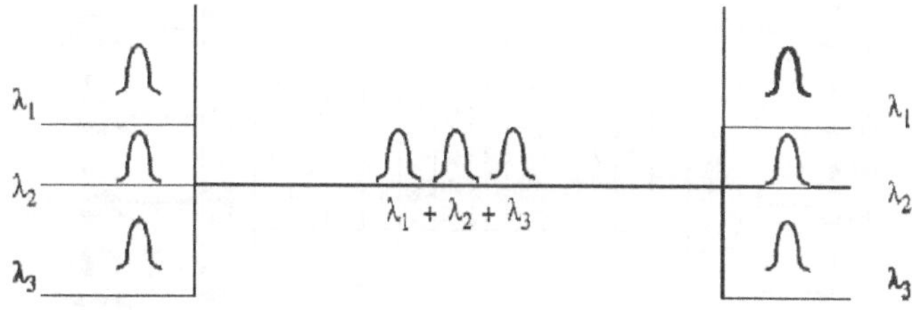

Wavelength Division Multiplexing

5) The difference between FDM and WDM is that the frequencies are very high in WDM.
6) We want to combine multiple light sources into one single light at the multiplexer and do the reverse at the demultiplexer.
7) The combining and splitting of light sources are easily handled by a prism.
8) A prism bends a beam of light based on the angle of incidence and the frequency. Using this technique, a multiplexer can be made to combine several input beams of light, each containing a narrow band of frequencies, into one output beam of a wider band of frequencies.

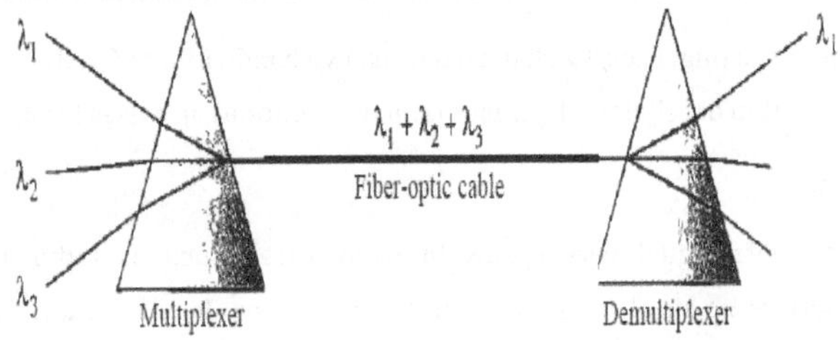

Prisms in Wavelength-Division Multiplexing and Demultiplexing

One **application** of WDM is the **SONET** network in which multiple optical fiber lines are multiplexed and demultiplexed.

Time-Division Multiplexing

1) TDM is a digital multiplexing technique. Digital data from different sources are combined into one timeshared link(Entire capacity of the link is taken by the users on time basis).
2) Instead of sharing a portion of the bandwidth as in FDM, time is shared. Each connection occupies a portion of time in the link.

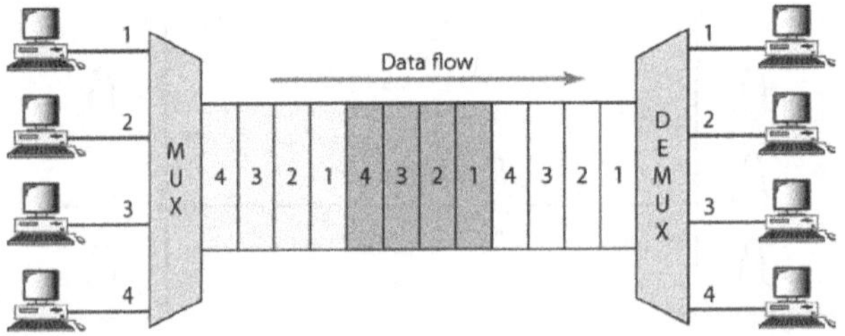

3) TDM is divided into two different schemes: synchronous TDM and statistical TDM.

Synchronous Time-Division Multiplexing

In synchronous TDM, each input connection has a timeslot allotment in the output even if it is not sending data.

Time Slots and Frames

In synchronous TDM, the data flow of each input connection is divided into units, where each input occupies one input time slot. A unit can be 1 bit, one character, or one block of data.

Each input unit becomes one output unit and occupies one output time slot.

In synchronous TDM, the data rate of the link is n times faster than the input rate. The unit duration of the link is *n* times shorter than input unit duration. (i.e) if an input time slot is *T* sec, the output time slot is *T/n* sec, where *n* is the number of connections.

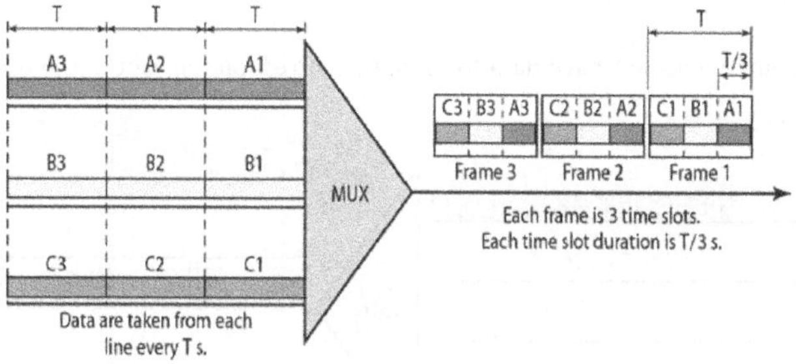

Synchronous Time-Division Multiplexing

1) In synchronous TDM, a round of data units from each input connection is collected into a frame
2) If we have n connections, a frame is divided into n time slots and one slot is allocated for each unit of data from each input line.
3) Time slots are grouped into frames. A frame consists of one complete cycle of time slots, with one slot dedicated to each sending device.

Interleaving

1) TDM can be visualized as two fast-rotating switches, one on the multiplexing side and the other on the demultiplexing side.
2) The switches are synchronized and rotate at the same speed, but in opposite directions.
3) On the multiplexing side, as the switch opens in front of a connection, that connection has the opportunity to send a unit onto the path. This process is called **interleaving.**
4) On the demultiplexing side, as the switch opens in front of a connection, that connection has the opportunity to receive a unit from the path.

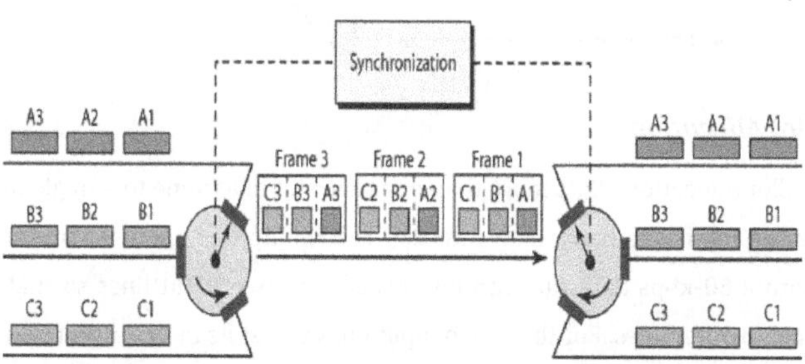

5) The data from the first connection at the multiplexer site go to the first connection at the demultiplexer.

Empty Slots

1) If a source does not have data to send, the corresponding slot in the output frame is empty.

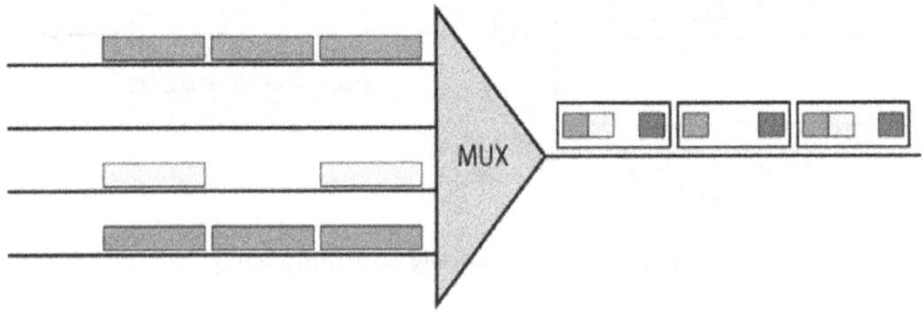

Data Rate Management

If data rates are not the same, three strategies, or a combination of them, can be used. The three strategies are: **multilevel multiplexing, multiple-slot allocation,** and **pulse stuffing.**

Multilevel Multiplexing

Multilevel multiplexing is a technique used when the data rate of an input line is a multiple of others.

In Figure, two inputs of 20 kbps and three inputs of 40 kbps. The first two input lines can be multiplexed together to provide a data rate equal to the last three (first level multiplexing). A second level of multiplexing can create an output of 160 kbps.

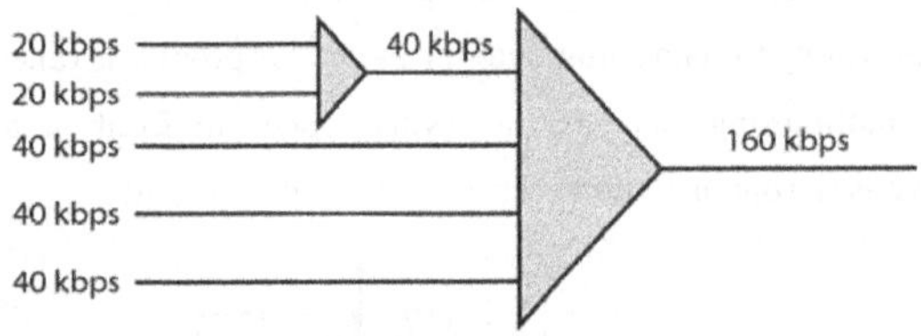

Multiple-Slot Allocation

Multiple-Slot Allocation allots more than one time slot in a frame to a single input line. This is used when an input line has a data rate that is a multiple of another input. In Figure, the input line with a 50-kbps data rate can be divided into two input lines so that its data rate becomes equal to other lines. For these two input lines two slots in the output will be given.

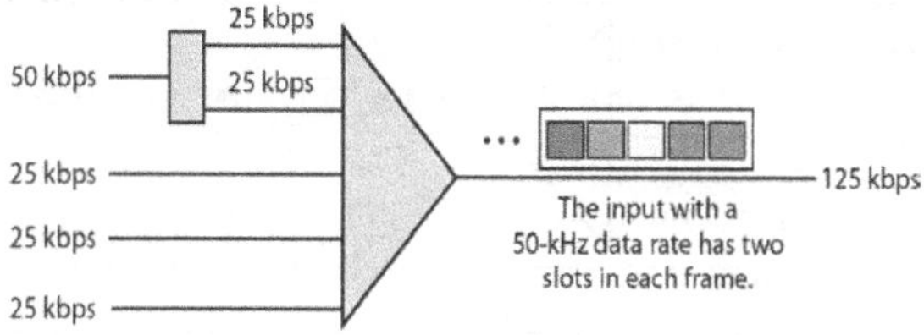

Pulse Stuffing Pulse stuffing can be used when the bit rates of sources are not multiple integers of each other. Here the highest input data rate is made the dominant data rate and then dummy bits are added to the input lines with lower rates. This technique is called pulse stuffing, bit padding, or bit stuffing.

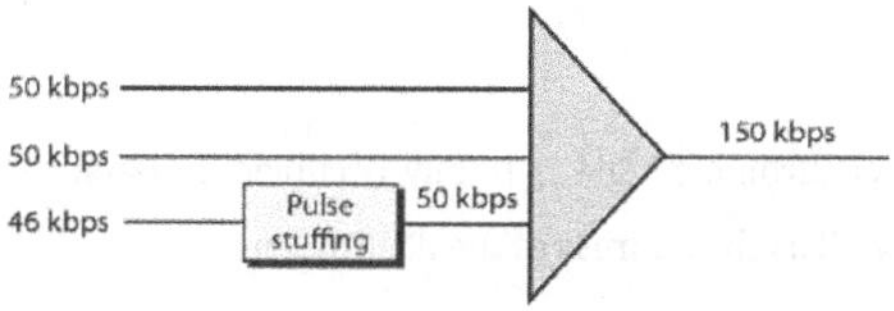

Frame Synchronizing

If the multiplexer and the demultiplexer are not synchronized, a bit belonging to one channel may be received by the wrong channel.

For this reason, one or more synchronization bits are usually added to the beginning of each frame. These bits, called framing bits, follow a pattern, frame to frame, that allows the demultiplexer to synchronize with the incoming stream so that it can separate the time slots accurately.

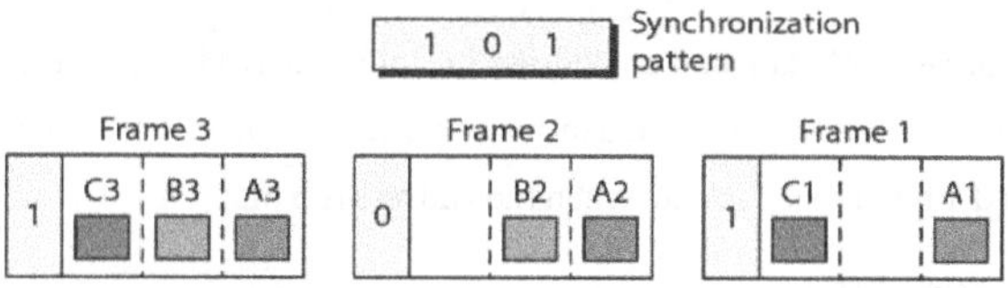

Statistical Time-Division Multiplexing

In synchronous TDM, each input has a reserved slot in the output frame which is inefficient if some input lines have no data to send. In statistical time-division multiplexing, slots are dynamically allocated to improve bandwidth efficiency. The multiplexer checks each input line in round robin fashion; it allocates a slot for an input line if the line has data to send; otherwise, it skips the line and checks the next line. In statistical multiplexing, the number of slots in each frame is less than the number of input lines.

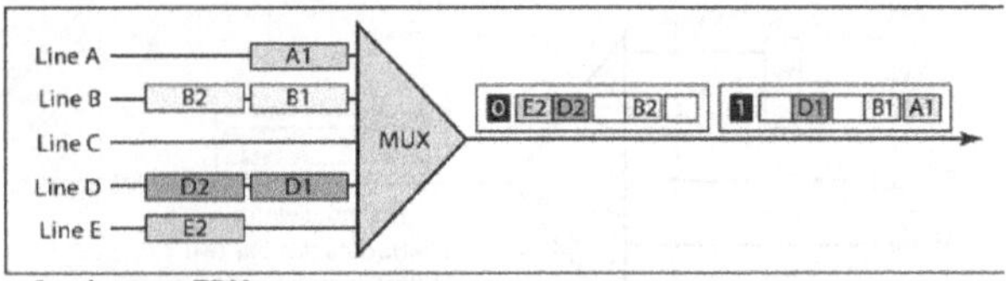

a. Synchronous TDM

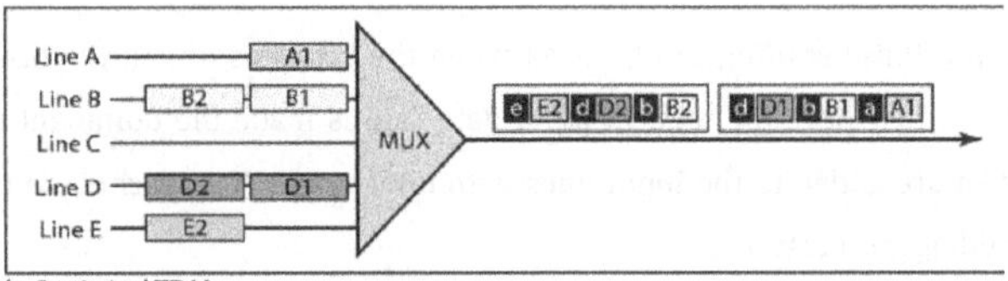

b. Statistical TDM

Addressing

An output slot in synchronous TDM is totally occupied by data; in statistical TDM, a slot needs to carry data as well as the address of the destination.

In synchronous TDM, there is no need for addressing; synchronization and preassigned relationships between the inputs and outputs serve as an address. In statistical multiplexing, there is no fixed relationship between the inputs and outputs because there are no pre-assigned or reserved slots. We need to include the address of the receiver inside each slot to show where it is to be delivered.

'n' bits are used for addressing N different output lines where n =log2 N. For example, for eight different output lines, we need a 3-bit address.

Slot Size

Since a slot carries both data and an address in statistical TDM, the ratio of the data size to address size must be reasonable to make transmission efficient. For example, it would be inefficient to send 1 bit per slot as data when the address is 3 bits.

No Synchronization Bit

The frames in statistical TDM need not be synchronized, so no need for synchronization bits.

Bandwidth

The designers of statistical TDM define the capacity of the link based on the statistics of the load for each channel. If on average only *x* percent of the input slots are filled, the capacity of the link reflects this.

Compare and Contrast Synchronous and Statistical TDM

Synchronous TDM	Statistical TDM
In synchronous TDM, each input has a reserved slot in the output frame which is inefficient if some input lines have no data to send. So empty slots can be there.	In statistical time-division multiplexing, slots are dynamically allocated only to the lines having data to send thus no empty slots.
Due to empty slots bandwidth efficiency is less	Improves bandwidth efficiency.
An output slot in synchronous TDM carries only data; no need for address bits	In statistical TDM addressing is required; a slot needs to carry data as well as the address of the destination.
Need for synchronization bits	No need for synchronization bits
The number of slots in each frame is equal to the number of input lines.	The number of slots in each frame may be lesser than the number of input lines.

2. Spread Spectrum

1) Privacy and anti-jamming can be achieved by spreading.
2) Spread spectrum techniques add redundancy; they spread the original spectrum needed for each station. If the required bandwidth for each station is B, spread spectrum expands it to Bss' such that Bss » B.
3) The expanded bandwidth allows the source to wrap its message in a protective envelope for a more secure transmission.

Spread Spectrum has Two Principles

1) The bandwidth allocated to each station needs to be larger than what is needed. This allows redundancy.
2) The expanding of the original bandwidth *B* to the bandwidth Bss must be done by a process that is independent of the original signal.

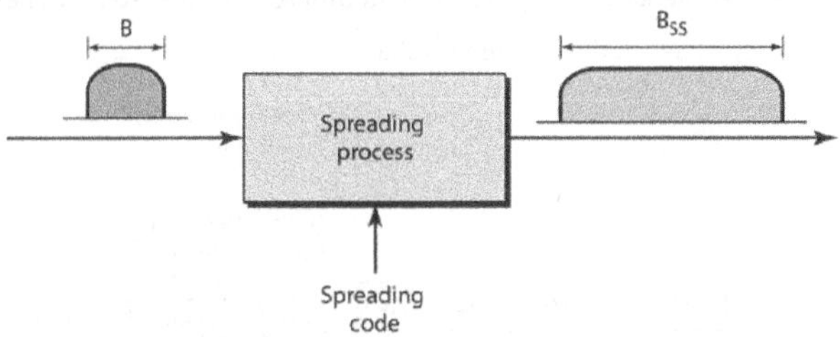

After the signal is created by the source, the spreading process uses a spreading code and spreads the bandwidth. The figure shows the original bandwidth *B* and the spreaded bandwidth *Bss.* The spreading code is a series of numbers that look random, but are actually a pattern. There are two techniques to spread the bandwidth: *frequency hopping spread spectrum (FHSS) and direct sequence spread spectrum (DSSS).*

Frequency Hopping Spread Spectrum (FHSS)

The frequency hopping spread spectrum (FHSS) technique uses *M* different carrier frequencies that are modulated by the source signal.

At one moment, the signal modulates one carrier frequency; at the next moment, the signal modulates another carrier frequency. Although the modulation is done using one carrier frequency at a time, *M* frequencies are used totally. The bandwidth occupied by a source after spreading is *BpHSS »B.*

Figure shows the general layout for FHSS. A pseudorandom code generator, called pseudorandom noise (PN), creates a k-bit pattern for every hopping period T_h.

The frequency table uses the pattern to find the frequency to be used for this hopping period and passes it to the frequency synthesizer. The frequency synthesizer creates a carrier signal of that frequency, and the source signal modulates the carrier signal.

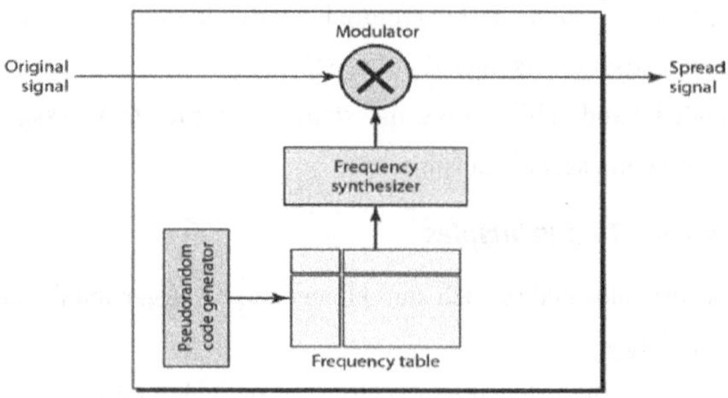

Suppose we have decided to have eight hopping frequencies. In this case, *M is* 8 and *k* is 3. The pseudorandom code generator will create eight different 3-bit patterns. These are mapped to eight different frequencies in the frequency table.

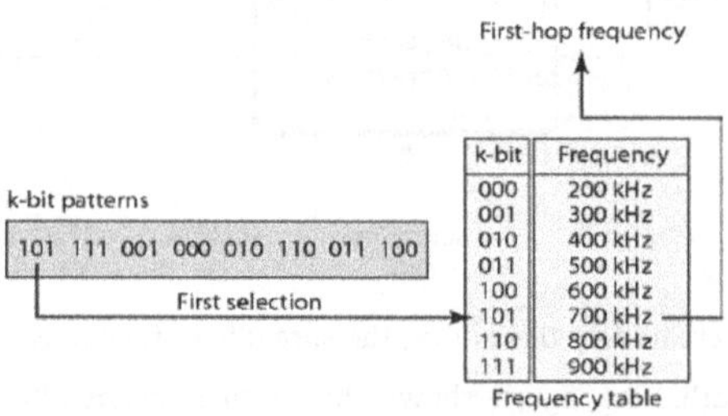

The pattern for this station is 101, 111, 001, 000, 010, all, 100. This means that at hopping period 1, the pattern is 101. The frequency selected is 700 kHz; the source signal modulates this carrier frequency. After eight hoppings, the pattern repeats, starting from 101 again.

If there are many k-bit patterns and the hopping period is short, a sender and receiver can have privacy. If an intruder tries to intercept the transmitted signal, she can only access a small piece of data because she does not know the spreading sequence to quickly adapt herself to the next hop.

The scheme has also an antijamming effect. A malicious sender may be able to send noise to jam the signal for one hopping period (randomly), but not for the whole period.

Bandwidth Sharing

If the number of hopping frequencies is *M*, we can multiplex *M* channels into one by using the same Bss bandwidth. This is possible because a station uses just one frequency in each hopping period; *M* - 1 other frequencies can be used by other *M* - 1 stations.

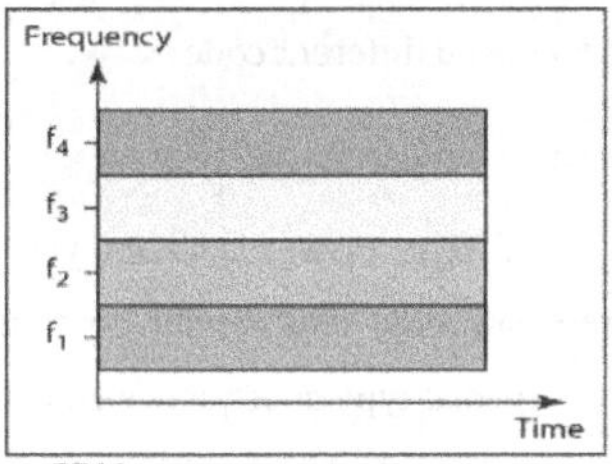

a. FDM

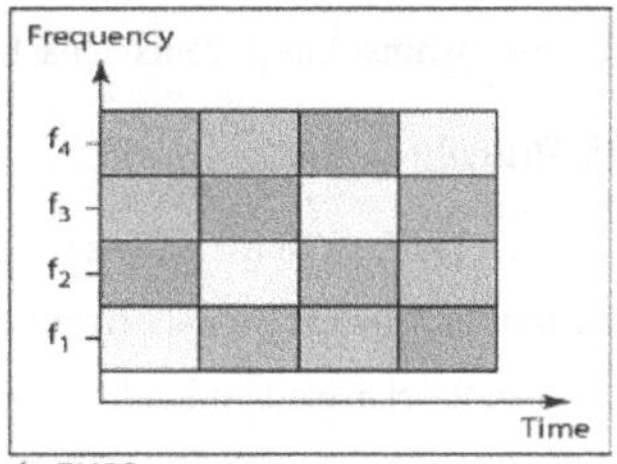

b. FHSS

Direct Sequence Spread Spectrum

The direct sequence spread spectrum (DSSS) technique also expands the bandwidth of the original signal, but the process is different.

In DSSS, each data bits is replaced with 11 bits using a spreading code. In other words, each bit is assigned a code of 11 bits, called chips, where the chip rate is 11 times that of the data bit.

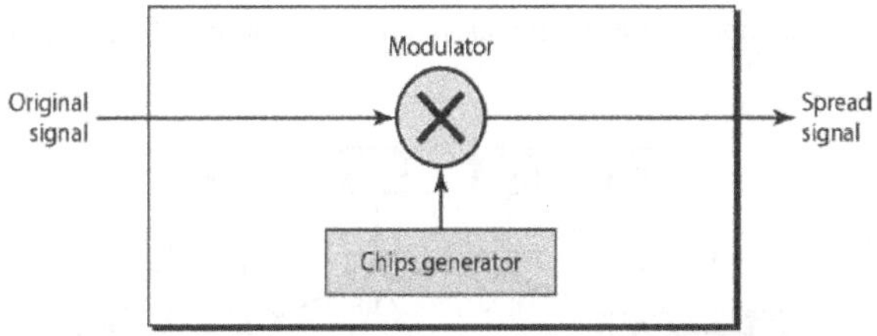

In Figure the spreading code is 11 chips having the pattern 10110111000 (in this case). If the original signal rate is *N*, the rate of the spread signal is l1N. This means that the required bandwidth for the spread signal is 11 times larger than the bandwidth of the original signal.

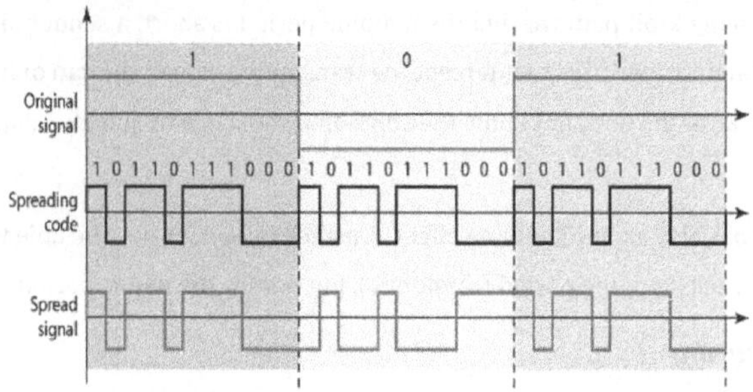

In the given example bits in original signal are multiplied with spreading code and the resultant signal is sent.

The spread signal can provide privacy if the intruder does not know the code. It can also provide immunity against interference if each station uses a different code.

Bandwidth Sharing

Can we share a bandwidth in DSSS as we did in FHSS? The answer is no and yes. If we use a spreading code that spreads signals (from different stations) that cannot be combined and separated, we cannot share a bandwidth. If we use a special type of sequence code that allows the combining and separating of spread signals, we can share the bandwidth.

3. Switching

A switched network consists of a series of interlinked nodes, called switches.

Switches are devices capable of creating temporary connections between two or more devices linked to the switch.

In a switched network, some of these nodes are connected to the end systems (computers or telephones, for example). Others are used only for routing. Figure shows a switched network.

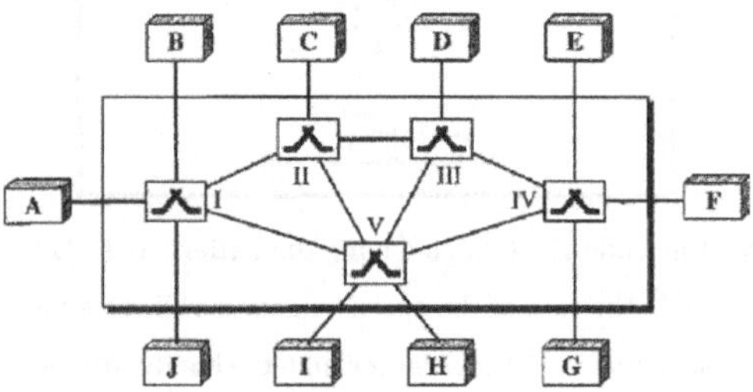

Three methods of switching have been important: **Circuit switching, Packet switching, and Message switching.**

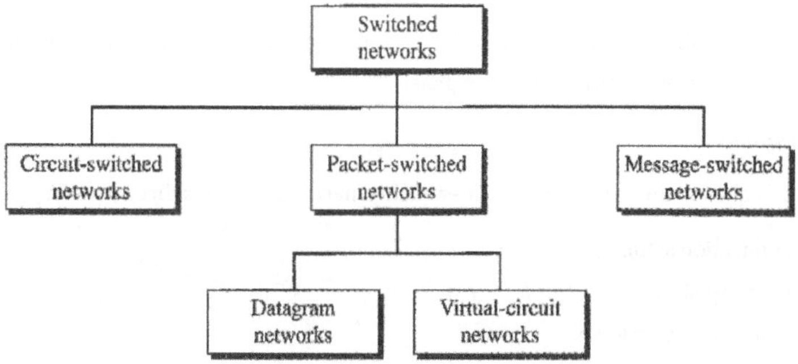

4. Circuit Switching

A circuit-switched network is made of a set of switches connected by physical links, in which each link is divided into *n* channels. Each connection uses only one dedicated channel on each link.

EX: Each link is divided into *n (n* is 3 in the figure) channels by using FDM or TDM.

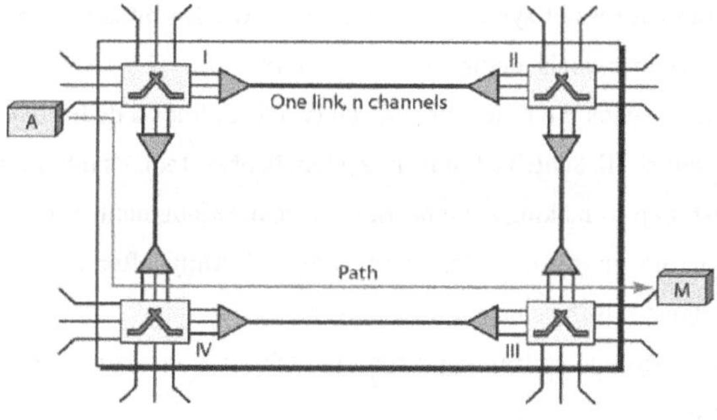

We Need to Emphasize Several Points here

1) Circuit switching takes place at the physical layer.
2) Data transferred between the two stations are not packetized (physical layer transfer of the signal). The data are a continuous flow sent by the source station and received by the destination station, although there may be periods of silence.
3) Before starting communication, the stations must make a reservation for the resources to be used during the communication. These resources, such as channels (bandwidth in FDM and time slots in TDM), switch buffers, switch processing time, and switch input/

output ports, must remain dedicated during the entire duration of data transfer until the teardown phase.

4) There is no addressing involved during data transfer. The switches route the data based on their occupied band (FDM) or time slot (TDM). Of course, there is end-to end addressing used during the setup phase.

Three Phases

The actual communication in a circuit-switched network requires three phases:

1) Connection setup.
2) Data transfer.
3) Connection teardown.

Setup Phase

1) Before the two parties (or multiple parties in a conference call) can communicate, a dedicated circuit (combination of channels in links) needs to be established.
2) The end systems are normally connected through dedicated lines to the switches, so connection setup means creating dedicated channels between all the switches. For example, when system A needs to connect to system M, it sends a setup request that includes the address of system M, to switch I. Switch I finds a channel between itself and switch IV that can be dedicated for this purpose.
3) Switch I then sends the request to switch IV, which finds a dedicated channel between itself and switch III. Switch III informs system M of system A's intention at this time.
4) In the next step to making a connection, an acknowledgment from system M needs to be sent in the opposite direction to system A. Only after system A receives this acknowledgment is the connection established.
5) Note that end-to-end addressing is required for creating a connection between the two end systems.

Data Transfer Phase

After the establishment of the dedicated circuit (channels), the two parties can transfer data. Data transferred between the two stations are not packetized. No need for addressing during data transfer since the circuit is already established.

Teardown Phase

When one of the parties needs to disconnect, a signal is sent to each switch to release the resources.

Circuit Switching Properties

1) Inefficiency
   - Channel capacity is dedicated for the whole duration of a connection.
   - If no data, capacity is wasted.
2) Delay
   - Long initial delay: circuit establishment takes time.
   - Low data delay: after the circuit establishment, information is transmitted at a fixed data rate with no delay other than the propagation delay. The delay at each node is negligible.

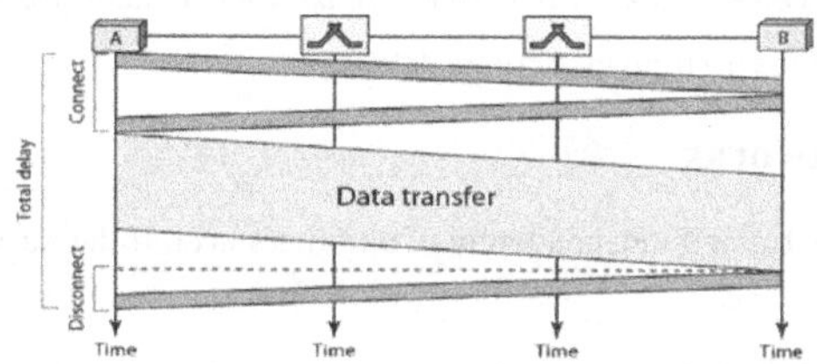

3) Developed for voice traffic (public telephone network) but can also applied to data traffic.
   - For voice connections, the resulting circuit will enjoy a high percentage of utilization because most of the time one party or the other is talking.
4) Data rate is fixed
   - Both ends must operate at the same rate during the entire period of connection

Ex: Public Circuit Switched Network

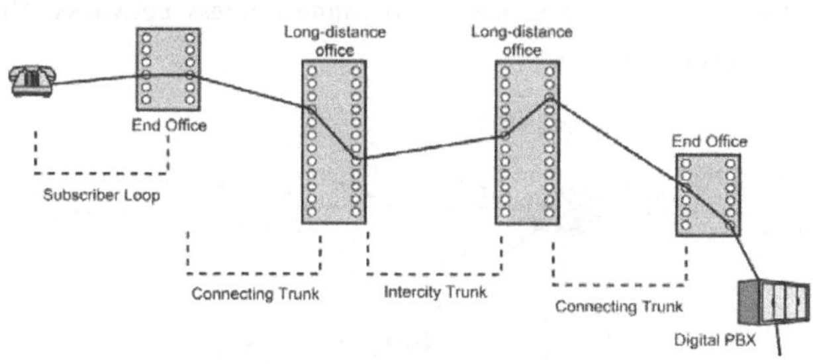

A good example of a circuit-switched network is the early telephone systems in which the path was established between a caller and a callee when the telephone number of the callee was dialed by the caller. When the callee responded to the call, the circuit was established. The voice message could now flow between the two parties, in both directions, while all of the connecting devices maintained the circuit. When the caller or callee hung up, the circuit was disconnected.

Packet Switched Network

The message going to pass through a packet-switched network it needs to be divided into packets of fixed or variable size. The size of the packet is determined by the network and the governing protocol.

In a packet-switched network, there is no resource reservation; resources are allocated on demand. The allocation is done first come, first served.

When a switch receives packets, the packet must wait if there are other packets being processed, this lack of reservation may create delay

5. Datagram Networks

1) Each packet is treated independently of all others even if the packets are parts of the same message.
2) All packets (or datagrams) belong to the same message may travel different paths to reach their destination. This is so because the links may be involved in carrying packets from other sources
3) Packets in this approach are referred to as datagrams. Datagram Switching is done at the network layer.
4) This approach can cause the datagrams of a transmission to arrive at their destination out of order with different delays between the packets.
5) Packets may also be lost or dropped because of a lack of resources.
6) The datagram networks are referred **to connectionless networks. There are no setup or teardown phases.**

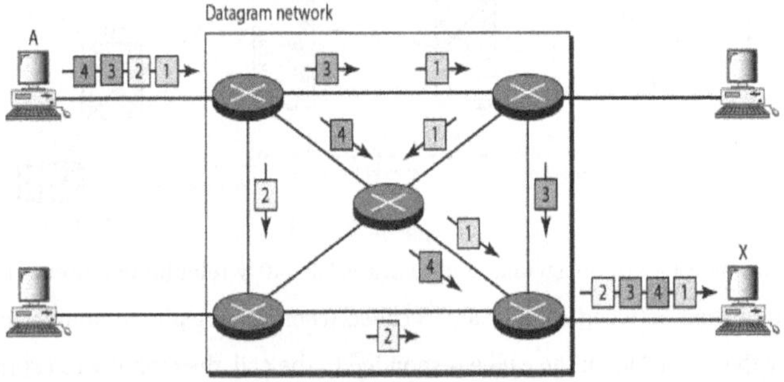

As shown in the above example packets 1,2,3,4 originating from A takes different routes and reach the destination. Each switch routes the packets by consulting a routing table.

Destination address	Output port
1232	1
4150	2
⋮	⋮
9130	3

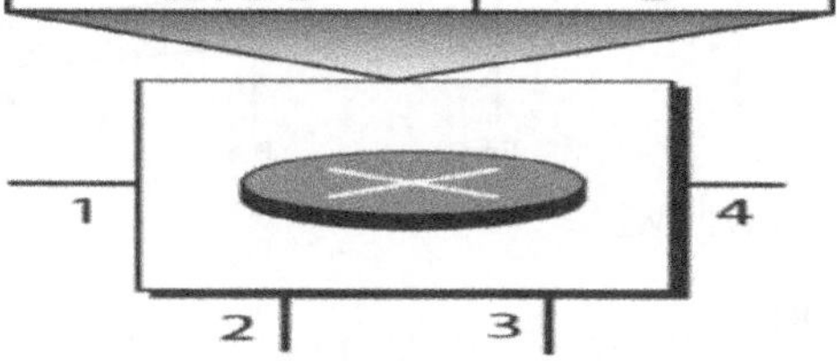

Each packet switch has a routing table which is based on the destination address.

1) The routing tables are dynamic and are updated periodically.
2) The destination addresses and the corresponding forwarding output ports are recorded in the tables.
3) This is different from the table of a circuit switched network in which each entry is created when the setup phase is completed and deleted when the teardown phase is over.

Addressing in Datagram

1) Every packet in a datagram network carries a header that contains the destination address of the packet.
2) When the switch receives the packet, this destination address is examined; the routing table is consulted to find the corresponding port through which the packet should be forwarded.
3) This address remains the same during the entire journey of the packet.

Efficiency

The efficiency of a datagram network is better than that of a circuit-switched network; resources are allocated only when there are packets to be transferred.

If a source sends a packet and there is a delay of a few minutes before another packet can be sent, the resources can be reallocated during these minutes for other packets from other sources.

Delay in a Datagram Network

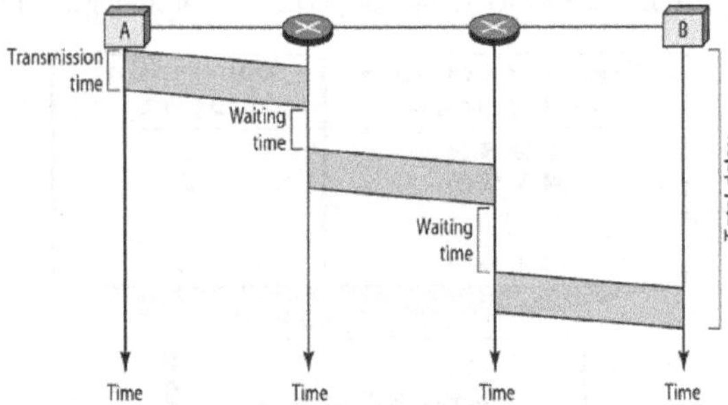

Total delay =3T + 3t + W1 + W2

T: transmission times

t: propagation delays

(W1 + w2) : waiting times ignore the processing time in each switch

6. Virtual-Circuit Switching

A virtual-circuit network is a combination of circuit-switched network and a datagram network. It has some characteristics of both. A source and destination need to go through three phases: setup, data transfer, and teardown.

1) In the setup phase, the source and destination use their global addresses to help switches make table entries for the connection.
2) Resources can be allocated during the setup phase, as in a circuit-switched network, or on demand, as in a datagram network.
3) Data are packetized and each packet carries an address in the header. However, the address in the header has local jurisdiction (it defines what should be the next switch and the channel on which the packet is being carried), not end-to-end jurisdiction. The reader may ask how the intermediate switches know where to send the packet if there is no final destination address carried by a packet.
4) All packets follow the same path established during the connection set up.
5) A virtual-circuit network is normally implemented in the data link layer while a circuit-switched network is implemented in the physical layer and a datagram network in the network layer.
6) In the teardown phase, the source and destination inform the switches to delete the corresponding entry.

Virtual-Circuit Network Addressing

In a virtual-circuit network, two types of addressing are involved: global and local (virtual-circuit identifier).

1) **Global Addressing** : A global address in virtual-circuit networks is used only to create a virtual-circuit identifier
2) Local Address (Virtual-circuit identifier).
    a) The identifier that is actually used for data transfer is VCI.
    b) A VCI, unlike a global address, is a small number used by a frame between two switches.
    c) When a frame arrives at a switch, it has a VCI; when it leaves, it has a different VCl.

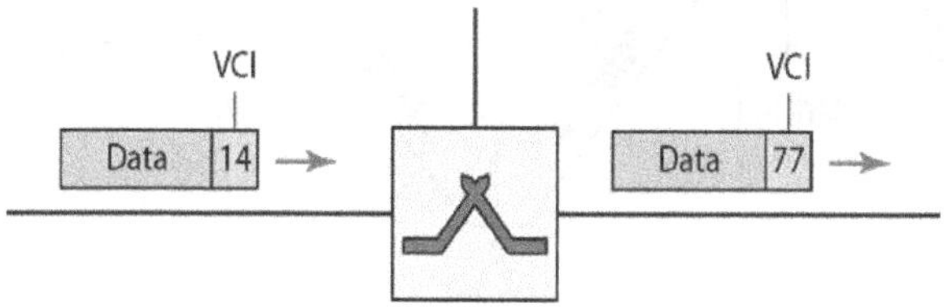

Three Phases

Three phases in a virtual-circuit network: setup, data transfer, and teardown.

Setup Phase

In the setup phase, a switch creates an entry for a virtual circuit. Two steps are required:

1) The setup request.
2) The acknowledgment.

Setup Request: A setup request frame containing global source and destination address is sent from the source to the destination.

a) Source A sends a setup frame to switch 1.
b) Switch 1 receives the setup request frame. It knows that a frame going from A to B goes out through port 3. The switch creates an entry in its routing table for this virtual circuit and assigns the incoming port (1) and chooses an available incoming VCI (14) and the outgoing port (3). It does not yet know the outgoing VCI, which will be found during the acknowledgment step. The switch then forwards the frame through port 3 to switch 2.
c) Switch 2 receives the setup request frame. Three columns of the table are completed: incoming port (l), incoming VCI (66), and outgoing port (2).

d) Switch 3 receives the setup request frame. Again, three columns are completed: incoming port (2), incoming VCI (22), and outgoing port (3).

e) Destination B receives the setup frame, and if it is ready to receive frames from A, it assigns a VCI to the incoming frames that come from A, in this case 77. This VCI lets the destination know that the frames come from A, and not other sources.

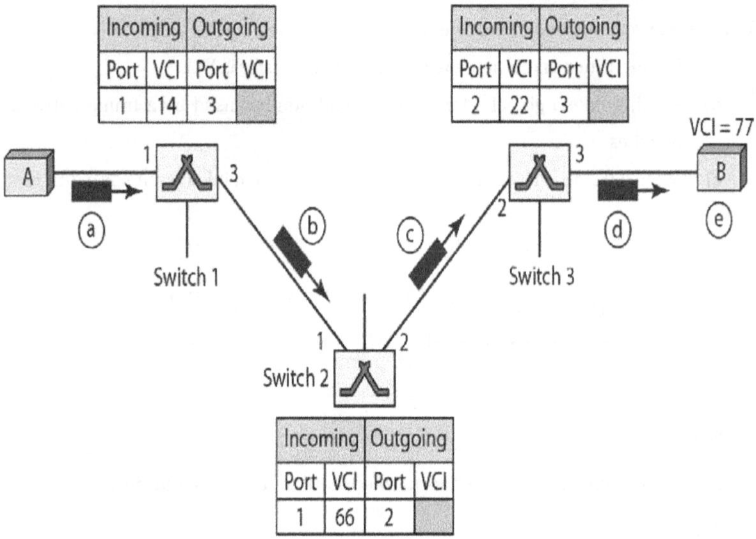

Acknowledgment: A special frame, called the acknowledgment frame containing global source and destination addresses, completes the entries in the switching tables.

1) The destination sends an acknowledgment to switch 3. The frame also carries VCI 77, chosen by the destination as the incoming VCI for frames from A. Switch 3 uses VCI 77 to complete the outgoing VCI column for this entry. Note that 77 is the incoming VCI for destination B, but the outgoing VCI for switch 3.
2) Switch 3 sends an acknowledgment to switch 2 that contains its incoming VCI(22). Switch 2 uses this as the outgoing VCI in the table.
3) Switch 2 sends an acknowledgment to switch 1 that contains its incoming VCI(66) in the table. Switch 1 uses 66 as the outgoing VCI in the table.
4) Finally switch 1 sends an acknowledgment to source A that contains its incoming VCI(14) in the table.
5) The source uses 14 as the outgoing VCI for the data frames to be sent to destination B.

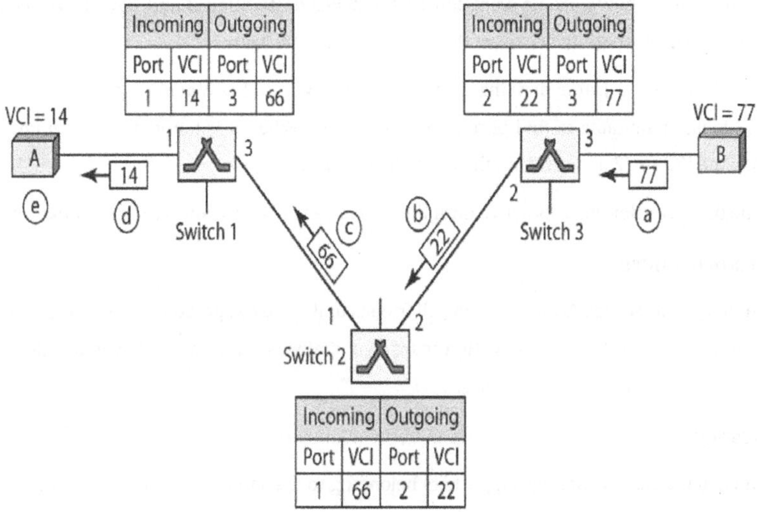

Data Transfer Phase

All switches need to have a table entry for this virtual circuit. The table, has four columns for each virtual circuit that is already set up.

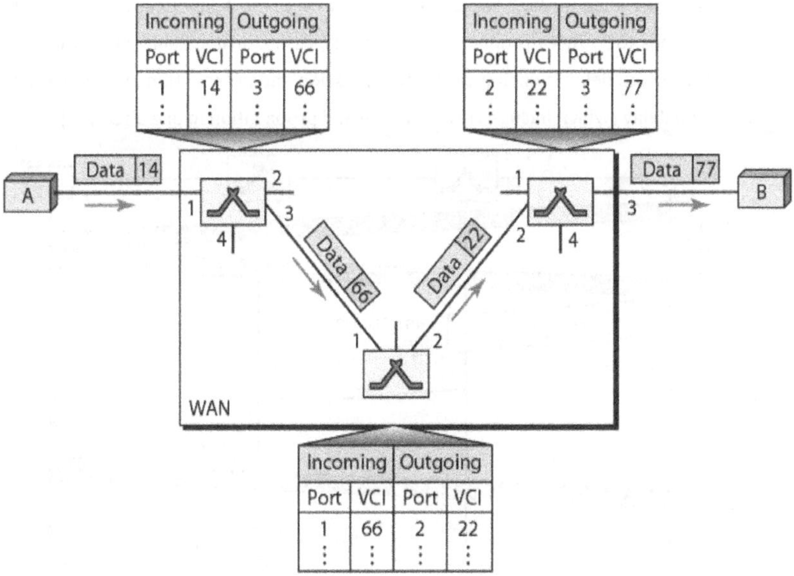

Figure shows how a frame from source A reaches destination B and how its VCI changes during the trip. Each switch changes the VCI and routes the frame.

For Example: a frame arriving at port 1 with a VCI of 14. When the frame arrives, the switch looks in its table to find port 1 and a VCI of 14. When it is found, the switch knows to change the VCI to 22 and send out the frame from port 3.

The data transfer phase is active until the source sends all its frames to the destination.

Teardown Phase

In this phase, source A, after sending all frames to B, sends a special frame called a *teardown request.* Destination B responds with a teardown confirmation frame. All switches delete the corresponding entry from their tables.

Efficiency

In virtual-circuit switching, all packets belonging to the same source and destination travel the same path; but the packets may arrive at the destination with different delays if resource allocation is on demand.

Delay in Virtual-Circuit Networks

The packet is traveling through two switches as shown in the below figure. There are three transmission times *(3T),* three propagation times (3t), data transfer depicted by the sloping lines, includes a setup delay (which includes transmission and propagation in two directions), and a teardown delay (which includes transmission and propagation in one direction).

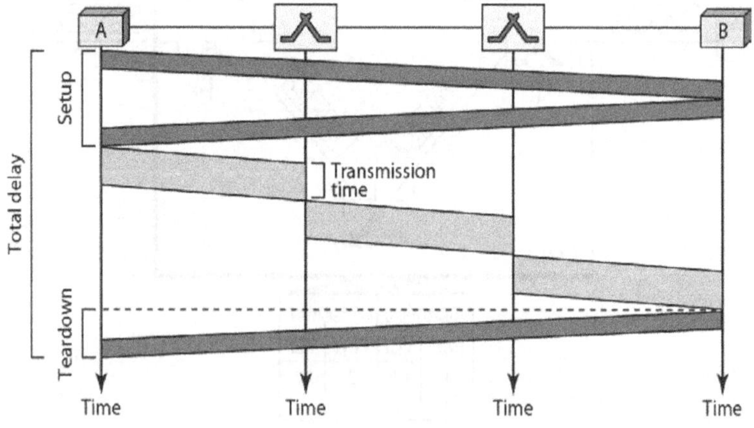

Total delay = 3T+ 3t +setup delay + teardown delay

Differentiate Circuit Switching and Packet Switching (8 marks)(Provide Diagram Wherever u can)

Circuit switching	Packet switching	
	Datagram switching	Virtual Circuit Switching
1. **Packetization (give circuit switching diagram)** In circuit switching data will flow like a stream without being divided into packets from sender to receiver	In packet switching the data will be divided into packets and provided with IDs.(give diagram)	In packet switching the data will be divided into packets and provided with IDs.
2. **Type of transmission :** Circuit switching is connection oriented.A circuit(connection) is established by reserving resources in all the switches on the way from the sender to the receiver before the actual transmission takes place.	Connection less transmission. No resource reservation. Resources are allocated on demand.	Connection oriented. Resources are reserved.
3. **Transmission Process** In circuit switching the communication process involves 3 phases: setup phase, data transfer phase and tear down phase	Only data transfer phase is there since it is connectionless.	Like circuit switching the communication involves 3 phases :setup phase, data transfer ansd tear down phase
4. **Addressing** No address is **required** because it is connection oriented The created circuit will uniquely identify the sender and the receiver.	Destination address is included in the header of the packet. A switch uses a routing table that is based on destination address.	Two types of addressing is used : Global ID and local vitual circuit id. The global Id will uniquely identify the receiver. The Local virtual circuit ID(VCI) will be used between only the switches to uniquely identify the transmission between the sender and receiver.
5. **Efficiency** Circuit switching is less efficient because the resources allocated during the entire connection even when there is no data transfer. Ex: telephone communication(voice transmission). Not suitable for data transmission	More efficient than circuit switching because the resource allocation will be done only when data transfer takes place.	More efficient than circuit switching. Resource allocation happens in setup phase but used only when there is a data to transfer.
6. **Delay :** In circuit switching the delay associated with the data transfer is less. The total delay is due to the time needed for creating connection, data transfer and termination the connection	Each datagram may experience a delay at switch before it is forwarded	The total delay is due to the time needed for creating connection, data transfer and termination the connection
7. **Data Rate** Circuit switching requires that all the links from source to destination needs to have same data rate.	In packet switching it is not required that all the links from source to destination needs to have same data rate.	Data rate may change form one network to another.
8. **Application** Switching at the physical layer in the **traditional telephone network** uses circuit switching approach	Switching in the **internet** is done by datagram approach at the network layer	Switching at the data link layer in a **switched WAN** is normally implemented by using virtual circuit approach.

Differentiate Frequency Division Multiplexing(FDM) from Time Division Multiplexing(TDM) (4 marks)

Frequency Division multiplexing(FDM)	Time Division Multiplexing(TDM)
The transmission path is divided into *n* no. of channels based on frequencies. Each channel carries one transmission of signals of frequencies of the corresponding channel. i.e portion of **bandwidth is shared** 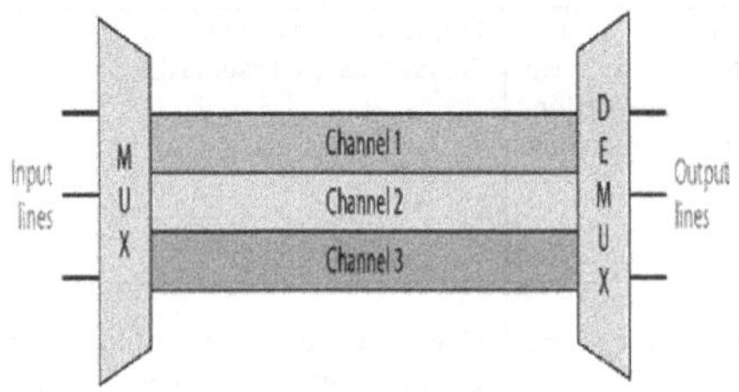 	The transmission path is shared among users based on time i.e the link is time-shared 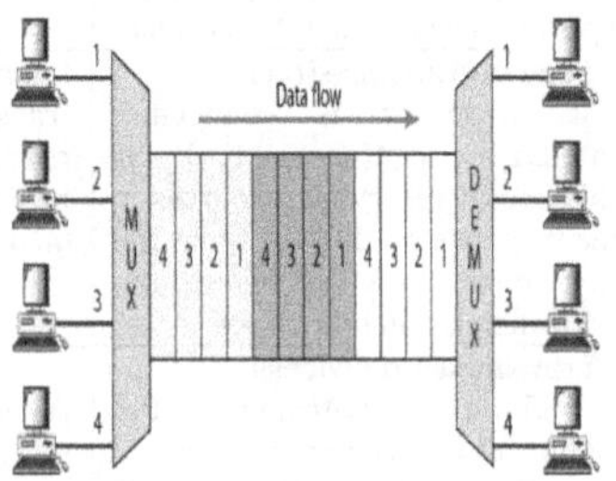
It is an analog multiplexing technique combining analog signals from different sources	TDM is a digital multiplexing technique.
The sender and receiver must be tuned to the same frequency for proper transmission and reception.	**Synchronous TDM:** The receiver must be synchronized in time with the sender for proper reception. Otherwise he will have to receive data sent for others. **Statistical TDM:** The receiver will recognize his address in the frame and receive the data.
Signals generated by each sending device modulate different carrier frequencies (same as their channel frequency). These modulates signals are then combined into a single composite signal that is transported over a single physical link	**Synchronous TDM**: A round of data units from each input connections is collected into a frame. **Statistical TDM:** The multiplexer checks each input line in round robin fashion; It allocates a slot if the line has data to send otherwise skips the line and checks the next line.

Solved Problems-TDM

Time Slots and Frames

In synchronous TDM, the data flow of each input connection is divided into units, where each input occupies one input time slot. A unit can be 1 bit, one character, or one block of data. Each input unit becomes one output unit and occupies one output time slot.

However, the duration of an output time slot is n times shorter than the duration of an input time slot. If an input time slot is T s, the output time slot is *Tin* s, where n is the number of connections. In other words, a unit in the output connection has a shorter duration; it travels faster.

Example

The data rate for 3 input connection is 1 kbps. If 1 bit at a time is multiplexed (a unit is 1 bit), what is the duration of (a) each input slot, (b) each output slot, and (c) each frame?

Solution

We can answer the questions as follows:

1. The data rate of each input connection is 1 kbps. This means that the bit duration is 1/1000 s or 1 ms. The duration of the input time slot is 1 ms (same as bit duration).
2. The duration of each output time slot is one-third of the input time slot. This means that the duration of the output time slot is 1/3 ms.
3. Each frame carries three output time slots. So the duration of a frame is 3 x 113 ms, or 1 ms.

The duration of a frame is the same as the duration of an input unit.

Example

A synchronous TDM with 4 data stream with 1Mbps data rate for each connection. The unit of data is 1 bit.

Find (a) the input bit duration, (b) the output bit duration, (c) the output bit rate, and (d) the output frame rate.

We can Answer the Questions as Follows

1) The input bit duration is the inverse of the bit rate: 1/1 Mbps = 1 μs.
2) The output bit duration is one-fourth of the input bit duration, or 1/4μs.
3) The output bit rate is the inverse of the output bit duration or 1/4 μs, or 4 Mbps. This can also be deduced from the fact that the output rate is 4 times as fast as any input rate; so the output rate =4 x 1 Mbps =4 Mbps.
4) The frame rate is always the same as any input rate. So the frame rate is 1,000,000 frames per second. Because we are sending 4 bits in each frame, we can verify the result of the previous question by multiplying the frame rate by the number of bits per frame.

Example

Four l-kbps connections are multiplexed together. A unit is 1 bit. Find (a) the duration of 1 bit before multiplexing, (b) the transmission rate of the link, (c) the duration of a time slot, and (d) the duration of a frame.

Solution

We Can Answer the Questions as Follows

1) The duration of 1 bit before multiplexing is 1/1 kbps, or 0.001 s (l ms).
2) The rate of the link is 4 times the rate of a connection, or 4 kbps.
3) The duration of each time slot is one-fourth of the duration of each bit before multiplexing, or 1/4 ms. Note that we can also calculate this from the data rate of the link, 4 kbps. The bit duration is the inverse of the data rate, or 1/4 kbps or 250μ s.
4) The duration of a frame is always the same as the duration of a unit before multiplexing, or 1 ms. We can also calculate this in another way. Each frame in this case has fouf time slots. So the duration of a frame is 4 times 250 μs, or 1 ms.

Example

Four channels are multiplexed using TDM. If each channel sends 100 bytes/s and we multiplex 1 byte per channel, show the frame travelling on the link, the size of the frame, the duration of a frame, the frame rate, and the bit rate for the link.

Solution

The multiplexer is shown in Figure.

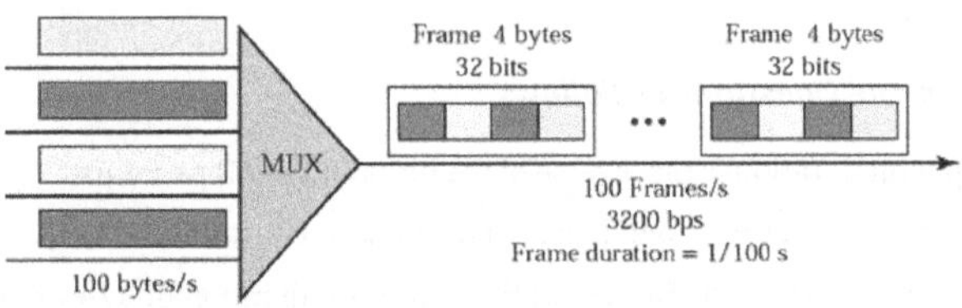

Each frame carries 1 byte from each channel; the size of each frame, therefore, is 4 bytes, or 32 bits. Because each channel is sending 100 bytes/s and a frame carries 1 byte from each channel, the frame rate must be 100 frames per second.

The duration of a frame is therefore 11100 s. The link is carrying 100 frames per second, and since each frame contains 32 bits, the bit rate is 100 x 32, or 3200 bps. This is actually 4 times the bit rate of each channel, which is 100 x 8 =800 bps.

Example

A multiplexer combines four 100-Kbps channels using a time slot of 2 bits. Show the output with four arbitrary inputs. What is the frame rate, the frame duration, bit rate &the bit duration?

Solution

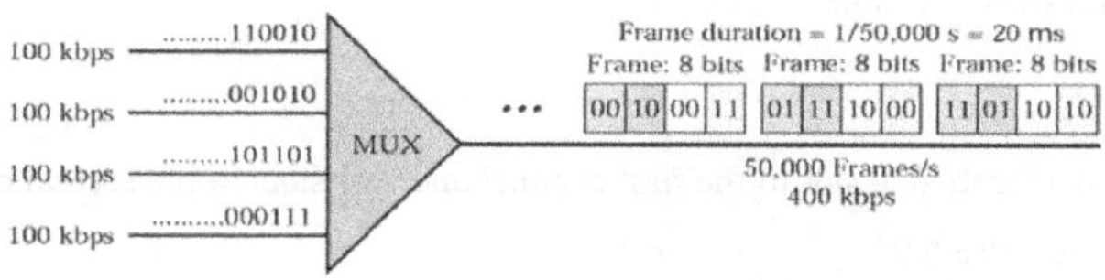

The link carries 50,000 frames per second since each frame contains 2 bits per channel. The frame duration is therefore 1/50,000 s or 20 μs.

The frame rate is 50,000 frames per second, and each frame carries 8 bits; the bit rate is 50,000 x 8 =400,000 bits or 400 kbps. The bit duration is 1/400,000 s, or 2.5 μs. Note that the frame duration is 8 times the bit duration because each frame is carrying 8 bits.

Example

We have four sources, each creating 250 characters per second. If the interleaved unit is a character and one synchronizing bit is added to each frame, find (1) the data rate of each source, (2) the duration of each character in each source, (3) the frame rate, (4) the duration of each frame, (5) the number of bits in each frame, and (6) the data rate of the link.

Solution

1) The data rate of each source is 250 x 8 = 2000 bps = 2 kbps.
2) Each source sends 250 characters per second; therefore, the duration of a character is 1/250 s, or4 ms.
3) Each frame has one character from each source, which means the link needs to send 250 frames per second to keep the transmission rate of each source.
4) The duration of each frame is 1/250 s, or 4 ms. Note that the duration of each frame is the same as the duration of each character coming from each source.
5) Each frame carries 4 characters and I extra synchronizing bit. This means that each frame is 4 x 8 + 1 =33 bits.
6) The link sends 250 frames per second, and each frame contains 33 bits. This means that the data rate of the link is 250 x 33, or 8250 bps. Note that the bit rate of the link is greater than the combined bit rates of the four channels. If we add the bit rates of four

channels, we get 8000 bps. Because 250 frames are traveling per second and each contains 1 extra bit for synchronizing, we need to add 250 to the sum to get 8250 bps.

Example

Two channels, one with a bit rate of 100 kbps and another with a bit rate of 200 kbps, are to be multiplexed. How this can be achieved? What is the frame rate? What is the frame duration? What is the bit rate of the link?

Solution

1) We can allocate one slot to the first channel and two slots to the second channel. Each frame carries 3 bits.
2) The frame rate is 100,000 frames per second because it carries 1 bit from the first channel.
3) The frame duration is 1/100,000 s, or 10 ms.
4) The bit rate is 100,000 frames/s x 3 bits per frame, or 300 kbps.

Note that because each frame carries 1 bit from the first channel, the bit rate for the first channel is preserved. The bit rate for the second channel is also preserved because each frame carries 2 bits from the second channel.

UNIT-4

Data Link Layer-1: Error Detection & Correction: Introduction, Block coding, Linear block codes, Cyclic codes, Checksum.

1) Error Detection & Correction: Introduction

Data can be corrupted during transmission. Some applications require that errors be detected and corrected.

Types of Errors

Whenever bits flow from one point to another, they are subject to unpredictable changes because of interference. This interference can change the shape of the signal. There are two types of errors:

1) Single bit error.
2) Burst Error.

1) Single-Bit Error

The term single-bit error means that only 1 bit of a given data unit (such as a byte, character, or packet) is changed from 1 to 0 or from 0 to 1.

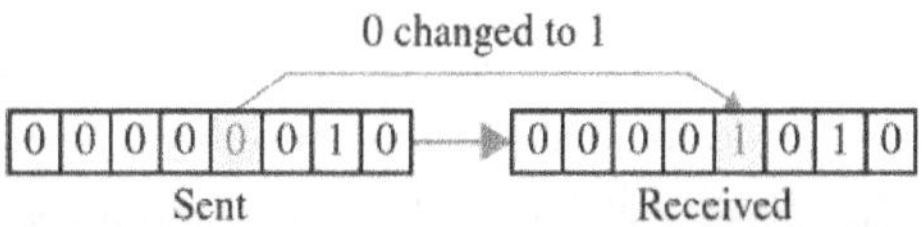

Single-bit errors are the least likely type of error in serial data transmission. Imagine data sent at 1 Mbps. This means that each bit lasts only 1/1,000,000 s, or 1 μs.

For a single-bit error to occur, the noise must have a duration of only 1 μs, which is very rare; noise normally lasts much longer than this.

2) Burst Error

A burst error means that 2 or more bits in the data unit have changed.

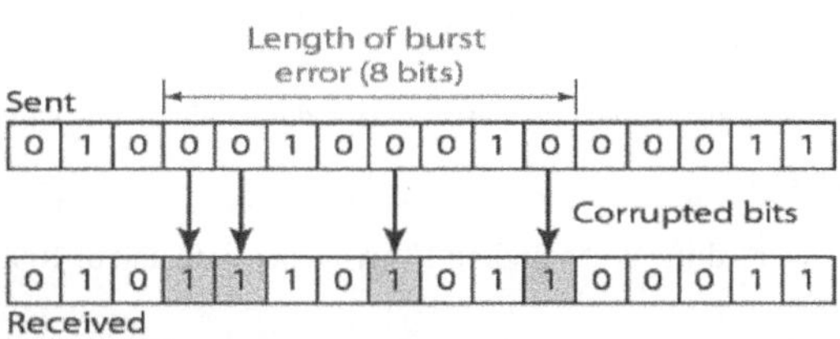

Figure shows the effect of a burst error on a data unit.

In this case, 0100010001000011 was sent, but 0101110101100011 was received.

Note that a burst error does not necessarily mean that the errors occur in consecutive bits.

The length of the burst is measured from the first corrupted bit to the last corrupted bit. Some bits in between may not have been corrupted.

A burst error is more likely to occur than a single-bit error.

The duration of noise is normally longer than the duration of 1 bit, which means that when noise affects data, it affects a set of bits. The number of bits affected depends on the data rate and duration of noise.

For example, if we are sending data at 1 kbps, a noise of 1/100 s can affect 10 bits; if we are sending data at 1 Mbps, the same noise can affect 10,000 bits.

Redundancy

The central concept in detecting or correcting errors is redundancy. To be able to detect or correct errors, we need to send some extra bits with our data. These redundant bits are added by the sender and removed by the receiver.

Detection versus Correction

The correction of errors is more difficult than the detection. In error detection, the receiver is checking to see if any error has occurred. The answer is a simple yes or no.

In error detection, the number of errors are not even interested. A single-bit error is the same for as a burst error.

Error Correction

In error correction, the receiver needs to know the exact number of bits that are corrupted and more importantly, their location in the message.

The number of the errors and the size of the message are important factors. If the receiver needs to correct one single error in an 8-bit data unit, it needs to consider eight possible error locations;

If the receiver needs to correct two errors in a data unit of the same size, it needs to consider 28 possibilities.

Imagine the receiver's difficulty in finding 10 errors in a data unit of 1000 bits.

Forward Error Correction versus Retransmission

There are two main methods of error correction. Forward error correction is the process in which the receiver tries to guess the message by using redundant bits. This is possible if the number of errors is small.

Correction by retransmission is a technique in which the receiver detects the occurrence of an error and asks the sender to resend the message. Resending is repeated until a message arrives that the receiver believes is error-free.

Coding

Coding is the Process of adding redundancy for error detection or correction.

The sender adds redundant bits through a process that creates a relationship between the redundant bits and the actual data bits. The receiver checks the relationships between the two sets of bits to detect or correct the errors.

The ratio of redundant bits to the data bits and the robustness of the process are important factors in any coding scheme. Figure shows the general idea of coding.

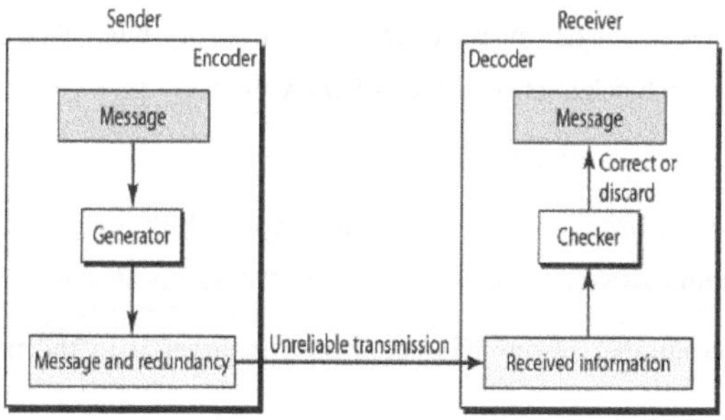

The coding schemes are divided into two broad categories: block coding and convolution coding.

1) Block Codes

1) Divides the data to be sent into a set of blocks.
2) Extra information attached to each block.
3) Memoryless .

2) Convolutional Codes

1) Treats data as a series of bits, and computes a code over a continuous series
2) The code computed for a set of bits depends on the current and previous input

Modular Arithmetic

Modulo-2 Arithmetic

In this arithmetic, the modulus *N* is 2. We can use only 0 and 1. Operations in this arithmetic are very simple. The following shows how we can add or subtract 2 bits.

Adding: 0+0=0 0+1=1 1+0=1 1+1=0

Subtracting: 0-0=0 0-1=1 1-0=1 1-1=0

In this arithmetic we use the XOR (exclusive OR) operation for both addition and subtraction. The result of an XOR operation is 0 if two bits are the same; the result is I if two bits are different. Figure 10.4 shows this operation.

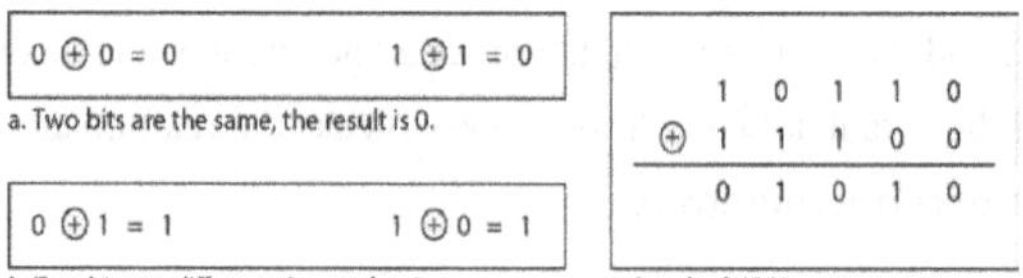

a. Two bits are the same, the result is 0.

b. Two bits are different, the result is 1.

c. Result of XORing two patterns

2) Block Coding

In block coding, we divide our message into blocks, each of *k* bits, called datawords. We add r redundant bits to each block to make the length $n = k + r$.

The resulting *n-bit* blocks are called code words.

With *k* bits, 2^k datawords can be created combination. With *n* bits, 2^n code words can be created a combination.

Since $n > k$, the number of possible codewords is larger than the number of possible datawords.

The block coding process is one-to-one; the same dataword is always encoded as the same codeword. This means that we have *2n - 2k* codewords that are not used. These codewords will be invalid or illegal.

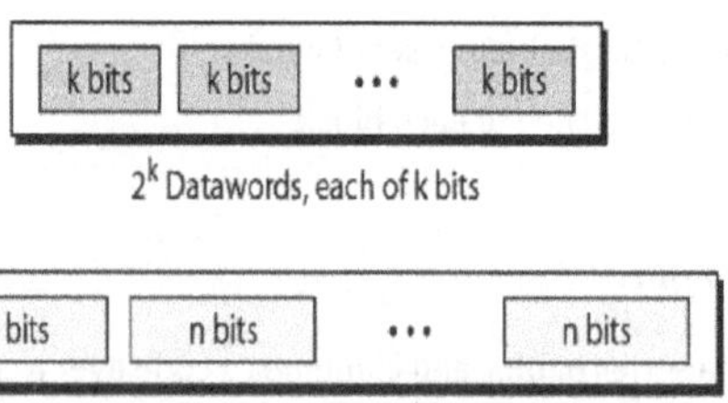

2^k Datawords, each of k bits

2^n Codewords, each of n bits (only 2^k of them are valid)

Example

The 4B/5B block coding is a good example of this type of coding. In this coding scheme, *k* =4 and *n* =5. As we saw, we have *2k* =16 datawords and *2n* =32 codewords. We saw that 16 out of 32 codewords are used for message transfer and the rest are either used for other purposes or unused.

Data	Code	Data	Code
0000	11110	1000	10010
0001	01001	1001	10011
0010	10100	1010	10110
0011	10101	1011	10111
0100	01010	1100	11010
0101	01011	1101	11011
0110	01110	1110	11100
0111	01111	1111	11101

Error Detection in Block Coding

How can errors be detected by using block coding? If the following two conditions are met, the receiver can detect a change in the original codeword.

1) The receiver has (or can find) a list of valid codewords.
2) The original codeword has changed to an invalid one.

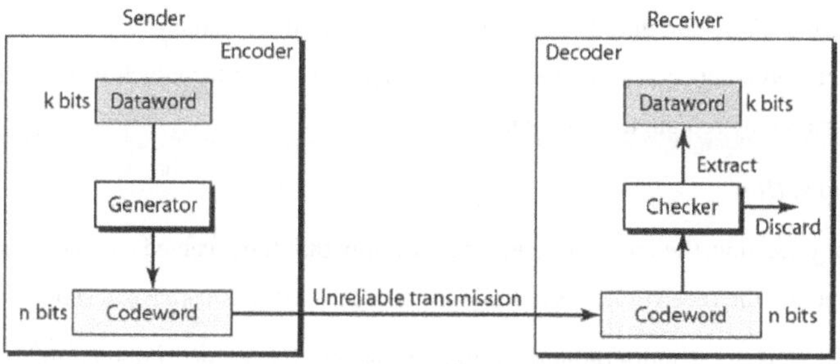

The sender creates codewords out of datawords by using a generator that applies the rules and procedures of encoding.

Each codeword sent to the receiver may change during transmission. If the received codeword is the same as one of the valid codewords, the word is accepted; the corresponding dataword is extracted for use.

If the received codeword is not valid, it is discarded. However, if the codeword is corrupted during transmission but the received word still matches a valid codeword, the error remains undetected.

Example

Let us assume that k =2 and n =3. Table shows the list of data words and code words.

Datawords	*Codewords*
00	000
01	011
10	101
11	110

Assume the sender encodes the data word 01 as 011 and sends it to the receiver. Consider the following cases:

1) The receiver receives 01l. It is a valid codeword. The receiver extracts the data word 01 from it.
2) The codeword is corrupted during transmission, and 111 is received (the leftmost bit is corrupted).

This is not a valid codeword and is discarded.

3) The codeword is corrupted during transmission, and 000 is received (the right two bits are corrupted). This is a valid codeword. The receiver incorrectly extracts the data word 00. Two corrupted bits have made the error undetectable.

An error-detecting code can detect only the types of errors for which it is designed; other types of errors may remain undetected.

Error Correction

In error detection, the receiver needs to know only that the received codeword is invalid; in error correction the receiver needs to find (or guess) the original codeword sent.

For error correction more redundant bits are needed than for error detection.

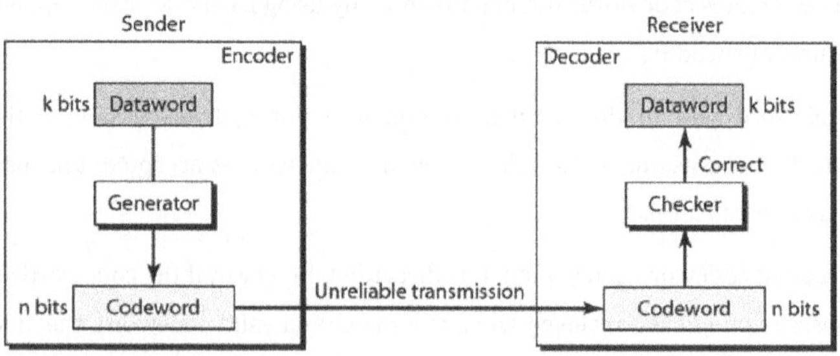

Example: Error Correction Code

Dataword	*Codeword*
00	00000
01	01011
10	10101
11	11110

Assume the dataword is 01. The sender consults the table (or uses an algorithm) to create the codeword 01011. The codeword is corrupted during transmission, and 010**0**1 is received (error in the second bit from the right). First, the receiver finds that the received codeword is not in the table.

This means an error has occurred. (Detection must come before correction.) The receiver, assuming that there is only 1 bit corrupted, uses the following strategy to guess the correct dataword.

1) Comparing the received codeword with the first codeword in the table (01001 versus 00000), the receiver decides that the first codeword is not the one that was sent because there are two different bits.
2) By the same reasoning, the original codeword cannot be the third or fourth one in the table.
3) The original codeword must be the second one in the table because this is the only one that differs from the received codeword by 1 bit. The receiver replaces 01001 with 01011 and consults the table to find the dataword 01.

Hamming Distance

The Hamming distance between two words (of the same size) is the number of differences between the corresponding bits. We show the Hamming distance between two words *x* and *y* as *d(x, y)*.

The Hamming distance can easily be found if we apply the XOR operation on the two words and count the number of 1s in the result. Let us find the Hamming distance between two pairs of words.

The Hamming distance d(000, 011) is 2 because

$$000 \oplus 011 \text{ is } 011 \text{ (two 1s)}$$

The Hamming distance d(10101, 11110) is 3 because

$$10101 \oplus 11110 \text{ is } 01011 \text{ (three 1s)}$$

Minimum Hamming Distance

The minimum Hamming distance is the smallest Hamming distance between all possible pairs in a set of words.

Find the Minimum Hamming Distance of the Coding Scheme in Table 1

A code for error detection (Example)

Datawords	Codewords
00	000
01	011
10	101
11	110

Solution

We first find all Hamming distances.

$d(000, 011) = 2$ $d(000, 101) = 2$ $d(000, 110) = 2$ $d(011, 101) = 2$
$d(011, 110) = 2$ $d(101, 110) = 2$

The d_{min} in this case is 2.

Find the Minimum Hamming Distance of the Coding Scheme in Table 2

Dataword	Codeword
00	00000
01	01011
10	10101
11	11110

Solution

We first find all the Hamming Distances

$d(00000, 01011) = 3$	$d(00000, 10101) = 3$	$d(00000, 11110) = 4$
$d(01011, 10101) = 4$	$d(01011, 11110) = 3$	$d(10101, 11110) = 3$

The d_{min} in this case is 3.

Three Parameters

Any coding scheme needs to have at least three parameters: the codeword size *n,* the dataword size *k,* and the minimum Hamming distance *dmin.* A coding scheme C is written as *C(n, k)* with a separate expression for *dmin.* For example, first coding scheme *C(3, 2)* with dmin =2 and second coding scheme *C(5,* 2) with dmin= 3.

Hamming Distance and Error

When a codeword is corrupted during transmission, the Hamming distance between the sent and received codewords is the number of bits affected by the error. For example, if the codeword 00000 is sent and 01101 is received, 3 bits are in error and the Hamming distance between the two is *d(00000,* 01101) =3.

Minimum Distance for Error Detection

To guarantee the detection of up to s errors in all cases, the minimum Hamming distance in a block code must be dmin =S + 1. The minimum Hamming distance for the first code scheme (Table 1) is 2. This code guarantees detection of only a single error. For example, if the third codeword (l0 1) is sent and one error occurs, the received codeword does not match any valid codeword. If two errors occur, the received codeword may match a valid codeword and the errors are not detected.

Minimum Distance for Error Correction

Error correction is more complex than error detection; a decision is involved. When a received codeword is not a valid codeword, the receiver needs to decide which valid codeword was actually sent.

To guarantee correction of up to t errors in all cases, the minimum Hamming distance in a block code must be dmin == 2t + 1.

Example

A code scheme has a Hamming distance dmin == 4. What is the error detection and correction capability of this scheme?

Solution

This code guarantees the detection of up to three errors *(s* == 3), but it can correct up to one error. In other words, if this code is used for error correction, part of its capability is wasted. Error correction codes need to have an odd minimum distance (3, 5, 7, ...).

3) Linear Block Codes

In a linear block code, the exclusive OR (XOR) of any two valid codewords creates another valid codeword.

Example

Let us see if the two codes we defined in Table 1 and Table 2 belong to the class of linear block codes.

1) The scheme in Table1 is a linear block code because the result of XORing any codeword with any other codeword is a valid codeword. For example, the XORing of the second and third codewords creates the fourth one.
2) The scheme in Table 2 is also a linear block code. We can create all four codewords by XORing two other codewords.

Minimum Distance for Linear Block Codes

The minimum Hamming distance is the number of 1s in the nonzero valid codeword with the smallest number of 1s.

Example

In our first code (Table 1), the numbers of 1s in the nonzero codewords are 2, 2, and 2. So the minimum Hamming distance is *dmin* =2. In our second code (Table 2), the numbers of 1s in the nonzero codewords are 3, 3, and 4. So in this code we have *dmin* =3.

Linear Block Codes

Simple Parity-Check Code

The most familiar error-detecting code is the simple parity-check code. In this code, a *k-bit* dataword is changed to an n-bit codeword where $n = k + 1$. The extra bit, called the parity bit, is selected to make the total number of 1s in the codeword even.

The minimum Hamming distance for this category is dmin =2, which means that the code is a single-bit error-detecting code; it cannot correct any error.

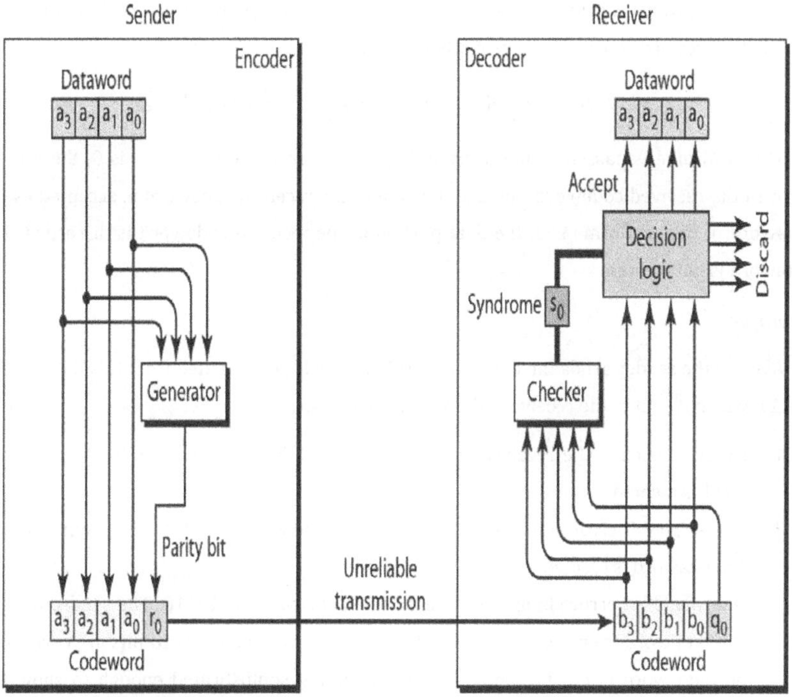

Steps for Simple Parity Check

The encoder uses a generator that takes a copy of a 4-bit dataword(here k=4) (a0, a1, a2, and a3) and generates a parity bit *r0.*

The dataword bits and the parity bit create the 5-bit codeword. The parity bit that is added makes the number of 1s in the codeword even.

This is normally done by adding the 4 bits of the dataword (modulo-2); the result is the parity bit. In other words,

$$r_0 = a_3 + a_2 + a_1 + a_0 \qquad \text{(modulo-2)}$$

If the number of 1s is even, the result is 0; if the number of 1s is odd, the result is 1. In both cases, the total number of 1s in the codeword is even. The sender sends the codeword which may be corrupted during transmission.

The receiver receives a 5-bit word. The checker at the receiver does the addition over all 5 bits.

The result, which is called the syndrome, is just 1 bit. The syndrome is 0 when the number of 1s in the received codeword is even; otherwise, it is 1.

$$s_0 = b_3 + b_2 + b_1 + b_0 + q_0 \qquad \text{(modulo-2)}$$

The syndrome is passed to the decision logic analyzer. If the syndrome is 0, there is no error in the received codeword; the data portion of the received codeword is accepted as the dataword; if the syndrome is 1, the data portion of the received codeword is discarded. The dataword is not created.

Example

Assume the sender sends the dataword 1011. The codeword created from this dataword is 10111, which is sent to the receiver. We examine five cases:

1) No error occurs; the received codeword is 10111. The syndrome is 0. The dataword 1011 is created.
2) One single-bit error changes a_1. The received codeword is 10**0**11. The syndrome is 1. No dataword is created.
3) One single-bit error changes r_0. The received codeword is 1011**0**. The syndrome is 1. No data word is created. Note that although none of the data word bits are corrupted, no data word is created because the code is not sophisticated enough to show the position of the corrupted bit.
4) An error changes r_0 and a second error changes a_3. The received codeword is **0**011**0**. The syndrome is 0. The wrong data word 0011 is created at the receiver The simple parity-check decoder cannot detect an even number of errors. The errors cancel each other out and give the syndrome a value of 0.
5) Three bits-a3, *a2,* and a1-are changed by errors. The received codeword is **01011.** The syndrome is 1. The dataword is not created. This shows that the simple parity check, guaranteed to detect one single error, can also find any odd number of errors.

Two-Dimensional Parity Check

In this method, the dataword is organized in a table (rows and columns). In Figure , the data to be sent, five 7-bit bytes, are put in separate rows. For each row and each column, 1 parity-check bit is calculated. The whole table is then sent to the receiver, which finds the syndrome for each row and each column.

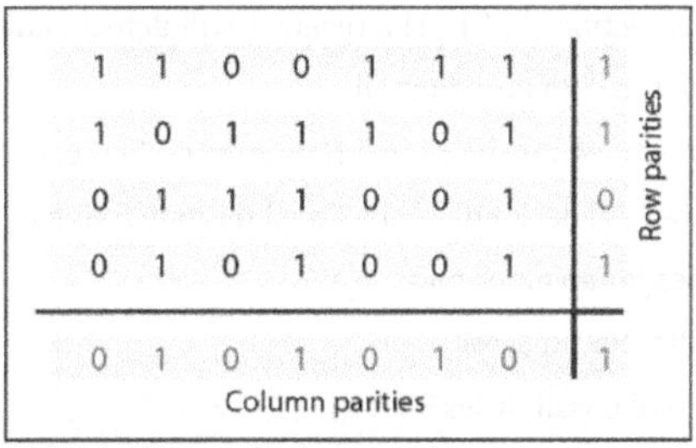

a. Design of row and column parities

As Figure b,c,d,e shows, the two-dimensional parity check can detect up to three errors that occur anywhere in the table (arrows point to the locations of the created nonzero syndromes in the corresponding rows and columns). However, errors affecting 4 bits may not be detected.

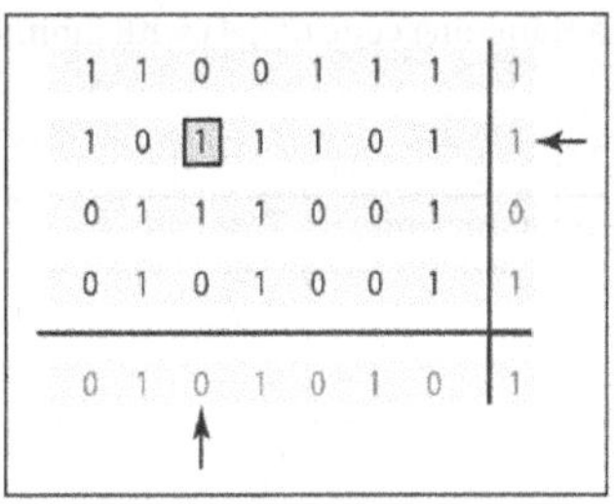

b. One error affects two parities

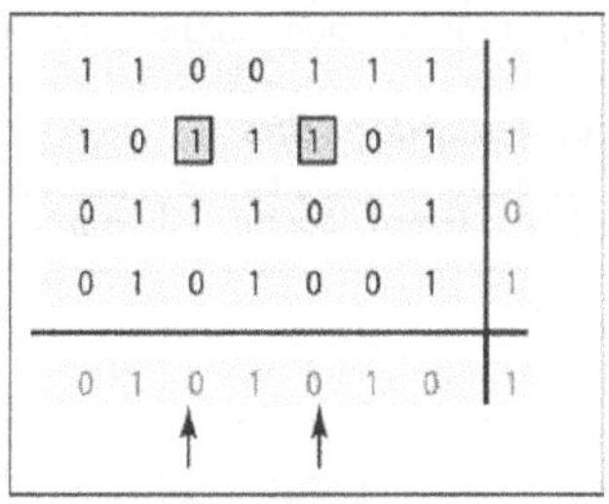

c. Two errors affect two parities

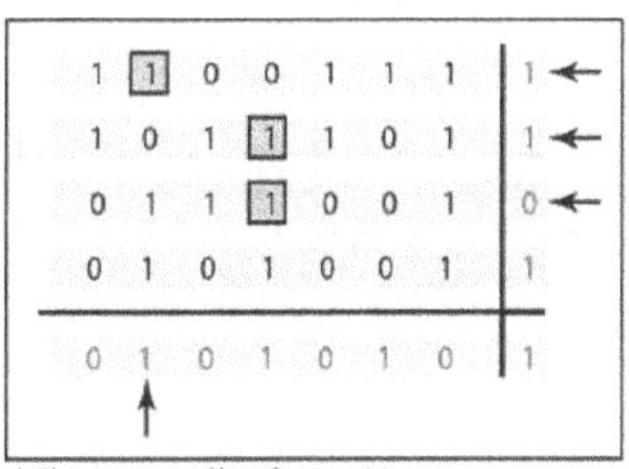

d. Three errors affect four parities

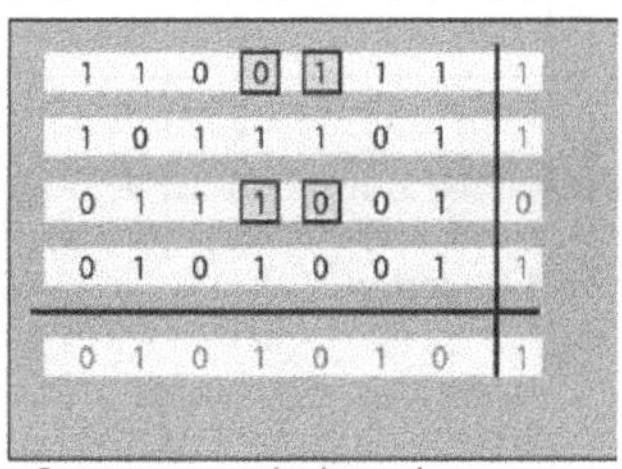

e. Four errors cannot be detected

Hamming Codes

Hamming Code is a Forward Error correction code. These codes were originally designed with *dmin* = 3, which means that they can detect up to two errors or correct one single error. Although. Two methods for error correction:

1) Retransmission after detecting error: After the receiver detected some errors in the received data Sender will retransmit the data till the receiver error free data. Suitable if more no. of bits are affected.

2) Forward error correction (FEC) : The receiver will detect and try to correct errors. Not suitable if most of the data is corrupted.

3) The relationship between n and m in a Hamming code is calculated from n= $2^m - 1$ and k=n-m. The number of check bits r = m. Consider only a single-bit error in k bits of data

   a) k possibilities for an error bit.

   b) One possibility for no error.

   c) Therefore no.of possibilities = k + 1.

4) Add r redundant bits to distinguish these possibilities where r is chosen such that the condition $2^r \geq k+1$ is satisfied.

5) But the r bits are also transmitted along with data; hence $2^r \geq k+r+1$

6) the relationship between r and k in a Hamming code is $2^r \geq k+r+1$

For example, if k=4 then r=3 then n=7. This is a Hamming code $C(7, 4)$ with dmin =3.

Number of Redundant Bits

Number of data bits k	Number of redundancy bits r	Total bits $k + r$
1	2	3
2	3	5
3	3	6
4	3	7
5	4	9
6	4	10
7	4	11

Encoder and Decoder

Steps

A copy of a 4-bit dataword(here k=4) is fed into the generator that creates three parity checks *ro,* rl,and *r2* as shown below:

$r_0 = a_2 + a_1 + a_0$ (modulo-2)

$r_1 = a_3 + a_2 + a_1$ (modulo-2)

$r_2 = a_1 + a_0 + a_3$ (modulo-2)

The total number of 1s in each 4-bit combination (3 dataword bits and 1 parity bit) must be even. *Any three equations that involve 3 of the 4 bits in the dataword and create independent equations (a combination of two cannot create the third) are valid.*

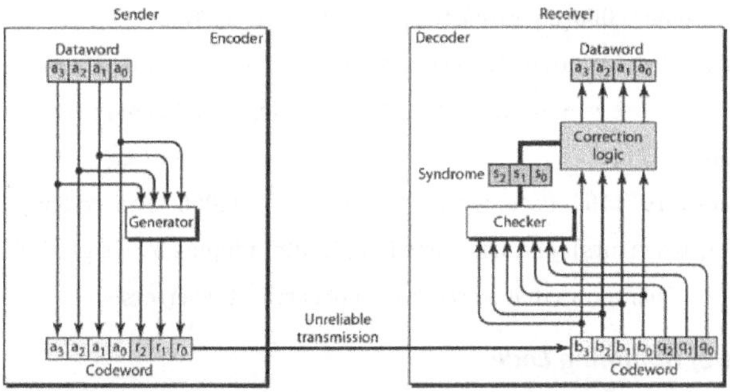

The Structure of the Encoder and Decoder for a Hamming Code

The checker in the decoder creates a 3-bit syndrome (s2s1s0) in which each bit is the parity check for 4 out of the 7 bits in the received codeword:

$$s_0 = b_2 + b_1 + b_0 + q_0 \qquad \text{modulo-2}$$
$$s_1 = b_3 + b_2 + b_1 + q_1 \qquad \text{modulo-2}$$
$$s_2 = b_1 + b_0 + b_3 + q_2 \qquad \text{modulo-2}$$

The 3-bit syndrome creates eight different bit patterns (000 to 111) that can represent eight different conditions. These conditions define a lack of error or an error in 1 of the 7 bits of the received codeword as shown below.

Syndrome	000	001	010	011	100	101	110	111
Error	None	q_0	q_1	b_2	q_2	b_0	b_3	b_1

Example

Let us trace the path of three datawords from the sender to the destination:

1. The dataword 0100:

   r0 = a0 + a1+ a2 = 0+0+1 = 1

   r1 = a1+a2+a3 = 0+1+0 = 1

   r2 = a3 + a0+a1 = 0+0+0 = 0

   Now the data word becomes the codeword(a3,a2,a1,a0,r2,r1,r0) 0100011. The codeword 0100011 is received. The syndrome is calculated as follows :

   s0 = r0 + a0 + a1+ a2 = 1+0+0+1 = 0

   s1 = r1+ a1+ a2+ a3 = 1+ 0+1+0 = 0

   s2 =r2+ a3 + a0+a1 =0+ 0 + 0+ 0 = 0

The syndrome is 000(no error), the final dataword is 0100.

2. Similarly, the dataword 0111 becomes the codeword 0111001. The received codeword is: 0<u>0</u>11001. The syndrome is 011. After flipping b_2 (changing the 0 to 1), the final dataword is 0111.
3. The dataword 1101 becomes the codeword 1101000. The codeword 1101000 is received(two errors). The syndrome is 101. After flipping b_0, we get 0000, the wrong data word. This shows that our code cannot correct two errors.

Performance of Hamming Code

A Hamming code can only correct a single error or detect a double error.

However, there is a way to make it detect a burst error, as shown in Figure below.

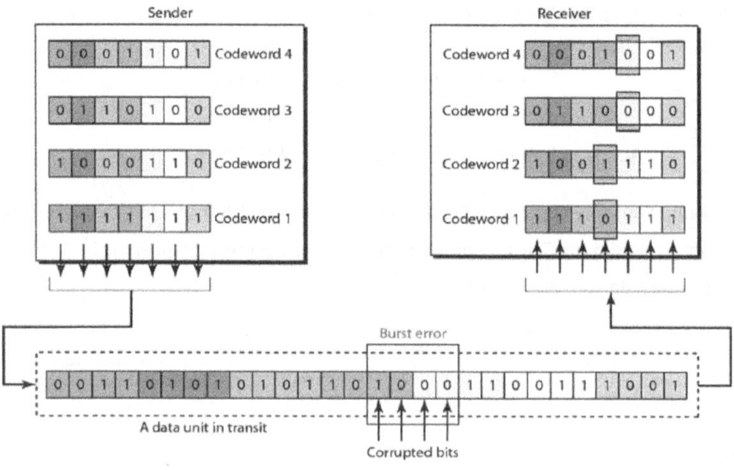

The key is to split a burst error between several codewords, one error for each codeword. In data communications, we normally send a packet or a frame of data. To make the Hamming code respond to a burst error of size *N*, we need to make *N* codewords out of our frame. Then, instead of sending one codeword at a time, we arrange the codewords in a table and send the bits in the table a column at a time.

In Figure, the bits are sent column by column (from the left). In each column, the bits are sent from the bottom to the top. In this way, a frame is made out of the four codewords and sent to the receiver. Figure shows that when a burst error of size 4 corrupts the frame, only 1 bit from each codeword is corrupted. The corrupted bit in each codeword can then easily be corrected at the receiver.

4) Cyclic Codes

In a cyclic code, if a codeword is cyclically shifted (rotated), the result is another codeword. For example, if 1011000 is a codeword and we cyclically left-shift, then 0110001 is also a codeword.

In the rightmost equation, the last bit of the first word is wrapped around and becomes the first bit of the second word.

Cyclic Redundancy Check

Cyclic codes called the cyclic redundancy check (CRC) that is used in networks such as LANs and WANs. We can create cyclic codes to correct errors.

CRC Encoder and Decoder

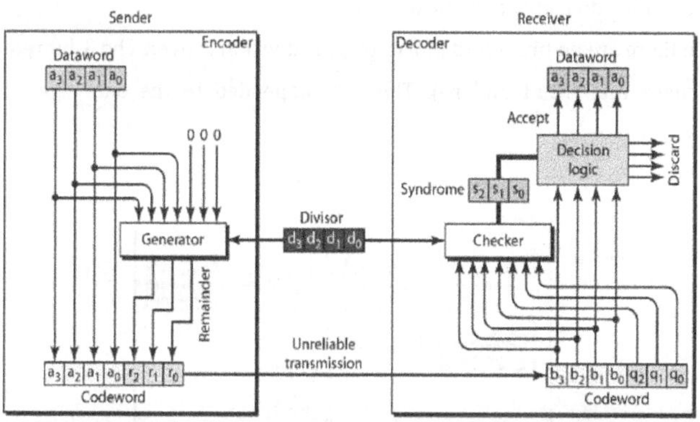

CRC Encoder and Decoder

In the encoder, the dataword has *k* bits (4 here); the codeword has *n* bits (7 here). The size of the dataword is augmented by adding *n* - *k* (3 here) 0s to the right-hand side of the word.

The n-bit result is fed into the generator. The generator uses a divisor of size *n* - *k* + 1 (4 here), predefined and agreed upon. The generator divides the augmented dataword by the divisor (modulo-2 division). The quotient of the division is discarded; the remainder *(r2r1r0)* is appended to the dataword to create the codeword.

The decoder receives the possibly corrupted codeword. A copy of all *n* bits is fed to the checker which is a replica of the generator.

The remainder produced by the checker is a syndrome of *n* - *k* (3 here) bits, which is fed to the decision logic analyzer.

The analyzer has a simple function. If the syndrome bits are all zeroes, the 4 leftmost bits of the codeword are accepted as the dataword (interpreted as no error); otherwise, the 4 bits are discarded (error).

Encoding Steps

1) The encoder takes the dataword and augments it with n-k number of 0s.
2) It then divides the augmented dataword by the divisor, as shown in Figure below.
3) In each step of division, a copy of the divisor is XORed with the 4 bits of the dividend.
4) The result of the XOR operation (remainder) is 3 bits (in this case), which is used as the dividend for the next step after pulling an extra bit down.
5) If the leftmost bit of the dividend (or the part used in each step) is 0, the step cannot use the regular divisor; we need to use an all-0s divisor.
6) Else continue division using the divisor.
7) When there are no bits left to pull down, the division is over. The 3-bit remainder forms the check Bits (r2,r1 and ro). They are appended to the data word to create the codeword.

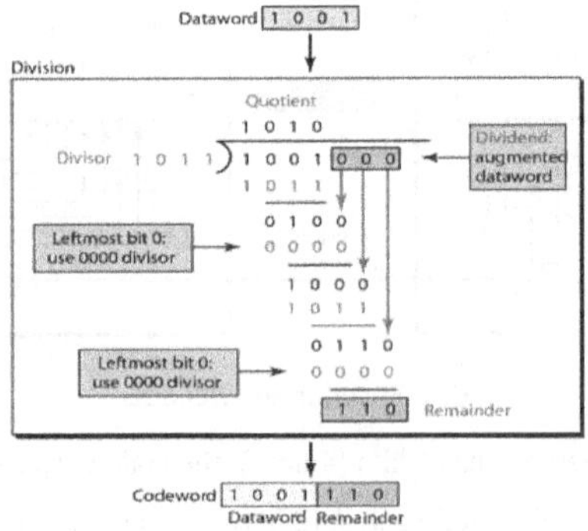

Decoding Steps

The codeword can change during transmission. The decoder does the same division process as the encoder. The remainder of the division is the syndrome.

If the syndrome is all 0s, there is no error; the data word is separated from the received codeword and accepted. Otherwise, everything is discarded.

Figure below shows two cases: The left hand figure shows the value of syndrome when no error has occurred; the syndrome is 000. The right-hand part of the figure shows the case in which there is one single error. The syndrome is not all 0s (it is 011).

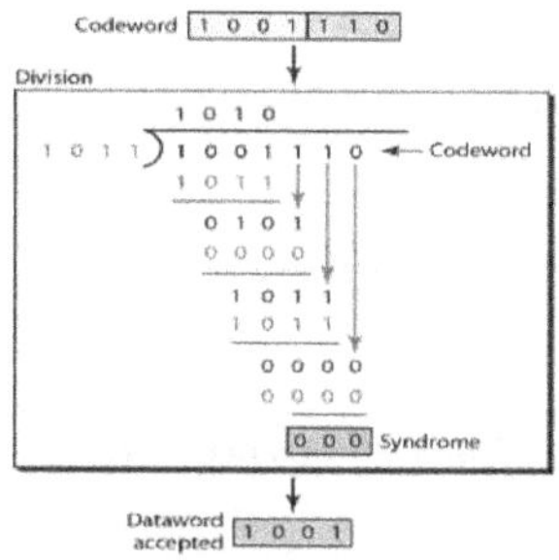

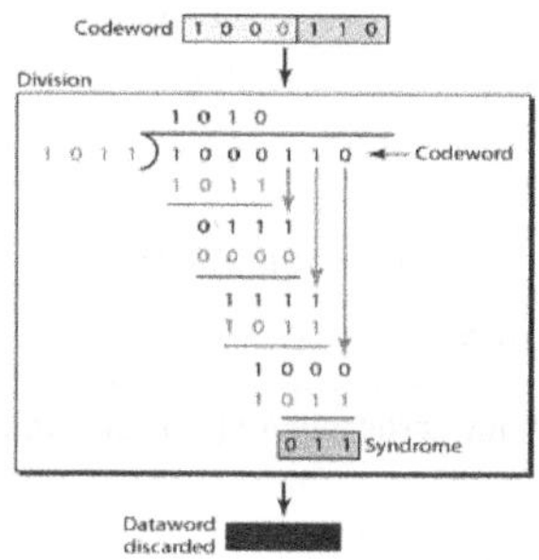

Polynomials

A better way to understand cyclic codes and how they can be analyzed is to represent them as polynomials. A pattern of 0s and 1s can be represented as a **polynomial** with coefficients of 0 and 1. The power of each term shows the position of the bit; the coefficient shows the value of the bit.

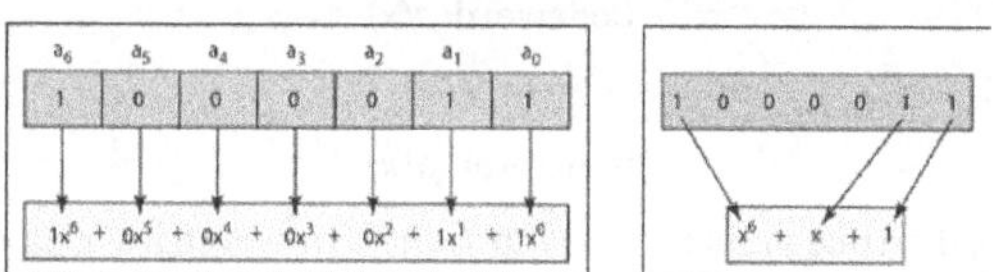

a. Binary pattern and polynomial   b. Short form

The divisor in a cyclic code is normally called the generator polynomial or simply the generator.

Properties of Good Polynomial

1) It should have at least two terms.
2) The coefficient of the term x^0 should be 1.
3) It should not divide $x^t + 1$, for t between 2 and $n - 1$.
4) It should have the factor $x + 1$.

Strength of CRC

1) Can be analyzed using polynomial

    a) $M(x)$ – Original message.

    b) $G(x)$ – Generator polynomial of degree n.

    c) $R(x)$ – Generated CRC.

$$\boxed{M(x) \cdot x^n = Q(x) \cdot G(x) + R(x)}$$

2) Transmitted message is

$$M(x) \cdot x^n - R(x)$$

which is divisible by G(x)

3) Received message is

$$M(x) \cdot x^n - R(x) + E(x)$$

where E(x) represents bit errors

4) Receiver does not detect any error when $E(x)$ is divisible by $G(x)$, which means either:

    a) $E(x) = 0 \rightarrow$ No error.

    b) $E(x) \neq 0 \rightarrow$ Undetectable error.

Cyclic Code Analysis

We define the following, *where f(x)* is a polynomial with binary coefficients.

Dataword: *d(x)*

Syndrome: *s(x)*

Codeword: *c(x)*

Error: *e(x)*

Generator: *g(x)*

If s(x) is not zero, then one or more bits is corrupted. However, if s(x) is zero, either no bit is corrupted or the decoder failed to detect any errors.

In a cyclic code, those e(x) errors that are divisible by g(x) are not caught.

Single-Bit Error: If the generator has more than one term and the coefficient ofx0 is 1, all single errors can be caught. Two Isolated Single-Bit Errors: If a generator cannot divide xt + 1 (t between 0 and n - 1), then all isolated double errors can be detected.

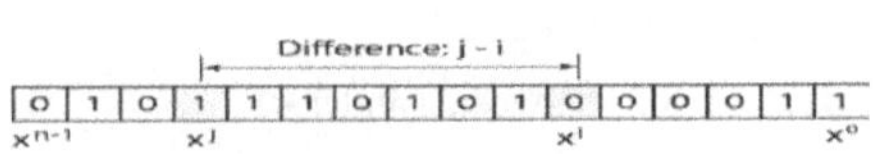

Odd Numbers of Errors: A generator that contains a factor of x + 1 can detect all odd-numbered errors.

Burst Errors

1) All burst errors with $L \leq n$ will be detected
2) All burst errors with $L = n + 1$ will be detected with probability $1 - (1/2)^{n-1}$
3) All burst errors with $L > n + 1$ will be detected with probability $1 - (1/2)^{n}$

5) Checksum

The checksum is based on the concept of redundancy. It is an error detection technique.

Suppose our data is a list of five 4-bit numbers that we want to send to a destination. In addition to sending these numbers, the sum of the numbers are also sent.

For example, if the set of numbers is (7, 11, 12, 0, 6), we send (7, 11, 12,0,6,36), where 36 is the sum of the original numbers.

The receiver adds the five numbers and compares the result with the sum. If the two are the same, the receiver assumes no error, accepts the five numbers, and discards the sum. Otherwise, there is an error somewhere and the data are not accepted.

We can make the job of the receiver easier if we send the negative (complement) of the sum, called the checksum. In this case, we send (7, 11, 12,0,6, -36). The receiver can add all the numbers received (including the checksum). If the result is 0, it assumes no error; otherwise, there is an error.

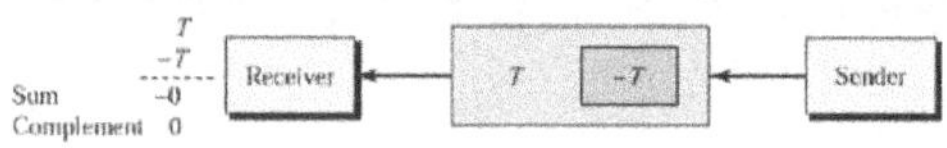

Example 1

Suppose the following block of 16 bits is to be sent using a checksum of 8 bits.

10101001 00111001

The numbers are added using one's complement

10101001

00111001

Sum 11100010

Checksum 00011101 (compliment of sum)

The pattern sent is 10101001 00111001 00011101

Now suppose the receiver receives the pattern sent and there is no error.

10101001 00111001 00011101

When the receiver adds the three sections, it will get all 1s, which, after complementing, is all 0s and shows that there is no error.

```
        10101001
        00111001
        00011101
--------------------------------
Sum     11111111
```

Complement 00000000 means that the pattern is OK.

Now suppose there is a burst error of length 5 that affects 4 bits.

10101111 11111001 00011101

When the receiver adds the three sections, it gets

```
                 1 0 1 0 1 1 1 1
                 1 1 1 1 1 0 0 1
                 0 0 0 1 1 1 0 1
- - - - - - - - - - - - - - - - - - -
Partial Sum    1 1 1 0 0 0 1 0 1
Carry                          1
Sum              1 1 0 0 0 1 1 0
Complement       0 0 1 1 1 0 0 1   the pattern is corrupted.
```

Example 2

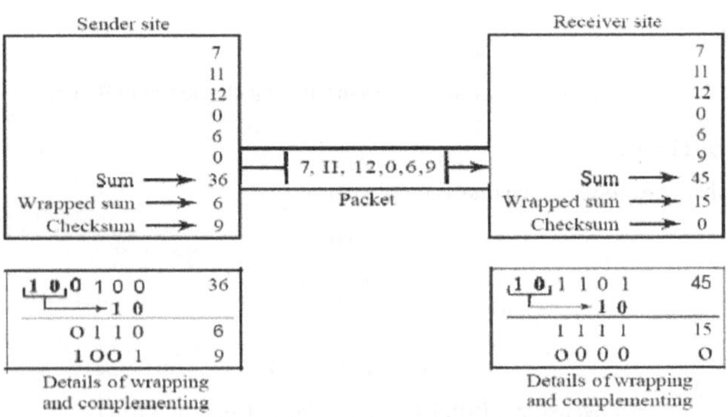

The sender initializes the checksum to 0 and adds all data items and the checksum (the checksum is considered as one data item and is shown in color). The result is 36. However, 36 cannot be expressed in 4 bits. The extra two bits are wrapped and added with the sum to create the wrapped sum value 6. In the figure, we have shown the details in binary.

The sum is then complemented, resulting in the checksum value 9 (15 - 6 = 9). The sender now sends six data items to the receiver including the checksum 9. The receiver follows the same procedure as the sender. It adds all data items (including the checksum); the result is 45. The sum is wrapped and becomes 15.

The wrapped sum is complemented and becomes 0. Since the value of the checksum is 0, this means that the data is not corrupted. The receiver drops the checksum and keeps the other data items. If the checksum is not zero, the entire packet is dropped.

6) Internet Checksum

Traditionally, the Internet has been using a 16-bit checksum. The sender and receiver calculates the checksum by following these steps.

Sender Site

1) The message is divided into 16-bit words.
2) The value of the checksum word is set to 0.
3) All words including the checksum are added using one's complement addition.
4) The sum is complemented and becomes the checksum.
5) The checksum is sent with the data.

Receiver Site

1) The message (including checksum) is divided into 16-bit words.
2) All words are added using one's complement addition.
3) The sum is complemented and becomes the new checksum.
4) If the value of checksum is 0, the message is accepted; otherwise, it is rejected.

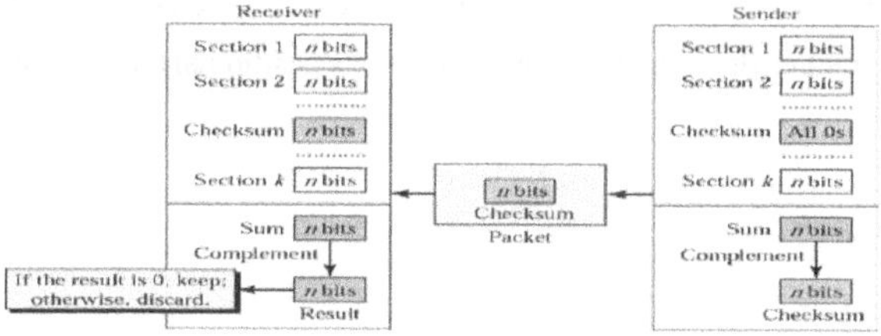

The nature of the checksum (treating words as numbers and adding and complementing them) is well-suited for software implementation.

Example

Let us calculate the checksum for a text of 8 characters ("Forouzan"). The text needs to be divided into 2-byte (16-bit) words. Each byte is changed to a 2-digit hexadecimal number using ASCII. For example, **F** is represented as 0x46 and **o** is represented as 0x6F. Figure shows how the checksum is calculated at the sender and receiver sites. In part a of the figure, the value of partial sum for the first column is 0x36. We keep the rightmost digit (6) and insert the leftmost dight (3) as the carry in the second column. The process is repeated for each column.

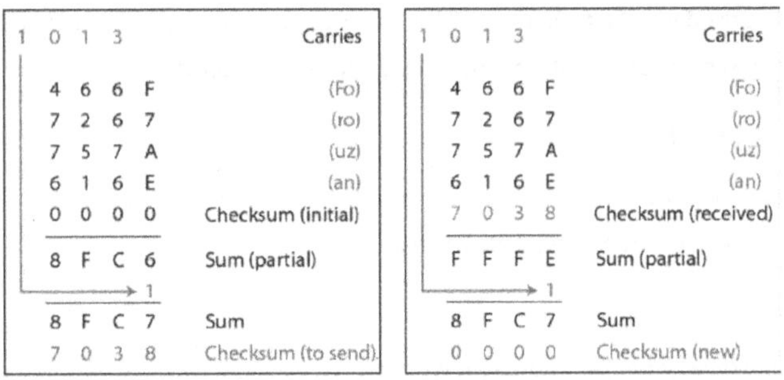

a. Checksum at the sender site a. Checksum at the receiver site

Performance

The traditional checksum uses a small number of bits (16) to detect errors in a message of any size (sometimes thousands of bits). However, it is not as strong as the CRC in error-checking capability. For example, if the value of one word is incremented and the value of another word is decremented by the same amount, the two errors cannot be detected because the sum and checksum remain the same.

Also if the values of several words are incremented but the total change is a multiple of 65535, the sum and the checksum does not change, which means the errors are not detected.

Fletcher and Adler have proposed some weighted checksums, in which each word is multiplied by a number (its weight) that is related to its position in the text. This will eliminate the first problem.

UNIT-5

Data Link Layer-2: Framing, Flow and Error Control, Protocols, Noiseless Channels, Noisy channels, HDLC, PPP (Framing, Transition phases only).

1. Data Link Control

Framing

The data link layer needs to pack bits into frames(framing) so that each frame is distinguishable from another. Framing in the data link layer separates a message from one source to a destination, or from other messages to other destinations, by adding a sender address and a destination address.

Although the whole message could be packed in one frame that is not normally done. One reason is that if a frame is very large, flow and error control are very inefficient. When a message is carried in one very large frame, even a single-bit error would require the retransmission of the whole message. When a message is divided into smaller frames, a single-bit error affects only that small frame. Frames can be of fixed or variable size.

Fixed-Size Framing: In fixed-size framing, all frames are of same size; there is no need for defining the boundaries of the frames. An example of this type of framing is the ATM wide-area network, which uses frames of fixed size called cells.

In variable-size framing, size of the frame is not fixed; so the end of the frame and the beginning of the next frame needs to be specified.

Character-Oriented Protocols

In a character-oriented protocol, data to be carried are 8-bit characters from a coding system such as ASCII. The header and the trailer are also multiples of 8 bits.

To separate one frame from the next, an 8-bit (1-byte) flag is added at the beginning and the end of a frame. The flag marks the start or end of a frame. Figure 1 shows the format of a frame in a character-oriented protocol.

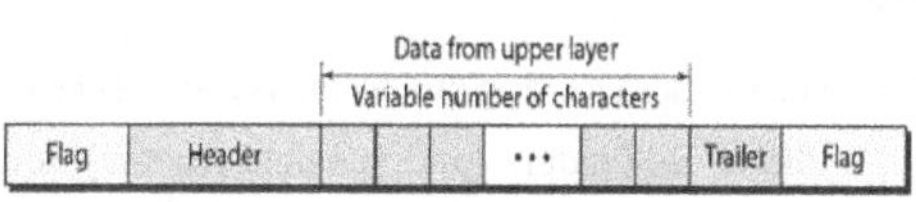

Figure 1: A Frame in a Character-Oriented Protocol

The flag could be any character not used for text communication. But any pattern used for the flag could also be part of the data. When the receiver encounters the flag like pattern in the middle of the data, it thinks it has reached the end of the frame.

To fix this problem, a **byte-stuffing** strategy was added to character-oriented framing. In byte stuffing (or character stuffing), the sender adds a special byte to the data section of the frame when there is a character with the same pattern as the flag.

The extra stuffed byte is called the escape character (ESC), which has a predefined bit pattern. Whenever the receiver encounters the ESC character, it removes it from the data section and treats the next character as data, not a delimiting flag. Byte stuffing by the escape character allows the presence of the flag like pattern in the data section of the frame, but it creates another problem. What happens if the text contains one or more escape characters followed by a flag? The receiver removes the escape character, but keeps the flag, which is incorrectly interpreted as the end of the frame.

To solve this problem, the escape characters that are part of the text must also be marked by another escape character.

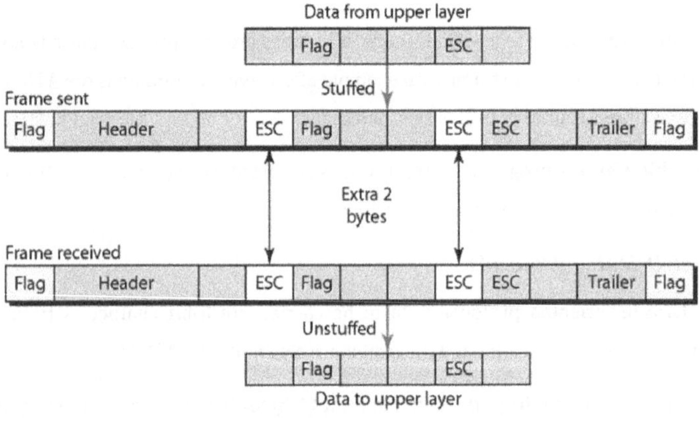

Figure 2: Byte Stuffing and Unstuffing

Bit-Oriented Protocols

In a bit-oriented protocol, the data section of a frame is a sequence of bits to be interpreted by the upper layer. In addition to headers (and possible trailers), a delimiter is needed to separate one frame from the other. Most protocols use a special 8-bit pattern flag **01111110** as the delimiter to define the beginning and the end of the frame, as shown in Figure 3.

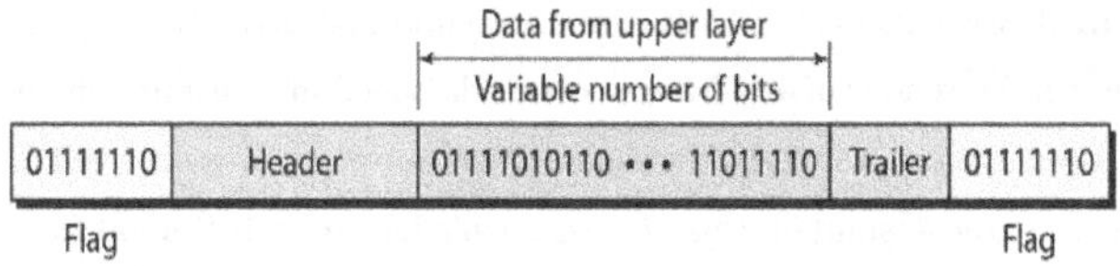

Figure 3: A Frame in a Bit-Oriented Protocol

If the flag pattern appears in the data, the receiver must be informed that this is not the end of the frame. To prevent the pattern from looking like a flag 1 single bit can be stuffed. The strategy is called **bit stuffing**.

In bit stuffing, if a 0 and five consecutive 1 bits are encountered, an extra 0 is added. This extra stuffed bit is eventually removed from the data by the receiver. Figure 11.4 shows bit stuffing at the sender and bit removal at the receiver. Note that even if we have a 0 after five 1s, we still stuff a 0. The 0 will be removed by the receiver.

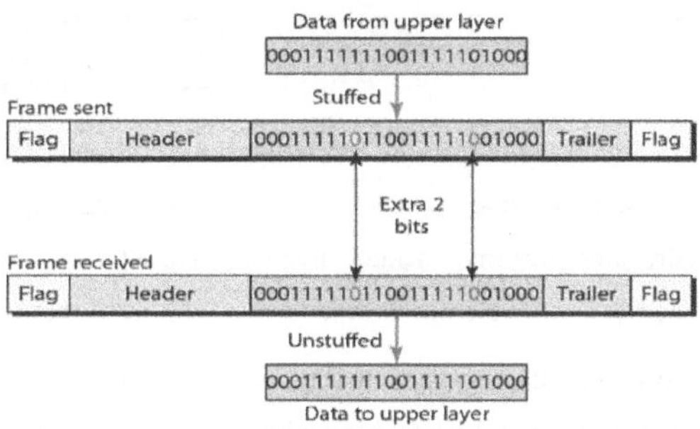

This means that if the flag like pattern 01111110 appears in the data, it will change to 011111010 (stuffed) and is not mistaken as a flag by the receiver. The real flag 01111110 is not stuffed by the sender and is recognized by the receiver.

2. Flow and Error Control

Flow control is a set of procedures that tells the sender how much data it can transmit before it must wait for an acknowledgment from the receiver.

The flow of data must not be allowed to overwhelm the receiver. Any receiving device might have a limited speed at which it can process incoming data and a limited amount of memory in which to store incoming data. Each receiving device has a block of memory, called a *buffer,* reserved for storing incoming data until they are processed. If the buffer begins to fill up, the receiver must be able to tell the sender to halt transmission until it is once again able to receive.

Error Control Error control is both error detection and error correction. It allows the receiver to inform the sender of any frames lost or damaged in transmission and coordinates the retransmission of those frames by the sender. Any time an error is detected in an exchange, specified frames are retransmitted. This process is called **Automatic Repeat Request (ARQ).**

3. Flow Control Protocols

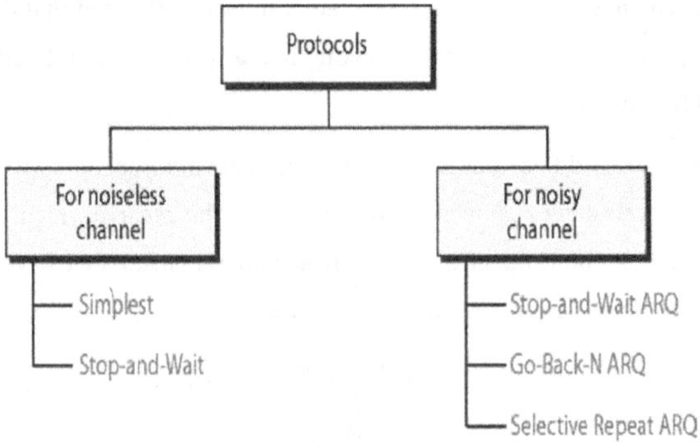

All the protocols are unidirectional, in the sense that the data frames travel from one node, called the sender, to another node, called the receiver. Although special frames, called acknowledgment (ACK) and negative acknowledgment (NAK) can flow in the opposite direction for flow and error control purposes, data flow in only one direction.

In a real-life network, data flow in both directions. In these protocols the flow and error control information such as ACKs and NAKs is included in the data frames in a technique called piggybacking.

4. Protocols for Noiseless Channels

The Simplest protocol is a protocol that does not use flow control; the stop and wait is the one that does use the flow control. Neither has error control because it is assumed that the channel is a perfect noiseless channel.

4.1.Simplest Protocol

Simplest Protocol is one that has no flow or error control.

It is a unidirectional protocol in which data frames are travelling in only one direction-from the sender to receiver. It is assumed that the receiver can immediately handle any frame it receives. The receiver can never be overwhelmed with incoming frames.

Example

Figure below shows an example of communication using this protocol. The sender sends a sequence of frames without even thinking about the receiver. To send three frames, three events occur at the sender site and three events at the receiver site.

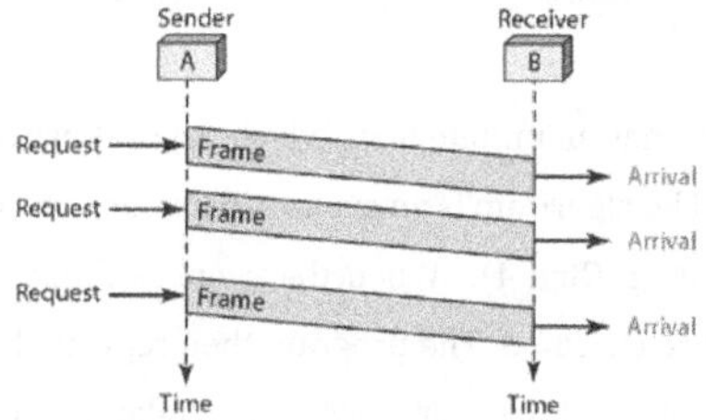

Design

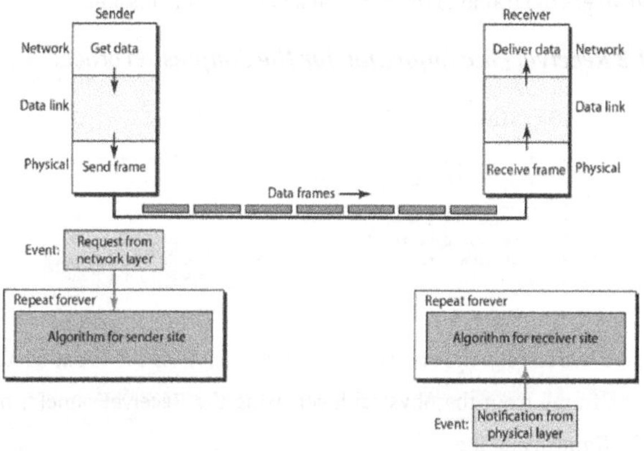

There is no need for flow control in this scheme. The data link layer at the sender site gets data from its network layer, makes a frame out of the data, and sends it. The data link layer at the receiver site receives a frame from its physical layer, extracts data from the frame, and delivers the data to its network layer. The sender site cannot send a frame until its network layer has a data packet to send. The receiver site cannot deliver a data packet to its network layer until a frame arrives.

The procedure at the sender site is constantly running; there is no action until there is a request from the network layer (event initiated by network layer). The procedure at the receiver site is also constantly running, but there is no action until notification from the physical layer arrives.

Algorithm 11.1 Sender-Site Algorithm for the Simplest Protocol

```
1  while(true)                    // Repeat forever
2  {
3    WaitForEvent();              // Sleep until an event occurs
4    if(Event(RequestToSend))     //There is a packet to send
5    {
6       GetData();
7       MakeFrame();
8       SendFrame();              //Send the frame
9    }
10 }
```

Analysis The algorithm has an infinite loop, which means lines 3 to 9 are repeated forever once the program starts. The algorithm is an event-driven one, which means that it *sleeps* (line 3) until an event wakes it *up* (line 4). When the event, a request from the network layer, occurs, lines 6 though 8 are executed. The program then repeats the loop and again sleeps at line 3 until the next occurrence of the event. Get Data( ) takes a data packet from the network layer, Make Frame( ) adds a header and delimiter flags to the data packet to make a frame, and Send Frame( ) delivers the frame to the physical layer for transmission.

Algorithm 11.2 Receiver-Site Algorithm for the Simplest Protocol

```
while(true)                          // Repeat forever
{
  WaitForEvent();                    // Sleep until an event occurs
  if(Event(ArrivalNotification))     //Data frame arrived
  {
     ReceiveFrame();
     ExtractData();
     DeliverData();                  //Deliver data to network layer
  }
}
```

Analysis The event here is the arrival of a data frame. After the event occurs, the data link layer receives the frame from the physical layer using the ReceiveFrame( ) process, extracts the data from the frame using the

Extract Data( )process, and delivers the data to the network layer using the DeliverData( ) process.

4.2.Stop-and-Wait Protocol

In Stop-and-Wait Protocol, the sender sends one frame, stops until it receives confirmation from the receiver, and then sends the next frame.

If data frames arrive at the receiver site faster than they can be processed, the frames must be stored until their use. Normally, the receiver does not have enough storage space, especially if it is receiving data from many sources. This may result in either the discarding of frames or denial of service. To prevent the receiver from becoming overwhelmed with frames there must be feedback from the receiver to the sender.

Example

Figure shows an example of communication using this protocol. The sender sends one frame and waits for feedback from the receiver. When the ACK arrives, the sender sends the next frame. Note that sending two frames in the protocol involves the sender in four events and the receiver in two events.

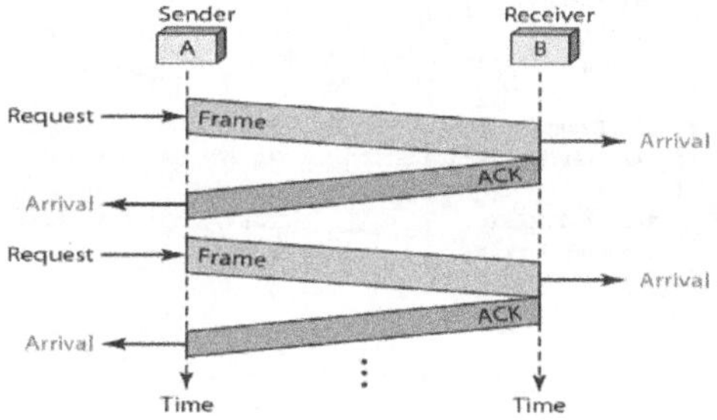

Design Figure illustrates the mechanism.

At any time, there is either one data frame on the forward channel or one ACK frame on the reverse channel. We therefore need a half-duplex link.

After the data frame arrives, the receiver sends an ACK frame to acknowledge the receipt and allow the sender to send the next frame.

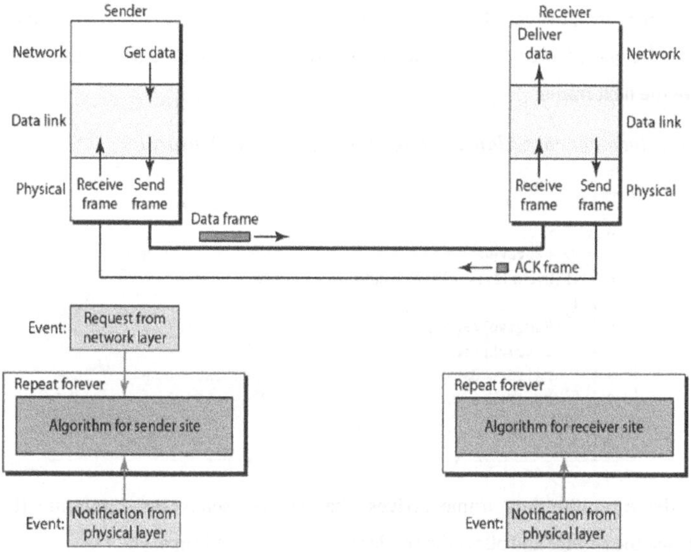

Algorithm Sender-Site Algorithm for Stop-and-Wait Protocol

```
while(true)                          //Repeat forever
canSend = true                       //Allow the first frame to go
{
  WaitForEvent();                    // Sleep until an event occurs
  if(Event(RequestToSend) AND canSend)
  {
     GetData();
     MakeFrame();
     SendFrame();                    //Send the data frame
     canSend = false;                //Cannot send until ACK arrives
  }
  WaitForEvent();                    // Sleep until an event occurs
  if(Event(ArrivalNotification)) // An ACK has arrived
   {
     ReceiveFrame();                 //Receive the ACK frame
     canSend = true;
   }
}
```

Analysis

Here two events can occur: a request from the network layer or an arrival notification from the physical layer. The responses to these events must alternate. In other words, after a frame is sent, the algorithm must ignore another network layer request until that frame is acknowledged. The requests from the network layer, however, may happen one after another without an arrival event in between. It needs to be prevented from the immediate sending of the data frame. So a simple *canSend* variable has been used that can either be true or false. When a frame is sent, the variable is set to false to indicate that a new network request cannot be sent until *canSend* is true. When an ACK is received, canSend is set to true to allow the sending of the next frame.

Algorithm Receiver-Site Algorithm for Stop-and-Wait Protocol

```
1  while(true)                          //Repeat forever
2  {
3    WaitForEvent();                    // Sleep until an event occurs
4    if(Event(ArrivalNotification)) //Data frame arrives
5    {
6       ReceiveFrame();
7       ExtractData();
8       Deliver(data);                  //Deliver data to network layer
9       SendFrame();                    //Send an ACK frame
10   }
11 }
```

Analysis: After the data frame arrives, the receiver sends an ACK frame (line 9) to acknowledge the receipt and allow the sender to send the next frame.

5. Noisy Channels

5.1.Stop-and-Wait Automatic Repeat Request

The Stop-and-Wait Automatic Repeat Request (Stop-and Wait ARQ) allows the sender to send a frame and waits for an acknowledgement(ACK) for a specific duration defined by its timer. If the sender receives the ACK before timeout occurs it will send the next frame. Otherwise it will retransmit the frame again.

The Stop-and Wait ARQ adds a simple error control mechanism to the Stop-and-Wait Protocol.

The Key Features of Stop-and-Wait Automatic Repeat Request

1) Sequence numbers are assigned to frames and ACK. Assume that the field is *m* bits long, the sequence numbers start from 0, go to 2^m - 1, and then are repeated. (Ex: if m=3 sequence no are from 0 to 7).
2) ACK no denotes the next frame expected by the Receiver.
3) Sender maintains a timer and starts it when a frame is transmitted and stopped when the ACK is received.
4) Sender keeps a copy of frame sent so that retransmission of the frame can be carried out when timer expires without ACK.
5) The sender maintains a control variable S_n -> Next frame to be sent.
6) The receiver maintains a control variable R_n -> Next frame to be received.
7) The receiver doesn't respond for the error corrupted/ lost frames. The silence of the receiver makes the timer at the sender expire without ACK thereby starting a retransmission.
8) Receiver doesn't accept duplicate frames.

Assume that the sender has sent the frame numbered *x*. Three things can happen.

1) The frame arrives safe and sound at the receiver site; the receiver sends an acknowledgment with an ACK no x+1, causing the sender to send the next frame numbered *x* + 1.
2) The frame arrives safe and sound at the receiver site; the receiver sends an acknowledgment, but the acknowledgment is corrupted or lost. The sender resends the frame (numbered *x)* after the time-out. The frame resent here is a duplicate. The receiver can discard this duplicate frame and send and ACK numbered *x* + 1.

3) The frame is corrupted or never arrives at the receiver site; the sender resends the frame (numbered *x)* after the time-out.

Example

Frame 0 is sent and acknowledged. Frame 1 is lost and resent after the time-out. The resent frame 1 is acknowledged and the timer stops. Frame0 is sent and acknowledged, but the acknowledgment is lost. The sender has no idea if the frame or the acknowledgment is lost, so after the time-out, it resends frame 0, which is acknowledged. The receiver receives duplicate copy of frame 0 and discards it and then send an ACK 1 to inform the sender that frame 0 received successfully.

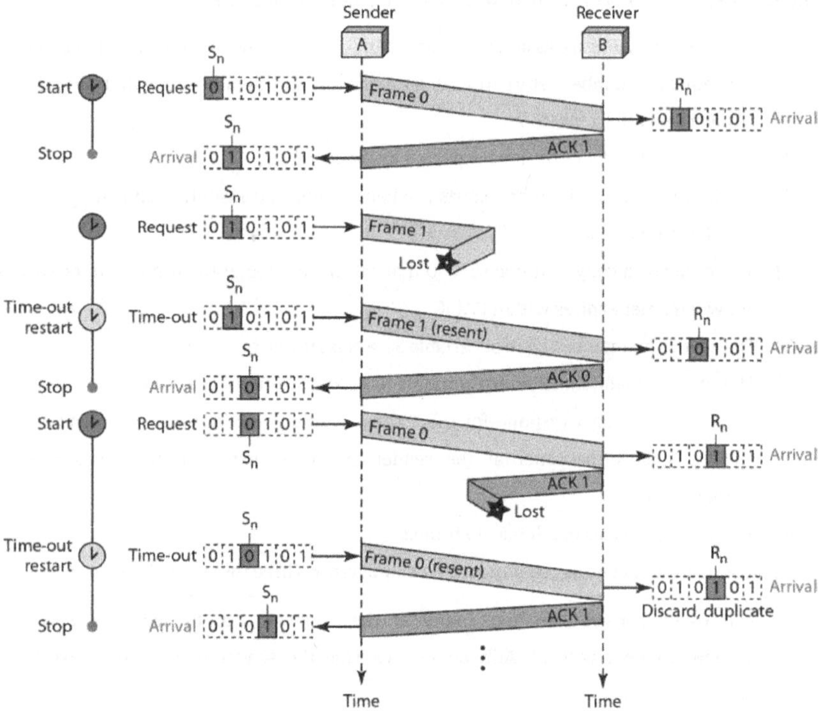

Design Figure shows the design of the Stop-and-WaitARQ Protocol. The sending device keeps a copy of the last frame transmitted until it receives an acknowledgment for that frame.A data frames uses a seqNo (sequence number); an ACK frame uses an ackNo (acknowledgment number). The sender has a control variable, which we call S_n (sender, next frame to send), that holds the sequence number for the next frame to be sent (0 or 1).

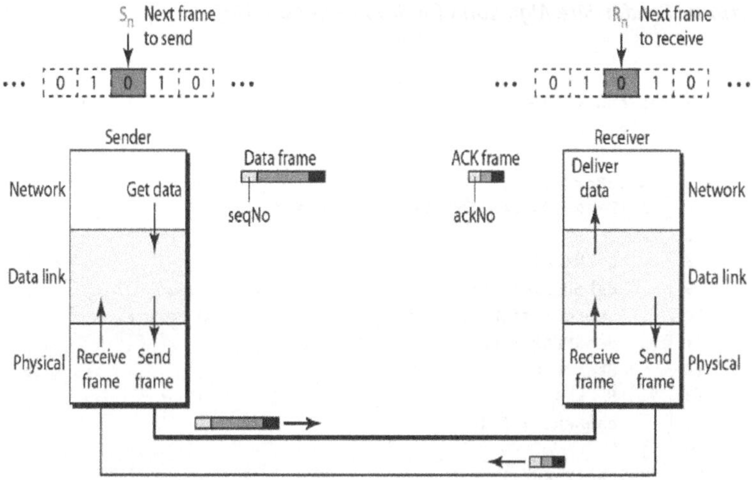

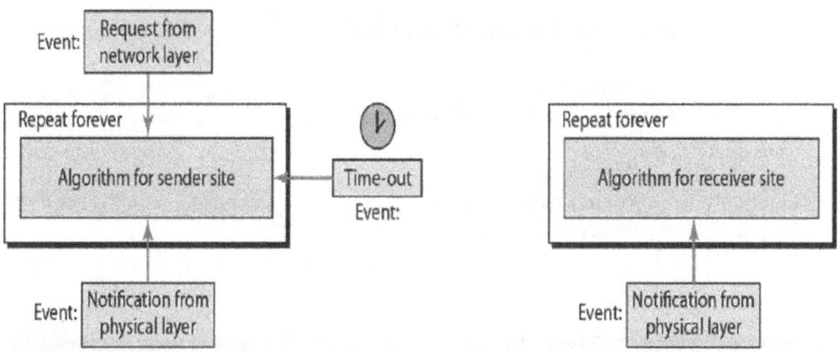

The receiver has a control variable, which we call R_n (receiver, next frame expected), that holds the number of the next frame expected. When a frame is sent, the value of *Sn* is incremented (modulo-2), which means if it is 0, it becomes 1 and vice versa. When a frame is received, the value of R_n is incremented (modulo-2), which means if it is 0, it becomes 1 and vice versa.

Three events can happen at the sender site:

1) Request from network layer when the data is ready to send
2) Notification from the Physical layer when the ACK is received
3) Timeout event when timer expires without any ACK.

One event can happen at the receiver site that occurs when the data frames are passed by the physical layer.

Algorithm: Sender-Site Algorithm for Stop-and-Wait ARQ

```
1  Sn = 0;                          // Frame 0 should be sent first
2  canSend = true;                  // Allow the first request to go
3  while(true)                      // Repeat forever
4  {
5    WaitForEvent();                // Sleep until an event occurs
6    if(Event(RequestToSend) AND canSend)
7    {
8       GetData();
9       MakeFrame(Sn);                        //The seqNo is Sn
10      StoreFrame(Sn);                       //Keep copy
11      SendFrame(Sn);
12      StartTimer();
13      Sn = Sn + 1;
14      canSend = false;
15   }
16   WaitForEvent();                          // Sleep
17   if(Event(ArrivalNotification)      // An ACK has arrived
18   {
19     ReceiveFrame(ackNo);             //Receive the ACK frame
20     if(not corrupted AND ackNo == Sn) //Valid ACK
21       {
22          Stoptimer();
23          PurgeFrame(Sn-1);           //Copy is not needed
24          canSend = true;
25       }
26   }
27
28   if(Event(TimeOut)                  // The timer expired
29   {
30    StartTimer();
31    ResendFrame(Sn-1);                //Resend a copy check
32   }
33 }
```

Analysis

We first notice the presence of *Sn'* the sequence number of the next frame to be sent. This variable is initialized once (line 1), but it is incremented every time a frame is sent (line 13) in preparation for the next frame. However, since this is modulo-2 arithmetic, the sequence numbers are 0, 1,0, 1, and so on.

Note that the processes in the first event (SendFrame, StoreFrame, and Purge Frame) use an S_n defining the frame sent out. We need at least one buffer to hold this frame until we are sure that it is received safe and sound. Line 10 shows that before the frame is sent, it is stored. The copy is used for resending a corrupt or lost frame. We are still using the canSend variable to prevent the network layer from making a request before the previous frame is received safe and sound. If the frame is not corrupted and the ackNo of theACK frame matches the sequence number of the next frame to send, we stop the timer and purge the copy of the data frame we saved. Otherwise, ignore this event and wait for the next event to happen. After each frame is sent, a timer is started. When the timer expires (line 28), the frame is resent and the timer is restarted.

Algorithm Receiver-Site Algorithm for Stop-and-Wait ARQ Protocol

```
Rn = 0;                          // Frame 0 expected to arrive first
while(true)
{
  WaitForEvent();                // Sleep until an event occurs
  if(Event(ArrivalNotification))  //Data frame arrives
  {
     ReceiveFrame();
     if(corrupted(frame));
        sleep();
     if(seqNo == Rn)               //Valid data frame
     {
      ExtractData();
       DeliverData();              //Deliver data
       Rn = Rn + 1;
     }
      SendFrame(Rn);               //Send an ACK
  }
}
```

Analysis

First, all arrived data frames that are corrupted are ignored. If the seqNo of the frame is the one that is expected *(Rn)*, the frame is accepted, the data are delivered to the network layer, and the value of *Rn* is incremented. Even if the sequence number of the data frame does not match the next frame expected, an ACK is sent to the sender. This ACK, however, just reconfirms the previous ACK instead of confirming the frame received. This is done because the receiver assumes that the previous ACK might have been lost; the receiver is sending a duplicate frame. The resent ACK may solve the problem before the time-out does it.

Sample Problem1

Assume that, in a Stop-and-Wait ARQ system, the bandwidth of the line is 1 Mbps, and 1 bit takes 20 ms to make a round trip. What is the bandwidth-delay product? If the system data frames are 1000 bits in length, what is the utilization percentage of the link?

Solution

Gn Bandwidth = $1x10^6$

Delay = 20 X 10^{-3}

The bandwidth-delay product is

$$(1 \times 10^6) \times (20 \times 10^{-3}) = 20{,}000 \text{ bits}$$

The system can send 20,000 bits during the time it takes for the data to go from the sender to the receiver and then back again. However, the system sends only 1000 bits. We can say that the link utilization is only 1000/20,000, or 5 percent.

For this reason, for a link with a high bandwidth or long delay, the use of Stop-and-Wait ARQ wastes the capacity of the link.

Sample Problem 2

What is the utilization percentage of the link in Example1 if we have a protocol that can send up to 15 frames before stopping and worrying about the acknowledgments?

Solution

The bandwidth-delay product is still 20,000 bits. The system can send up to 15 frames or 15,000 bits during a round trip. This means the utilization is 15,000/20,000, or 75 percent. Of course, if there are damaged frames, the utilization percentage is much less because frames have to be resent.

Drawbacks

1) Efficiency

The Stop-and-WaitARQ is very inefficient if the channel has high bandwidth-delay product.

2) Pipelining

There is no pipelining in Stop-and-Wait ARQ because need to wait for a frame to reach the destination and be acknowledged before the next frame can be sent. Pipelining improves the efficiency of the transmission if the number of bits in transition is large with respect to the bandwidth-delay product.

5.2. Go-Back-N Automatic Repeat Request

To improve the efficiency of transmission (filling the pipe), multiple frames must be in transition (pipelining) while waiting for acknowledgment.

The Go-Back-N Automatic Repeat Request can send several frames before receiving acknowledgments. The Go-Back-N Automatic Repeat Request is a sliding window protocol.

Key Features

1) It allows pipelining to improve efficiency.
2) Frames assigned with sequence numbers in the range 0 to2^m-1 where m -> no.of bits used for sequence numbers. Ex: For example, if m is 4, the only sequence numbers are 0 through 15 inclusive.
3) The sender keeps a copy of these frames until the acknowledgments arrive.
4) Sliding window Protocol: The sender sliding window size :2^m-1) and receiver sliding window size =1
5) Timers are maintained at the sender side and started when a frame is sent.
6) Cumulative ACK: The receiver can send cumulative ACK to inform the sender about the safe reception of multiple frames.
7) If a frame is damaged or is received out of order, the receiver is silent and will discard all subsequent frames until it receives the one it is expecting. The silence of the receiver causes the timer of the unacknowledged frame at the sender site to expire.
8) If the timer at the sender expire without any ACK then the sender goes back and resend all N unacknowledged frames. That is why it is called Go Back N ARQ.
   For example, suppose the sender has already sent frame 6, but the timer for frame 3 expires. This means that frame 3 has not been acknowledged; the sender goes back and sends frames 3, 4,5, and 6 again.

Sliding Window The sliding window is an abstract concept that defines the range of sequence numbers that is the concern of the sender and receiver.

The range which is the concern of the sender is called the **send sliding window**; the range that is the concern of the receiver is called the **receive sliding window**.

The **send window** covers the sequence numbers of the data frames which can be in transit. The maximum size of the window is $2^m - 1$.

Figure(a) shows a sliding window of size 15 *(m* =4).

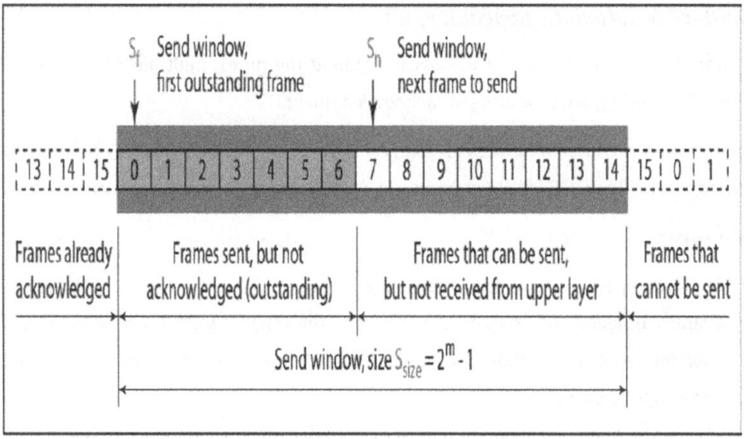

a. Send window before sliding

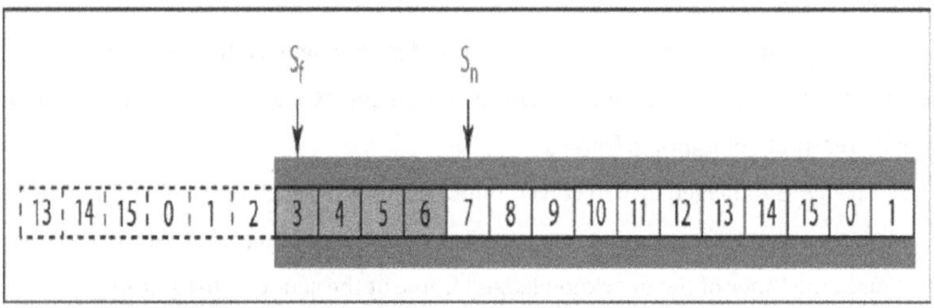

b. Send window after sliding

Three control variables used are :

Sf: The variable *Sf* defines the sequence number of the first (oldest) outstanding frame.

Sn: The variable *Sn* holds the sequence number that will be assigned to the next frame to be sent

Ssize: The variable Ssize defines the size of the window, which is fixed in our protocol.

Figure(b) shows how a send window can slide one or more slots to the right when an acknowledgment arrives from the other end.

The acknowledgments in this protocol are cumulative, meaning that more than one frame can be acknowledged by an ACK frame. In Figure b, frames 0, 1, and 2 are acknowledged, so the window has slid to the right three slots. Note that the value of *Sf* is 3 because frame 3 is now the first outstanding frame.

The **receive window** makes sure that the correct data frames are received and that the correct acknowledgments are sent. The size of the receive window is always 1.

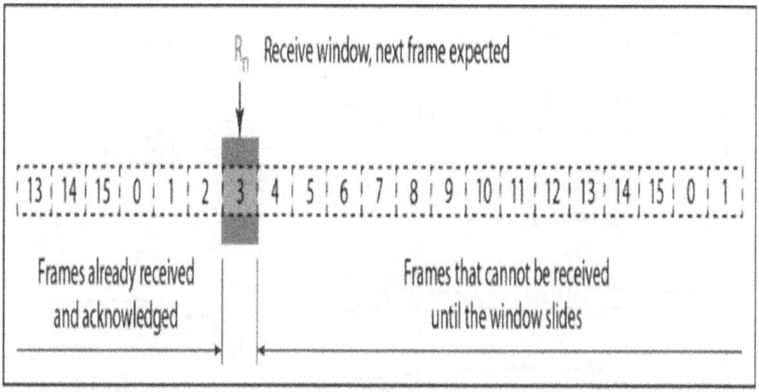

a. Receive window

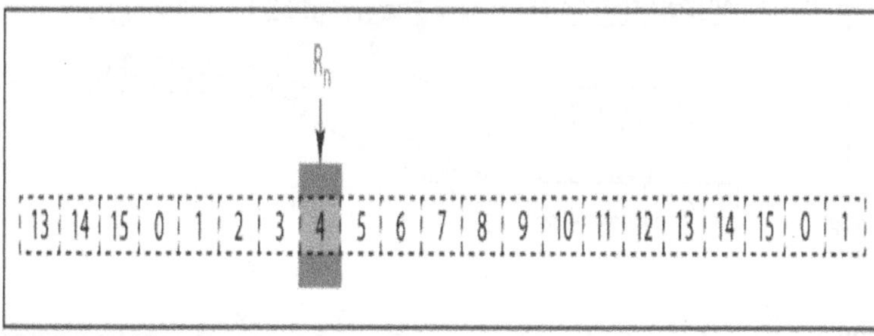

b. Window after sliding

The receiver needs only one variable R_n (receive window, next frame expected) to define this abstraction. Only a frame with a sequence number matching the value of *Rn* is accepted and acknowledged. Other frames are discarded.

The receive window also slides, but only one slot at a time. When a correct frame is received (and a frame is received only one at a time), the window slides.

Example

The example shows how cumulative acknowledgments can help if acknowledgments are delayed or lost. Note that although ACK 2 is lost, ACK 3 serves as both ACK 2 and ACK 3.

Upon sending each frame (except retransmission) Sn is incremented and the sending window is sliding for every ACK.

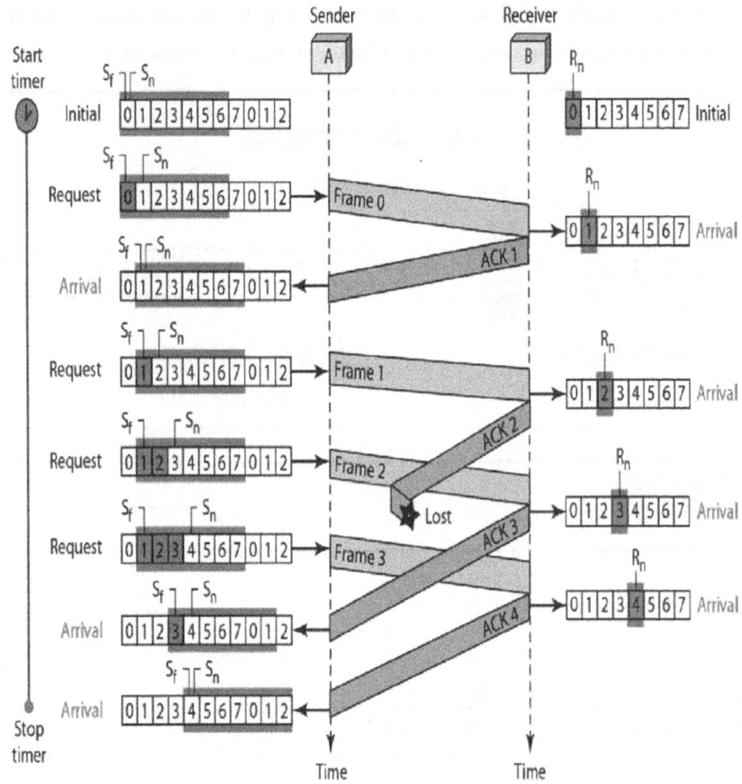

Example

The next Figure shows what happens when a frame is lost. Frames 0, 1, 2, and 3 are sent. However, frame 1 is lost. The receiver receives frames 2 and 3, but they are discarded because they are received out of order. The sender receives no acknowledgment about frames 1, 2, or 3. Its timer finally expires. The sender sends all outstanding frames (1, 2, and 3) because it does not know what is wrong.

Note that the resending of frames 1, 2, and 3 is one single event. When the sender is responding to this event, it cannot accept the triggering of other events. This means that when ACK 2 arrives, the sender is still busy with sending frame 3.

The physical layer must wait until this event is completed and the data link layer goes back to its sleeping state. We have shown a vertical line to indicate the delay. It is the same story with ACK 3; but when ACK 3 arrives, the sender is busy responding to ACK 2. It happens again when ACK 4 arrives.

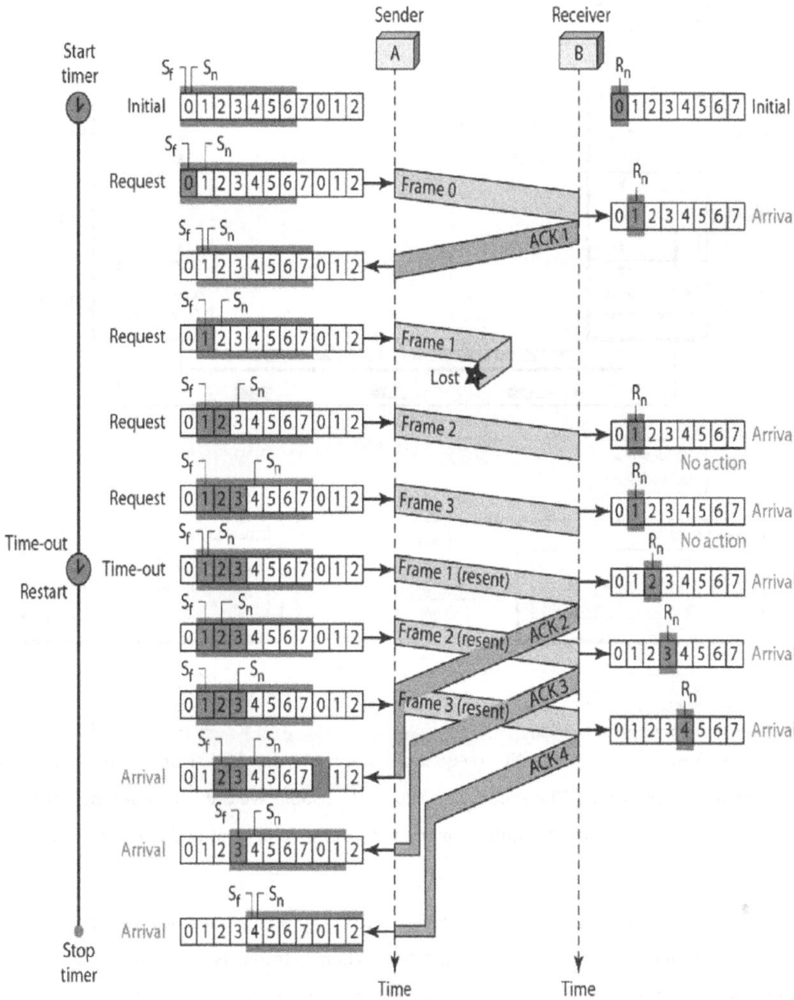

Design

Figure below shows the design for this protocol. Here, multiple frames can be in transit in the forward direction, and multiple acknowledgments in the reverse direction. The send window allows us to have as many frames in transition as there are slots in the send window.

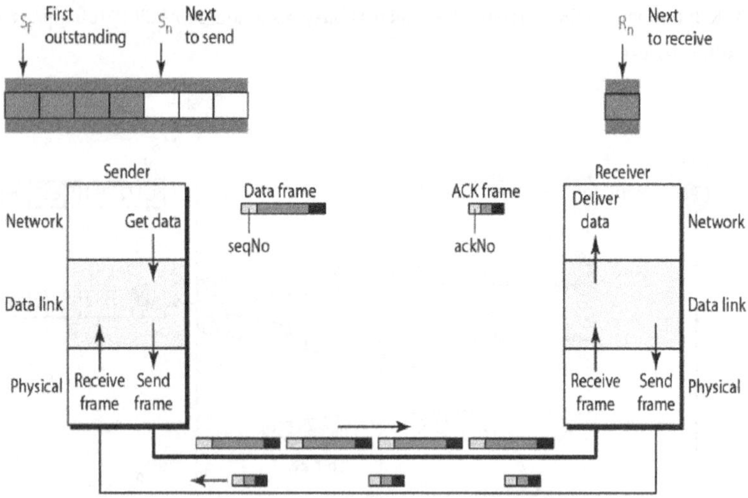

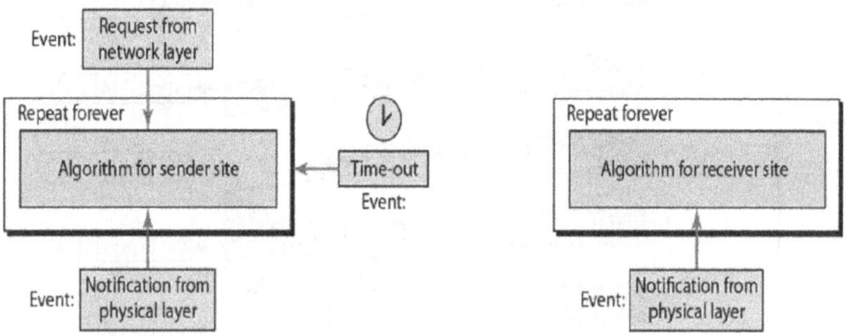

A data frames uses a seqNo (sequence number); an ACK frame uses an ackNo (acknowledgment number). The sender has a control variable, we call S_n (sender, next frame to send), that holds the sequence number for the next frame to be sent and S_f (first frame in the window)

The receiver has a control variable, which we call R_n (receiver, next frame expected), that holds the number of the next frame expected. When a frame is sent, the value of *Sn* is incremented (modulo-2 When a frame is received, the value of R_n is incremented (modulo-2),

Three events can happen at the sender site:

1) Request from network layer when the data is ready to send
2) Notification from the Physical layer when the ACK is received
3) Timeout event when timer expires without any ACK.

One event can happen at the receiver site that occurs when the data frames are passed by the physical layer.

Send Window Size

We can now show why the size of the send window must be less than *2^m^*. As an example, we choose *m* =2, which means the size of the window can be *2^m^* - 1, or 3. Figure below compares a window size of 3 against a window size of 4. If the size of the window is (less than 22) and all three acknowledgments are lost, the frame timer expires and all three frames are resent. The receiver is now expecting frame 3, not frame 0, so the duplicate frame is correctly discarded.

On the other hand, if the size of the window is 4 (equal to 22) and all acknowledgments are lost, the sender will send a duplicate of frame 0. However, this time the window of the receiver expects to receive frame 0, so it accepts frame 0, not as a duplicate, but as the first frame in the next cycle. This is an error.

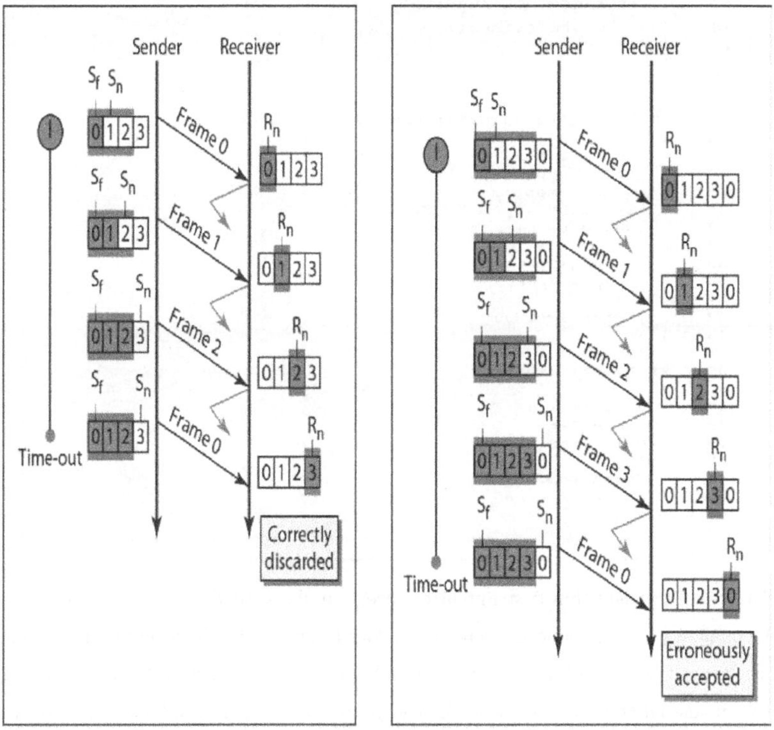

a. Window size $< 2^m$ b. Window size $= 2^m$

Algorithm

Sender Algorithm

```
Sw = 2^m - 1;
Sf = 0;
Sn = 0;

while (true)                               //Repeat forever
{
 WaitForEvent();
   if(Event(RequestToSend))                //A packet to send
   {
      if(Sn-Sf >= Sw)                      //If window is full
            Sleep();
      GetData();
      MakeFrame(Sn);
      StoreFrame(Sn);
      SendFrame(Sn);
      Sn = Sn + 1;
      if(timer not running)
           StartTimer();
   }

   if(Event(ArrivalNotification))          //ACK arrives
   {
      Receive(ACK);
      if(corrupted(ACK))
           Sleep();
      if((ackNo>Sf)&&(ackNo<=Sn))          //If a valid ACK
      While(Sf <= ackNo)
        {
         PurgeFrame(Sf);
         Sf = Sf + 1;
        }
        StopTimer();
   }

   if(Event(TimeOut))                      //The timer expires
   {
    StartTimer();
    Temp = Sf;
    while(Temp < Sn);
      {
       SendFrame(Sf);
       Sf = Sf + 1;
      }
   }
}
```

Analysis This algorithm first initializes three variables. Unlike Stop-and-Wait ARQ, this protocol allows several requests from the network layer without the need for other events to occur; we need to be sure that the window is not full . In our approach, if the window is full, the request is just ignored and the network layer needs to try again. The handling of the arrival event is more complex than in the previous protocol. If we receive a corrupted ACK, we ignore it. If the ACK belongs to one of the outstanding frames, we use a loop to purge the buffers and move the left wall to the right. The time-out event is also more complex. We first start a new timer. We then resend all outstanding frames.

Receiver Algorithm

This algorithm is simple. We ignore a corrupt or out-of-order frame. If a frame arrives with an expected sequence number, we deliver the data, update the value of *Rn,* and send an ACK with the ackNo showing the next frame expected.

```
Rn = 0;

while (true)                               //Repeat forever
{
  WaitForEvent();

  if(Event(ArrivalNotification)) /Data frame arrives
  {
     Receive(Frame);
     if(corrupted(Frame))
          Sleep();
     if(seqNo == Rn)                       //If expected frame
     {
       DeliverData();                      //Deliver data
       Rn = Rn + 1;                        //Slide window
       SendACK(Rn);
     }
  }
}
```

Advantages

Pipelining improves bandwidth utilization

Drawbacks

1) Inefficient
2) all out of order received packets are discarded
3) This is a problem in a noisy link

In a noisy link a frame has a higher probability of damage, which means the resending of multiple frames. This resending uses up the bandwidth and slows down the transmission.

Solution

Re-send only the damaged frames

Selective Repeat Automatic Repeat Request

For noisy links, there is no need resend *N* frames when just one frame is damaged; only the damaged frame is resent. This mechanism is called Selective Repeat ARQ. It is more efficient for noisy links, but the processing at the receiver is more complex.

When the frames are received out of order, then the receiver marks the missing frame and sends a negative acknowledgement (NAK) numbered with the missing frame number. On receiving the NAK, the sender resends only the frame mentioned in the NAK.

An ACK or a NAK frame may arrive. If a valid NAK frame arrives, resend the corresponding frame. If a valid ACK arrives stop the corresponding timer and move the left wall of the window. The time-out event is simpler here; only the frame which times out is resent

Key Features

1. It allows multiple frames in transition(pipelining) before receiving a n ACK
2. Frames assigned with sequence numbers in the range 0 to2^m-1 where m -> no.of bits used for sequence numbers. Ex: For example, if *m* is 4, the only sequence numbers are 0 through 15 inclusive.
3. The sender keeps a copy of outstanding frames until the acknowledgments arrive.
4. Sliding window Protocol:
   The sender sliding window size :2^{m-1} and receiver sliding window size =2^{m-1}
5. Timers are maintained at the sender side and started when a frame is sent.
6. Cumulative ACK: The receiver can send cumulative ACK to inform the sender about the safe reception of multiple frames. ACK number denotes the next frame expected by the receiver.
7. Negative ACK (NAK): The receiver can send negative ACK to indicate the lost/damaged frame to be retransmitted. NAK number denotes the frame to be retransmitted.
8. Receiver will accept out of order frames and buffer them and marks the missing frame then sends the NAK.
9. The data link layer of the Receiver will deliver a set of received frames to network layer only when a there is a set of in-order frames staring from the beginning of receiver window are ready.
10. The sender selectively retransmits only the frame for which NAK is received.

Windows

Size of the sending window is 2^{m-1} and Three control variables used are :

Sf: The variable *Sf* defines the sequence number of the first (oldest) outstanding frame.

Sn: The variable *Sn* holds the sequence number that will be assigned to the next frame to be sent.

Ssize: The variable Ssize defines the size of the window, which is fixed in our protocol.

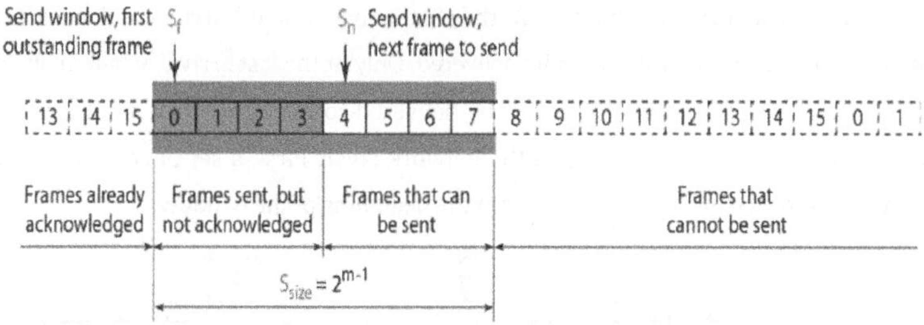

The size of the receive window is the same as the size of the send window 2^{m-1} .The Selective Repeat Protocol allows as many frames as the size of the receive window to arrive out of order and be kept until there is a set of in-order frames to be delivered to the network layer. The receiver never delivers packets out of order to the network layer.

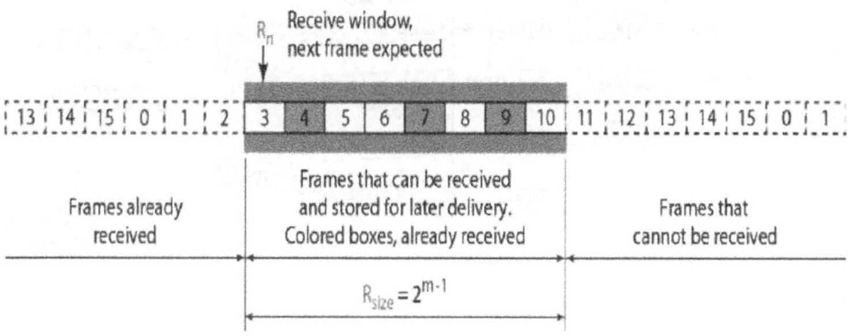

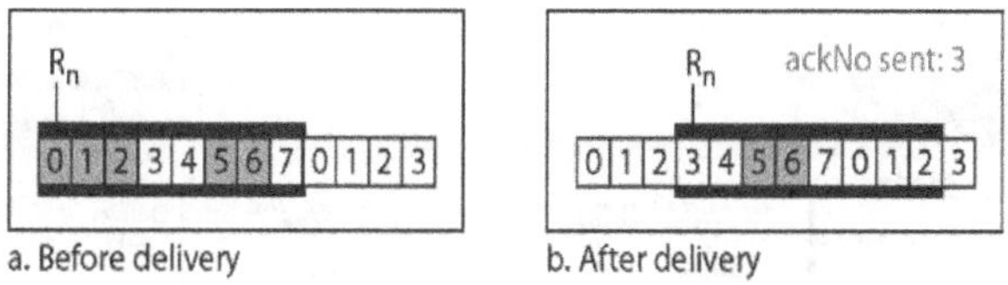

Example

This example shows how Selective Repeat behaves in case if a frame is lost. Figure below shows the situation. One main difference is the number of timers. Here, each frame sent or resent needs a timer, which means that the timers need to be numbered (0, 1, 2, and 3). The timer for frame 0 starts at the first request, but stops when the ACK for this frame arrives. The timer for frame 1 starts at the second request, restarts when a NAK arrives, and finally stops when the last ACK arrives. The other two timers start when the corresponding frames are sent and stop at the last arrival event. At the receiver site when frame 0 arrives it is stored and delivered to the upper layer. But when frame 2 arrives and is stored and marked, but it cannot be delivered because frame 1 is missing. At the next arrival, frame 3 arrives and is marked and stored, but still none of the frames can be delivered. Only at the last arrival, when finally a copy of frame 1 arrives, can frames 1, 2, and 3 be delivered to the network layer. There are two conditions for the delivery of frames to the network layer: First, a set of consecutive frames must have arrived. Second, the set starts from the beginning of the window.

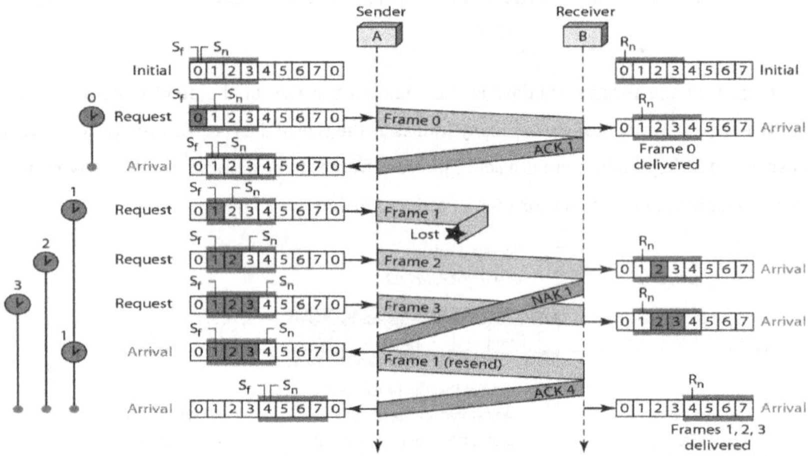

Design

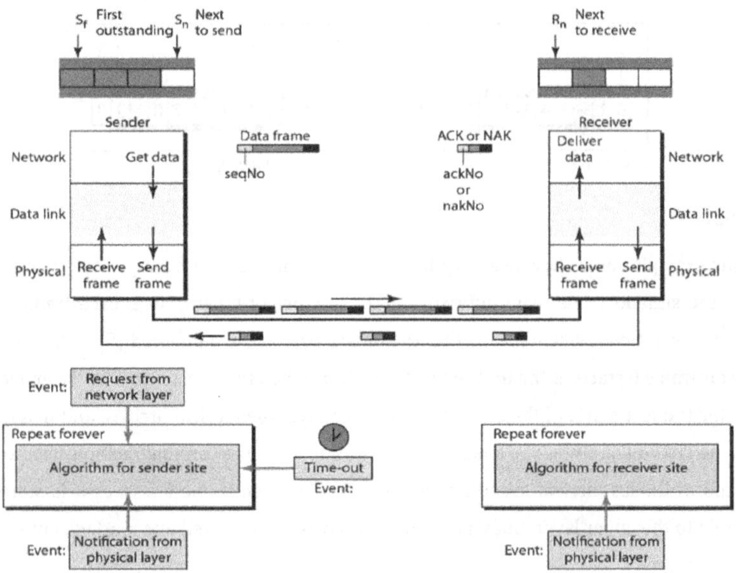

A data frames uses a seqNo (sequence number): an ACK frame uses an ackNo (acknowledgment number) or NAK number. The sender has a control variable, we call S_n (sender, next frame to send), that holds the sequence number for the next frame to be sent and S_f (first frame in the window)

The receiver has a control variable, which we call R_n (receiver, next frame expected), that holds the number of the next frame expected. When a frame is sent, the value of *Sn* is incremented (modulo-2 When a frame is received, the value of R_n is incremented (modulo-2),

Three events can happen at the sender site:

1) Request from network layer when the data is ready to send.
2) Notification from the Physical layer when the ACK is received.
3) Timeout event when timer expires without any ACK.

One event can happen at the receiver site that occurs when the data frames are passed by the physical layer.

Window Sizes

Windows must be at most 2^{m-1}. For an example, we choose m = 2, which means the size of the window is 2. Figure below compares a window size of 2 with a window size of 3. If the size of the window is 2 and all acknowledgments are lost, the timer for frame 0 expires and frame 0 is resent. However, the window of the receiver is now expecting frame 2, not frame 0, so this duplicate frame is correctly discarded. When the size of the window is 3 and all acknowledgments are lost, the sender sends a duplicate of frame 0. However, this time, the window of the receiver expects to receive frame 0 (0 is part of the window), so it accepts frame 0, not as a duplicate, but as the first frame in the next cycle. This is clearly an error.

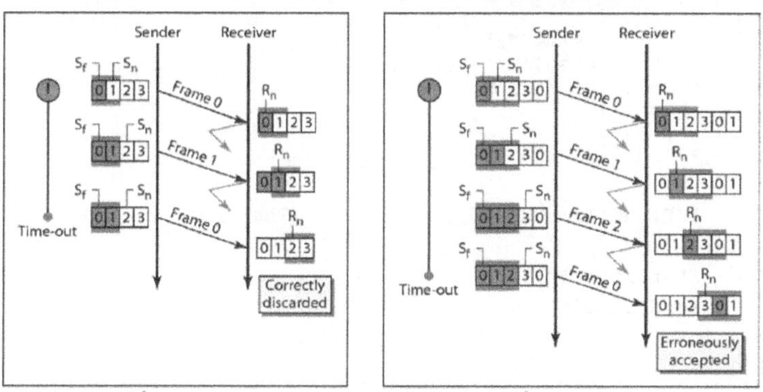

a. Window size = 2^{m-1} b. Window size > 2^{m-1}

Algorithm

Sender Algorithm

```
Sw = 2^(m-1) ;
Sf = 0;
Sn = 0;

while (true)                            //Repeat forever
{
  WaitForEvent();
  if(Event(RequestToSend))              //There is a packet to send
  {
     if(Sn-Sf >= Sw)                    //If window is full
          Sleep();
     GetData();
     MakeFrame(Sn);
     StoreFrame(Sn);
     SendFrame(Sn);
     Sn = Sn + 1;
     StartTimer(Sn);
  }

  if(Event(ArrivalNotification)) //ACK arrives
  {
     Receive(frame);                    //Receive ACK or NAK
     if(corrupted(frame))
          Sleep();
     if (FrameType == NAK)
        if (nakNo between Sf and Sn)
        {
         resend(nakNo);
         StartTimer(nakNo);
        }
     if (FrameType == ACK)
        if (ackNo between Sf and Sn)
        {
          while(sf < ackNo)
          {
           Purge(sf);
           StopTimer(sf);
           Sf = Sf + 1;
          }
        }
  }

  if(Event(TimeOut(t)))                 //The timer expires
  {
   StartTimer(t);
   SendFrame(t);
  }
}
```

Receiver Algorithm

```
Rn = 0;
NakSent = false;
AckNeeded = false;
Repeat(for all slots)
    Marked(slot) = false;

while (true)                                   //Repeat forever
{
  WaitForEvent();

  if(Event(ArrivalNotification))              /Data frame arrives
  {
     Receive(Frame);
     if(corrupted(Frame))&& (NOT NakSent)
     {
      SendNAK(Rn);
      NakSent = true;
      Sleep();
     }
     if(seqNo <> Rn)&& (NOT NakSent)
     {
      SendNAK(Rn);
      NakSent = true;
      if ((seqNo in window)&&(!Marked(seqNo))
      {
       StoreFrame(seqNo)
       Marked(seqNo)= true;
       while(Marked(Rn))
       {
        DeliverData(Rn);
        Purge(Rn);
        Rn = Rn + 1;
        AckNeeded = true;
       }
        if(AckNeeded);
        {
        SendAck(Rn);
        AckNeeded = false;
        NakSent = false;
        }
      }
     }
  }
}
```

Piggybacking

Piggybacking is a method to combine a data frame with an ACK. Both stations A & B can send as well as receive data.

Transmission process can be achieved using piggybacking, which combines data & ACK into one frame.

In reality, data frames are normally flowing in both directions: From node A to node B and from node B to node A. This means that the control information also needs to flow in both directions.

Piggybacking is used to improve the efficiency of the bidirectional protocols. When a frame is carrying data from A to B, it can also carry control information about arrived (or lost) frames from B; when a frame is carrying data from B to A, it can also carry control information about the arrived (or lost) frames from A.

Piggybacking for Duplex Stop-and-Wait ARQ

Piggybacking

1) combine data with ACK (less overhead saves bandwidth)

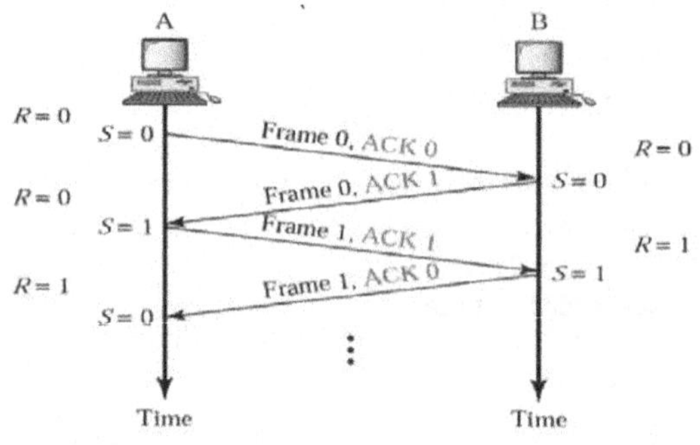

Piggybacking for Duplex Go-Back-N ARQ

Note that each node now has two windows: one send window and one receive window. Both also need to use a timer. Both are involved in three types of events: request, arrival, and time-out. The arrival event here is complicated; when a frame arrives, the site needs to handle control information as well as the frame itself.

Frame flows in both directions. Each frame has both sequence number field and also ACK/NAK field.

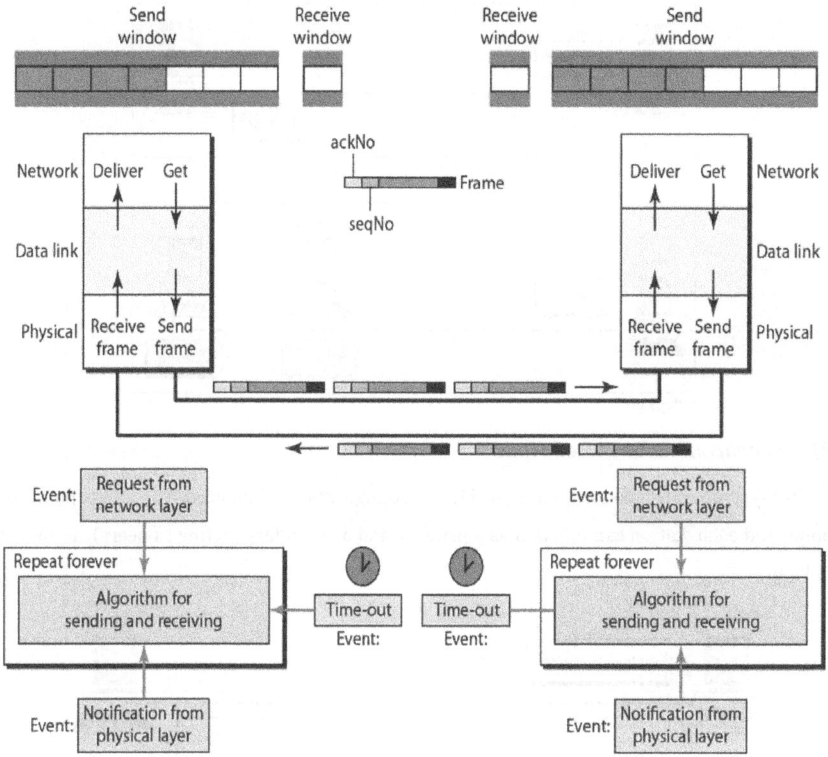

6. HDLC

High-level Data Link Control (HDLC) is a bit-oriented protocol for communication over point-to-point and multipoint links.

Configurations and Transfer Modes

HDLC provides two common transfer modes that can be used in different configurations: normal response mode (NRM) and asynchronous balanced mode (ABM).

1) Normal Response Mode

In normal response mode (NRM), the station configuration is unbalanced.

Assume there is one primary station and multiple secondary stations. A primary station can send commands; a secondary station can only respond. The NRM is used for both point-to-point and multiple-point links, as shown in Figure.

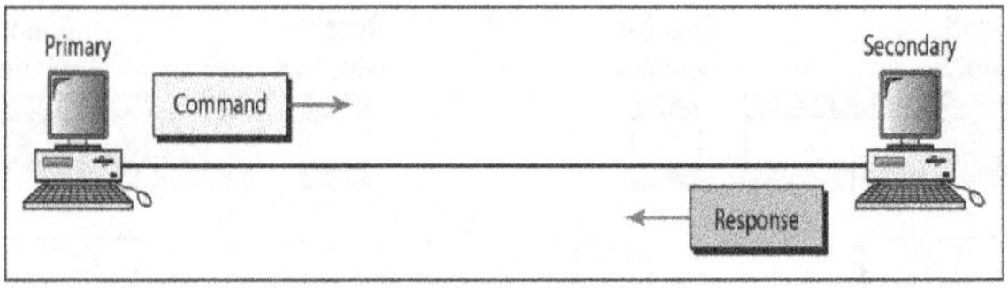

a. Point-to-point

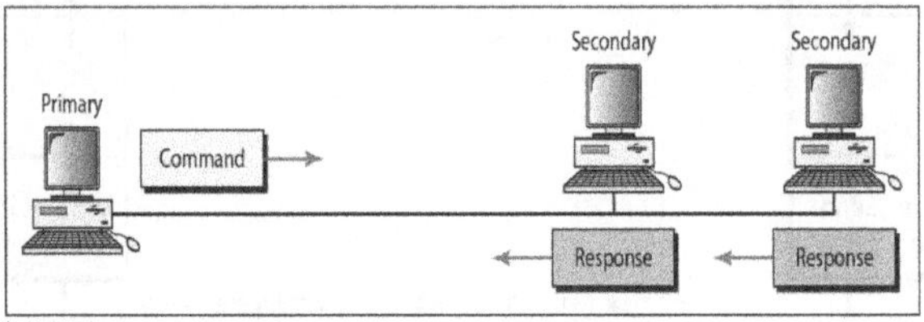

b. Multipoint

2) Asynchronous Balanced Mode

In asynchronous balanced mode (ABM), the configuration is balanced. The link is point-to-point, and each station can function as a primary and a secondary (acting as peers), as shown in Figure.

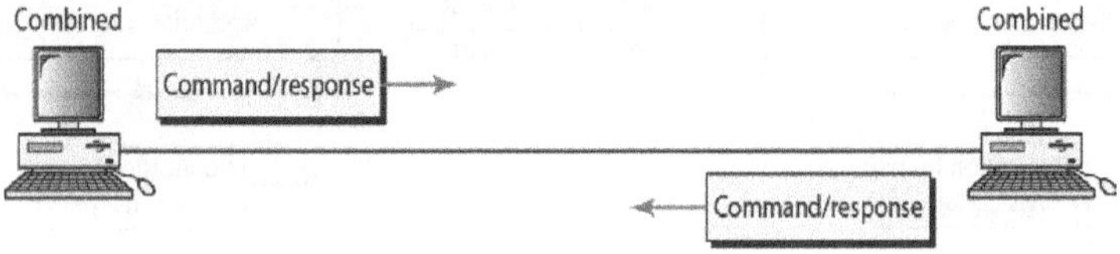

Frames

HDLC defines three types of frames

1) Information Frames (I-Frames): I-frames are used to transport user data and control information relating to user data (piggybacking).
2) Supervisory Frames (S-Frames): S-frames are used only to transport control information.
3) Unnumbered Frames (V-Frames):V-frames are reserved for system management. Information carried by V-frames is intended for managing the link itself.

Frame Format

Each frame in HDLC may contain up to six fields: a beginning flag field, an address field, a control field, an information field, a frame check sequence (FCS) field, and an ending flag field.

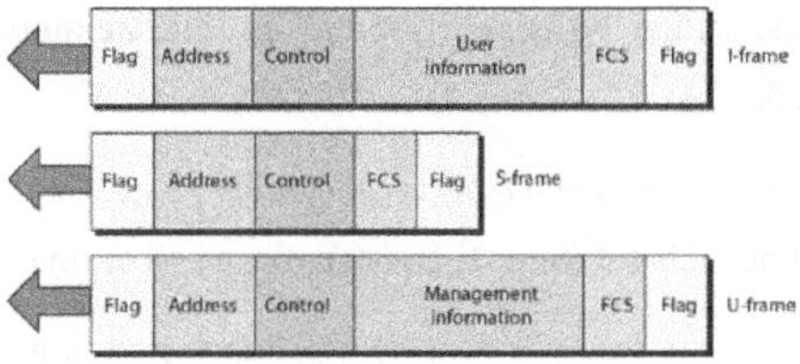

Fields

Flag Field: The flag field of an HDLC frame is an 8-bit sequence with the bit pattern 01111110 that identifies both the beginning and the end of a frame and serves as a synchronization pattern for the receiver.

Address Field: The second field of an HDLC frame contains the address of the secondary station. If a primary station created the frame, address field contains a *to* address. If a secondary creates the frame, it contains *a from* address. An address field can be 1 byte or several bytes long, depending on the needs of the network. One byte can identify up to 128 stations (l bit is used for another purpose).

Information Field: The information field contains the user's data from the network layer or management information. Its length can vary from one network to another.

FCS Field: The frame check sequence (FCS) is the HDLC error detection field. It can contain either a 2- or 4-byte ITU-T CRC(cyclic redundancy check).

Control Field: The control field is a 1- or 2-byte segment of the frame used for flow and error control. The interpretation of bits in this field depends on the frame type.

The control field determines the type of frame and defines its functionality. The format of control field for every frame type is given below:

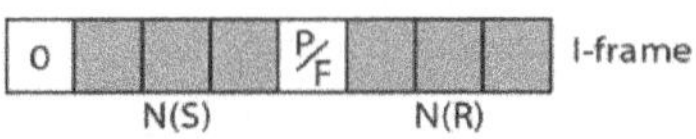

Control Field for I-Frames

I-frames are designed to carry user data from the network layer. The subfields in the control field are used to define flow and error control (piggybacking) functions.

The first bit defines the type. If the first bit of the control field is 0, this means the frame is an I-frame.

The next 3 bits, called ***N(S),*** define **the sequence number** of the frame. Note that with 3 bits, we can define a sequence number between 0 and 7.

The last 3 bits, called ***N(R)***, correspond to the **acknowledgment number** when piggybacking is used.

The single bit between *N(S)* and *N(R)* is called the ***P/F*** bit. The *P/F* field is a single bit which has meaning only when it is set (bit = 1) and can mean poll or final.

It means *poll* when the frame is sent by a primary station to a secondary. It means *final* when the frame is sent by a secondary to a primary.

Control Field for S-Frames

Supervisory frames are used for flow and error control whenever piggybacking is not done (e.g., when the station either has no data of its own to send or needs to send a command or response other than an acknowledgment).

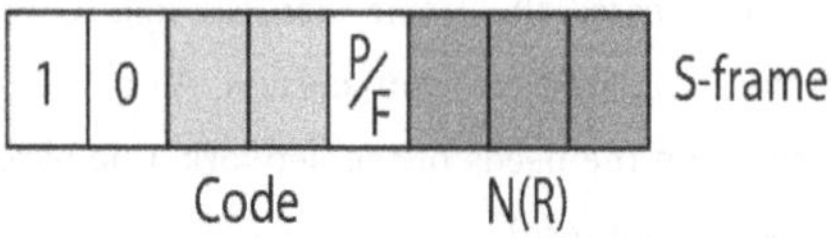

S-frames do not have information fields. If the first 2 bits of the control field is 10, this means the frame is an S-frame. The last 3 bits, called *N(R)*, corresponds to the acknowledgment number (ACK) or negative acknowledgment number (NAK) depending on the type of S-frame.

The 2 bits called code is used to define the four types of S-frame itself.

1) **Receive ready (RR):** If the value of the code subfield is **00**, it is an RR S-frame. This kind of frame acknowledges the receipt of a safe and sound frame or group of frames. In this case, the value *N(R)* field defines the acknowledgment number.
2) **Receive not ready (RNR):** If the value of the code subfield is **10**, it is an RNR S-frame. This frame acknowledges the receipt of a frame or group of frames, and it announces that the receiver is busy and cannot receive more frames. The value of *N(R)* is the acknowledgment number.
3) **Reject (REJ)**: If the value of the code subfield is **01**, it is a REJ S-frame. This is a NAK frame used in *Go-Back-N* ARQ to inform the sender, before the sender time expires, that the last frame is lost or damaged. The value of *N(R)* is the negative acknowledgment number.
4) **Selective reject (SREJ):** If the value of the code subfield is **11**, it is an SREJ S-frame. This is a NAK frame used in Selective Repeat ARQ. The value of *N(R)* is the negative acknowledgment number.

Control Field for U-Frames

Unnumbered frames are used to exchange session management and control information between connected devices. Unlike S-frames, U-frames contain an information field, but one used for system management information, not user data.

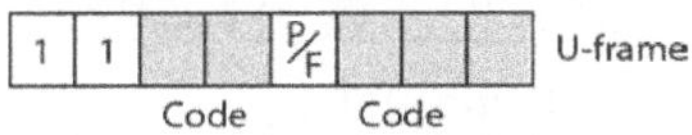

U-frame codes are divided into two sections: a 2-bit prefix before the P/F bit and a 3-bit suffix after the P/F bit. Together, these two segments (5 bits) can be used to create up to 32 different types of U-frames.

Code	*Command*	*Response*	*Meaning*
00 001	SNRM		Set normal response mode
11 011	SNRME		Set normal response mode, extended
11 100	SABM	DM	Set asynchronous balanced mode or disconnect mode
11 110	SABME		Set asynchronous balanced mode, extended
00 000	UI	UI	Unnumbered information
00 110		UA	Unnumbered acknowledgment
00 010	DISC	RD	Disconnect or request disconnect
10 000	SIM	RIM	Set initialization mode or request information mode
00 100	UP		Unnumbered poll
11 001	RSET		Reset
11 101	XID	XID	Exchange ID
10 001	FRMR	FRMR	Frame reject

Example

Connection/Disconnection: Figure shows how V-frames can be used for connection establishment and connection release. Node A asks for a connection with a set asynchronous balanced mode = (SABM) frame; node B gives a positive response with an unnumbered acknowledgment (VA) frame. After these two exchanges, data can be transferred between the two nodes (not shown in the figure). After data transfer, node A sends a DISC (disconnect) frame to release the connection; it is confirmed by node B responding with a VA (unnumbered acknowledgment).

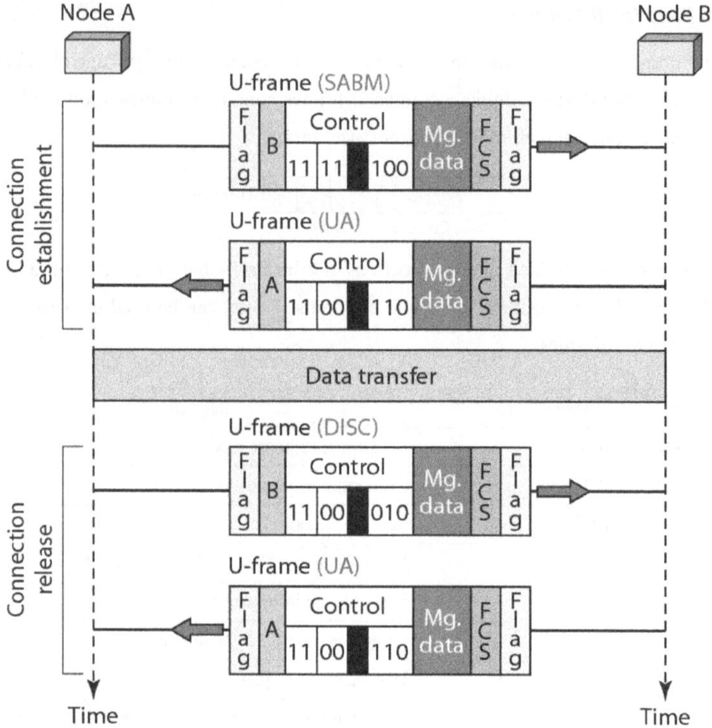

Example

Figure below shows an exchange using piggybacking without error. Node A begins the exchange of information with an I-frame numbered 0 followed by another I-frame numbered 1. Node B piggybacks its acknowledgment of both frames onto an I-frame of its own. Node B's first I-frame is also numbered 0 *[N(S)* field] and contains a 2 in its *N(R)* field, acknowledging the receipt of Ns frames 1 and 0 and indicating that it expects frame 2 to arrive next.

Node B transmits its second and third I-frames (numbered 1 and 2) before accepting further frames from node A. Its *N(R)* information, therefore, has not changed: B frames 1 and 2 indicate that node B is still expecting Ns frame 2 to arrive next.

Node A has sent all its data. Therefore, it cannot piggyback an acknowledgment onto an I-frame and sends an S-frame instead. The RR code indicates that A is still ready to receive. The number 3 in the *N(R)* field tells B that frames 0, 1, and 2 have all been accepted and that A is now expecting frame number 3.

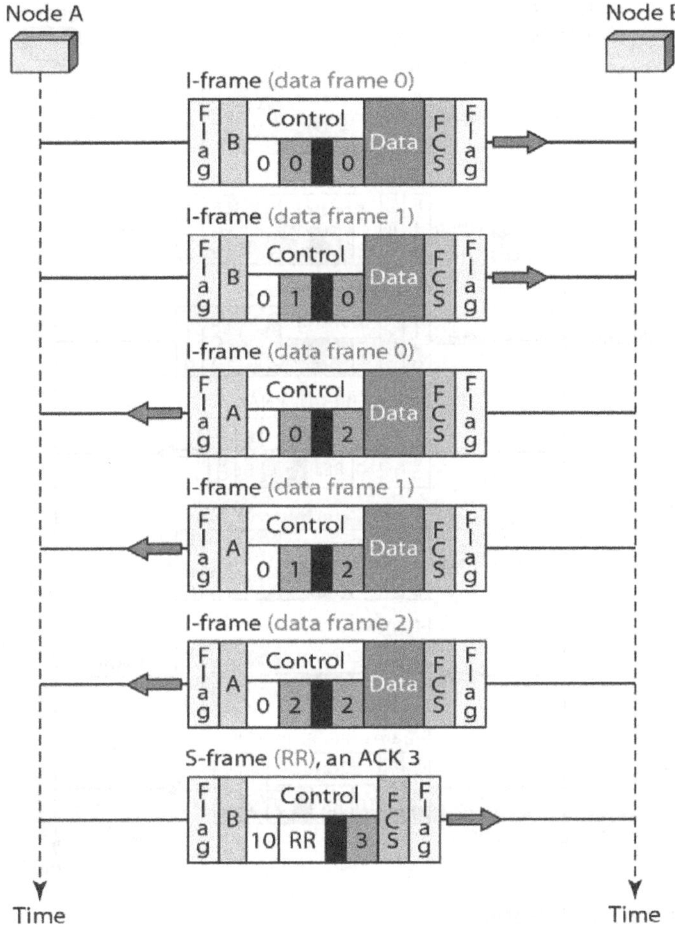

Example

Piggybacking with Error Figure shows an exchange in which a frame is lost. Node B sends three data frames (0, 1, and 2), but frame 1 is lost. When node A receives frame 2, it discards it and sends a REJ frame for frame 1. Note that the protocol being used is *Go-Back-N* with the special use of an REJ frame as a NAK frame. The NAK frame does two things here: It confirms the receipt of frame and declares that frame 1 and any following frames must be resent. Node B, after receiving the REJ frame, resends frames 1 and 2. Node A acknowledges the receipt by sending an RR frame (ACK) with acknowledgment number 3.

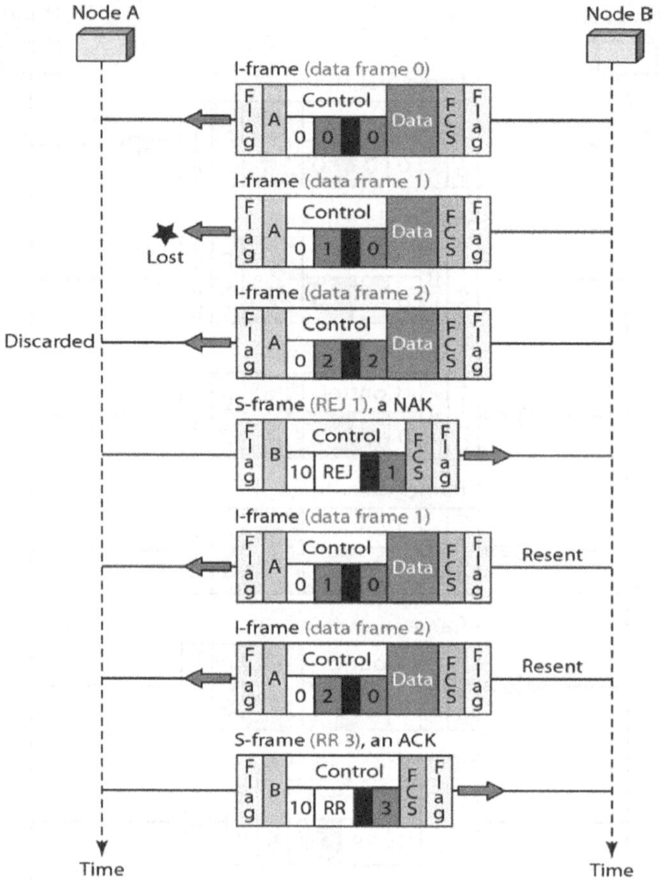

7. Point-to-Point Protocol

PPP is a byte oriented protocol.

PPP provides several services.

1) PPP defines the format of the frame to be exchanged between devices.
2) PPP defines how two devices can negotiate the establishment of the link and the exchange of data.
3) PPP defines how network layer data are encapsulated in the data link frame.
4) PPP defines how two devices can authenticate each other

5) PPP provides multiple network layer services supporting a variety of network layer protocols.
6) PPP provides connections over multiple links.
7) PPP provides network address configuration. This is particularly useful when a home user needs a temporary network address to connect to the Internet.

Drawbacks of PPP

1) PPP does not provide flow control. A sender can send several frames one after another with no concern about overwhelming the receiver.
2) PPP has a very simple mechanism for error control. A CRC field is used to detect errors. Lack of error control and sequence numbering may cause a packet to be received out of order.
3) PPP does not provide a sophisticated addressing mechanism to handle frames in a multipoint configuration.

Framing

PPP is a byte-oriented protocol.

Frame Format : Figure shows the format of a PPP frame.

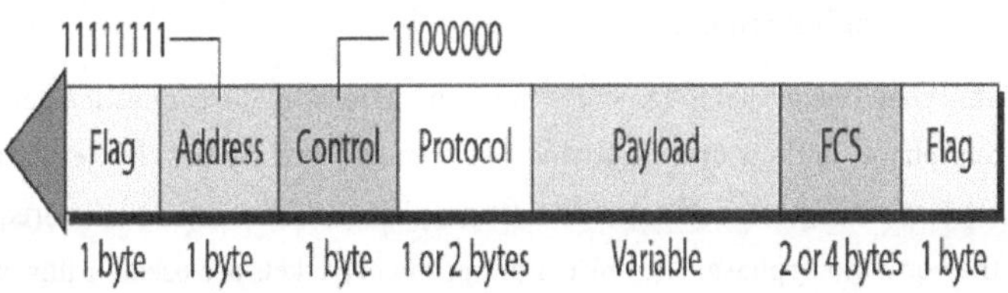

Flag

A PPP frame starts and ends with a 1-byte flag with the bit pattern 01111110. Although this pattern is the same as that used in HDLC, there is a big difference. PPP is a byte-oriented protocol; So the flag is treated as a byte.

Address: The address field in this protocol is a constant value and set to 11111111 (broadcast address). During negotiation, the two parties may agree to omit this byte.

Control: This field is set to the constant value 11000000 (imitating unnumbered frames in HDLC). PPP does not provide any flow control. Error control is also limited to error detection. This means that this field is not needed at all, the two parties can agree, during negotiation, to omit this byte.

Protocol: The protocol field defines what is being carried in the data field: either user data or other information. This field is by default 2 bytes long, but the two parties can agree to use only 1 byte.

Payload Field: This field carries either the user data or other information. The data field is a sequence of bytes with the default of a maximum of 1500 bytes; but this can be changed during negotiation. The data field is byte stuffed if the flag byte pattern appears in this field. Because there is no field defining the size of the data field, padding is needed if the size is less than the maximum default value or the maximum negotiated value.

FCS: The frame check sequence (FCS) is simply a 2-byte or 4-byte standard CRC.

Byte Stuffing: As a byte-oriented protocol, the flag in PPP is a byte and needs to be escaped whenever it appears in the data section of the frame. The escape byte is 01111101, which means that every time the flag like pattern appears in the data, this extra byte is stuffed to tell the receiver that the next byte is not a flag.

Transition Phases

A PPP connection goes through phases which can be shown in a transition phase diagram.

Dead: In the dead phase the link is not being used. There is no active carrier (at the physical layer) and the line is quiet.

Establish: When one of the nodes starts the communication, the connection goes into this phase. In this phase, options are negotiated between the two parties. If the negotiation is successful, the system goes to the authentication phase (if authentication is required) or directly to the networking phase. The link control protocol packets are used for this purpose.

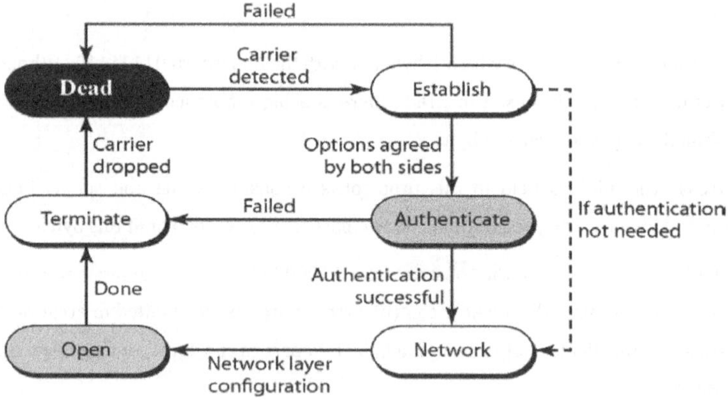

Authenticate: The authentication phase is optional; the two nodes may decide, during the establishment phase, not to skip this phase. However, if they decide to proceed with authentication, they send several authentication packets. If the result is successful, the connection goes to the networking phase; otherwise, it goes to the termination phase.

Network: In the network phase, negotiation for the network layer protocols takes place. PPP specifies that two nodes establish a network layer agreement before data at the network layer can be exchanged. The reason is that PPP supports multiple protocols at the network layer. If a node is running multiple protocols simultaneously at the network layer, the receiving node needs to know which protocol will receive the data.

Open: In the open phase, data transfer takes place. When a connection reaches this phase, the exchange of data packets can be started. The connection remains in this phase until one of the endpoints wants to terminate the connection.

Terminate: In the termination phase the connection is terminated. Several packets are exchanged between the two ends for closing the link.

UNIT-6

Multiple Access & Ethernet: Random access, Controlled Access, Channelization, Ethernet: IEEE standards, Standard Ethernet, Changes in the standard, Fast Ethernet, Gigabit Ethernet.

1. Multiple Access

Data link layer divided into two functionality-oriented sublayers.

The upper sublayer that is responsible for flow and error control is called the logical link control (LLC) or data link control layer.

The lower sublayer that is mostly responsible for multiple access resolution is called the media access control (MAC) layer.

IEEE has actually made this division for LANs.

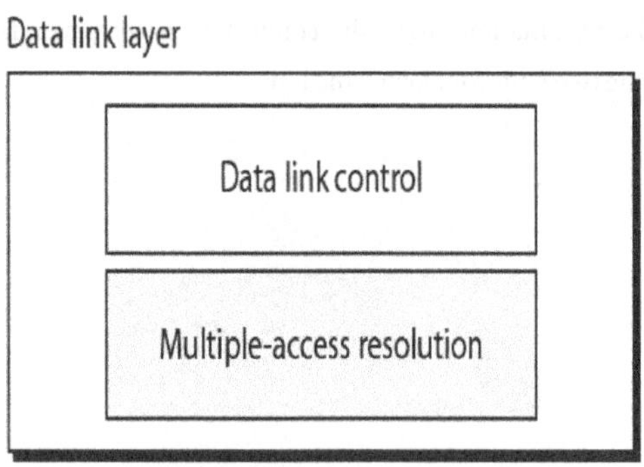

Logical Link Control (LLC)

In IEEE Project 802, flow control, error control, and part of the framing duties are collected into one sublayer called the logical link control. Framing is handled in both the LLC sublayer and the MAC sublayer. The LLC provides one single data link control protocol for all IEEE LANs.

The LLC is different from the media access control sublayer, which provides different protocols for different LANs.

Framing: LLC defines a protocol data unit (PDU) that is similar to that of HDLC. The header contains a control field that is used for flow and error control. The two other header fields, destination service access point (DSAP) and the source service access point (SSAP) define the upper-layer protocol at the source and destination that uses LLC.

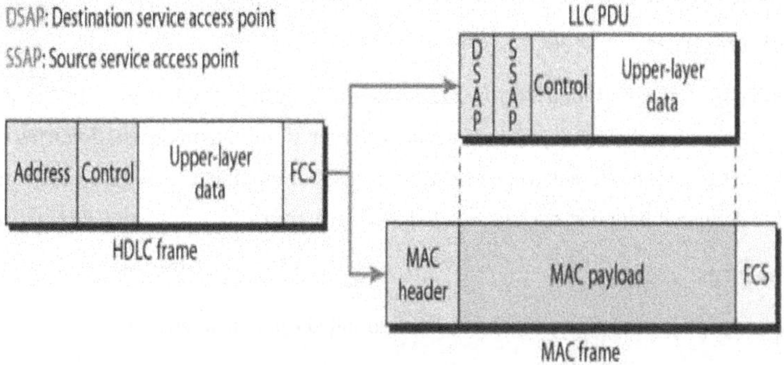

Need for LLC The purpose of the LLC is to provide flow and error control for the upper-layer protocols that actually demand these services.

Media Access Control (MAC)

IEEE Project 802 has created a sublayer called media access control that defines the specific access method for each LAN. For example, it defines *CSMA/CD* as the media access method for Ethernet LANs and the token passing method for Token Ring and Token Bus LANs.

In multiple access, multiple stations are connected to a shared link. Access to the shared link is coordinated by multiple access protocol. There are 3 categories of multiple access protocols.

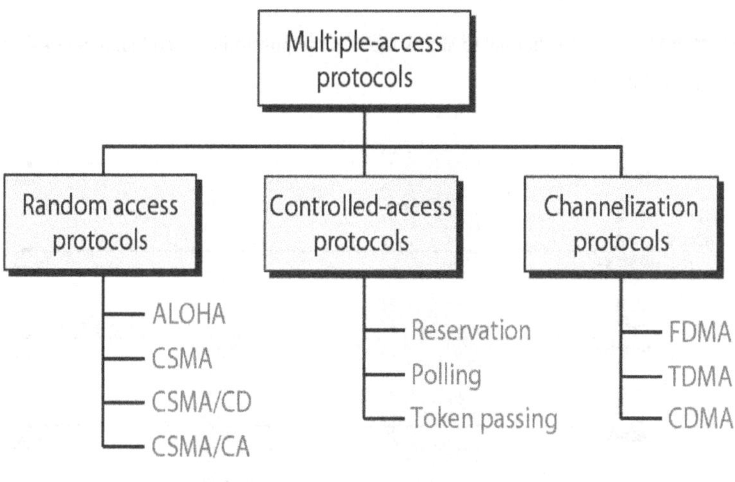

Taxonomy of Multiple-Access Protocols

2. Multiple Access Protocols

2.1. Random Access

In random access or contention methods, each station has the right to the medium without being controlled by any other station. However, if more than one station tries to send, collision occurs and the frames will be either destroyed or modified. To avoid access conflict or to resolve it when it happens, each station follows a procedure.

Two Features

Transmission is random among the stations so called *random access.*

Stations compete with one another to access the medium. So it is called *contention* methods.

2.1.1. ALOHA

ALOHA, the earliest random access method, was designed for a radio (wireless) LAN, but it can be used on any shared medium.

The medium is shared between the stations. When a station sends data, another station may attempt to do so at the same time. The data from the two stations collide and become garbled.

Pure ALOHA

The original ALOHA protocol is called pure ALOHA. The idea is that each station sends a frame whenever it has a frame to send.

Since there is only one channel to share, there is the possibility of collision between frames from different stations.

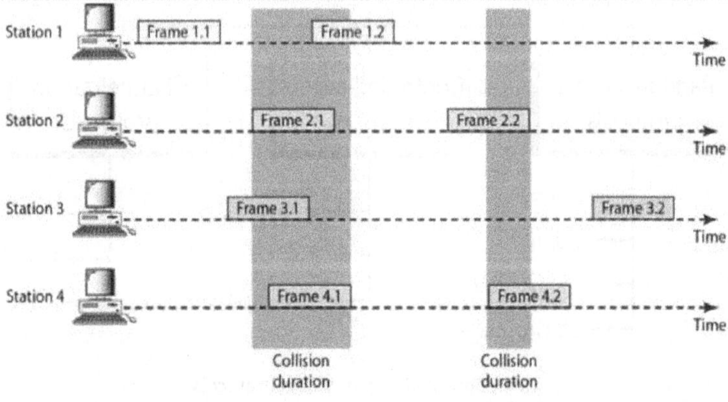

There are four stations that contend with one another for access to the shared channel. The figure shows that each station sends two frames; Some of these frames collide because multiple frames are in contention for the shared channel. If the frame is collided it is retransmitted again.

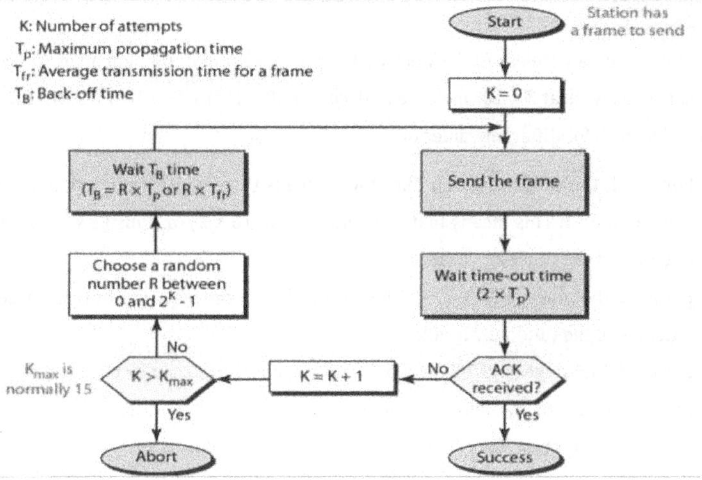

Procedure for Pure ALOHA

When a station sends a frame, it expects the receiver to send an acknowledgment. If the acknowledgment does not arrive after a time-out period, the station assumes that the frame (or the acknowledgment) has been destroyed and resends the frame.

A collision involves two or more stations. If all these stations try to resend their frames after the time-out, the frames will collide again.

Pure ALOHA dictates that when the time-out period passes, each station waits a random amount of time called **back-off time(T_B)** before resending its frame.

After a maximum number of retransmission attempts Kmax a station must give up and try later to prevent congesting the channel with retransmitted frames. The value of *Kmax* is usually chosen as 15.

The time-out period is equal to the maximum possible round-trip propagation delay, which is twice the amount of time required to send a frame between the stations at two ends of network (2 x *Tp)*. The back-off time T_B is a random value that normally depends on *K* (the number of attempted unsuccessful transmissions).

One common formula for backoff is the **binary exponential back-off.** In this method, for each retransmission, a multiplier in the range 0 to $2^K - 1$ is randomly chosen and multiplied by *Tp* (maximum propagation time) or T_{fr} (the average time required to send out a frame) to find T_B. The range of the random numbers increases after each collision.

Example

The stations on a wireless ALOHA network are a maximum of 600 km apart. If we assume that signals propagate at 3×10^8 m/s, we find $Tp = (600 \times 10^5) / (3 \times 10^8) = 2$ ms. Now we can find the value of T_B for different values of *K*.

1) For $K = 1$, the range is {0, 1}. The station needs to generate a random number with a value of 0 or 1. This means that T_B is either **0** ms (0 x 2) or 2 ms (1 x 2), based on the outcome of the random variable.
2) For $K = 2$, the range is {0, 1, 2, 3}. This means that T_B can be 0, 2, 4, or 6 ms, based on the outcome of the random variable.
3) For $K = 3$, the range is {0,1,2,3,4,5,6,7}. This means that T_B can be 0,2,4, ... , 14 ms, based on the outcome of the random variable.
4) We need to mention that if $K > 10$, it is normally set to 10.

Vulnerable Time

The vulnerable time is the length of time in which there is a possibility of collision. Assume that the stations send fixed-length frames with each frame taking T_{fr} Sec to send.

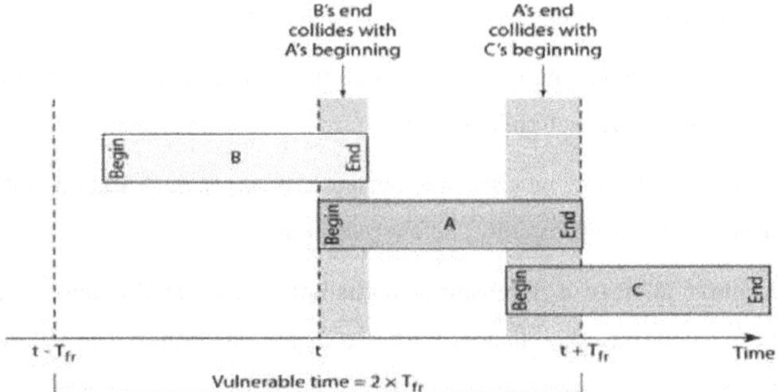

Vulnerable Time for Pure ALOHA Protocol

The vulnerable time, during which a collision may occur in pure ALOHA, is 2 times the frame transmission time.

Pure ALOHA vulnerable time = $2 \times T_{fr}$

Example

A pure ALOHA network transmits 200-bit frames on a shared channel of 200 kbps. What is the requirement to make this frame collision-free?

Solution

Average frame transmission time T_{fr} is 200 bits/200 kbps or 1 ms.

The vulnerable time is 2 × 1 ms = 2 ms.

1) This means no station should send later than 1 ms before this station starts transmission and no station should start sending during the one 1-ms period that this station is sending.

Throughput

Let G be the average number of frames generated by the system during one frame transmission time. Then the average number of successful transmissions for pure ALOHA is **S = G x** e^{-2G}. The maximum throughput Smax is 0.184, for G = 1.

Example

A pure ALOHA network transmits 200-bit frames on a shared channel of 200 kbps. What is the throughput if the system (all stations together) produces:

1) 1000 frames per second.
2) 500 frames per second.
3) 250 frames per second.

Solution

The frame transmission time is 200/200 kbps or 1 ms.

1) The system creates 1000 frames per second: G= 1000 x 10^{-3}= 1 frame per millisecond. The load is 1. S = G× e−2 G or S = 0.135 (13.5 percent). Throughput =1000 × 0.135 = 135 frames. Only 135 frames out of 1000 will probably survive.
2) If the system creates 500 frames per second, G= 500 x 10^{-3}=(1/2) frame per millisecond. The load is (1/2). S = G × e −2G or S = 0.184 (18.4 percent). This means that the throughput is 500×0.184 = 92 and that only 92 frames out of 500 will probably survive.
3) If the system creates 250 frames per second, G= 250 x 10 $^{-3}$ = (1/4) frame per millisecond. The load is (1/4). S = G × e −2G or S = 0.152 (15.2 percent). This means

that the throughput is 250 × 0.152 = 38. Only 38 frames out of 250 will probably survive.

Slotted ALOHA

Slotted ALOHA was invented to improve the efficiency of pure ALOHA. In slotted ALOHA the time slot is divided into T_{fr} sec and forces the station to send only at the beginning of the time slot.

Because a station is allowed to send only at the beginning of the synchronized time slot, if a station misses this moment, it must wait until the beginning of the next time slot.

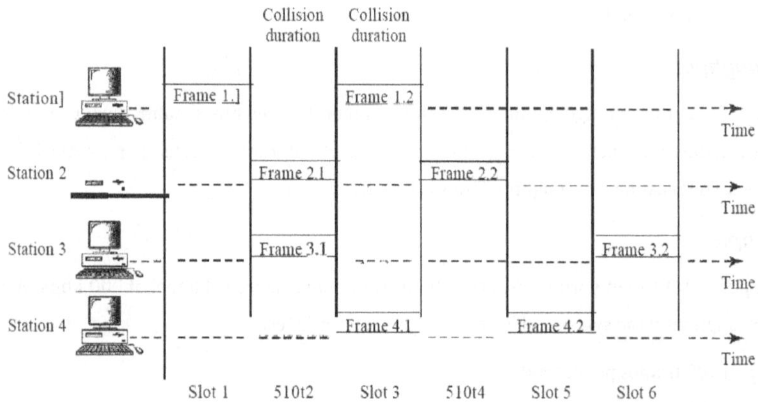

There is still the possibility of collision if two stations try to send at the beginning of the same time slot. The vulnerable time is now reduced to one-half, equal to T_{fr}.

Slotted ALOHA vulnerable time = T_{fr}

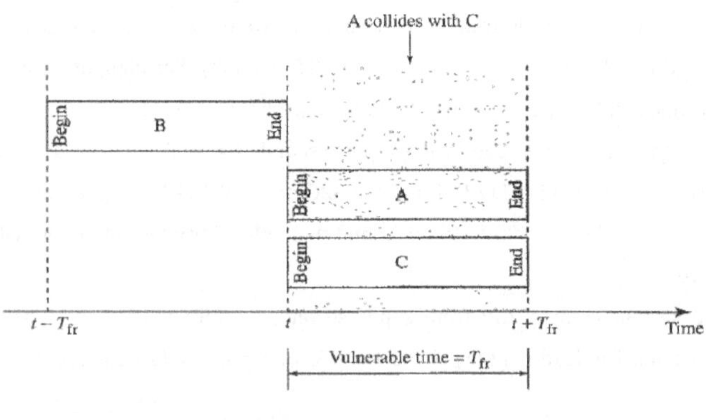

Throughput

The throughput for slotted ALOHA is S =: G x e^{-G}. The maximum throughput Smax is 0.368, when G = 1.

Example

A slotted ALOHA network transmits 200-bit frames using a shared channel with a 200-kbps bandwidth. Find the throughput if the system (all stations together) produces:

1) 1000 frames per second.
2) 500 frames per second.
3) 250 frames per second.

Solution

The frame transmission time is *200/200* kbps or 1 ms.

1) **If the system generates 1000 frames per second,** G =1000 x 10^{-3}= 1 frame per millisecond.

   So S =G x e^{-G} or S =0.368 (36.8 percent). This means that the throughput is 1000 x 0.0368 =368 frames. Only 368 out of 1000 frames will probably survive.
2) **If the system generates 500 frames per second,** G =500 x 10^{-3} = 1/2. In this case S =G x *e-G* or

   S =0.303 (30.3 percent). This means that the throughput is 500 x 0.0303 =151. Only 151 frames out of 500 will probably survive.
3) **If the system generates 250 frames per second,** G =250 x 10^{-3}1/4. In this case S =G x *e-G* or S =0.195 (19.5 percent). This means that the throughput is 250 x 0.195 = 49. Only 49 frames out of 250 will probably survive.

2.1.2. Carrier Sense Multiple Access (CSMA)

Carrier sense multiple access (CSMA) requires that each station first listen to the medium (or check the state of the medium) before sending.

CSMA can reduce the possibility of collision, but it cannot eliminate it. Stations are connected to a shared channel (usually a dedicated medium).

The possibility of collision still exists because of propagation delay; when a station sends a frame, it still takes time (although very short) for the first bit to reach every station and for every station to sense it.

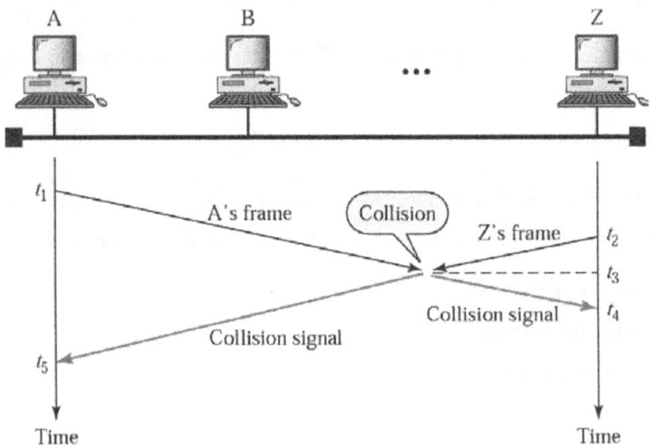

Space/time Model of the Collision in CSMA

At time t1, station A, sensed that medium is idle, so sends a frame. At time t2 (t2 > t1), station Z also senses the medium and finds idle because of propagation delay(time taken to reach Z) of A's frame and send its a frame. Two signals collide at t3 (t3>t2>t1). The garbled signal, reach Z in t4 (t4>t3>t2>t1) and station A at time t5 (t5>t4>t3>t2>t1)

Vulnerable Time

The vulnerable time for CSMA is the propagation time *Tp* . This is the time needed for a signal to propagate from one end of the medium to the other.

When a station sends a frame, and any other station tries to send a frame during this time, a collision will result. But if the first bit of the frame reaches the end of the medium, every station will already have heard the bit and will refrain from sending.

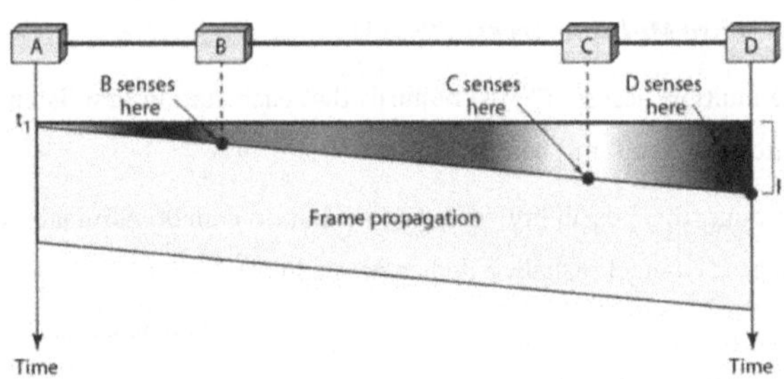

Vulnerable time = propagation time

Persistence Methods

What should a station do if the channel is busy? What should a station do if the channel is idle? Three methods have been devised to answer these questions:

1) The 1-persistent method.
2) The nonpersistent method.
3) The p-persistent method.

1-Persistent

In this method, the station senses the medium continuously if the medium is busy until it finds the medium as idle. After the station finds the line idle, it sends its frame immediately (with probability 1).

This method has the highest chance of collision (drawback) because two or more stations may find the line idle and send their frames immediately.

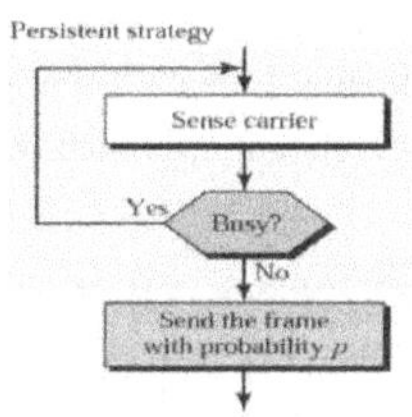

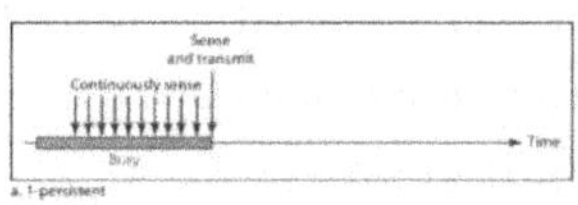

Nonpersistent: In the nonpersistent method, a station that has a frame to send senses the line. If the line is idle, it sends immediately. If the line is not idle, it waits a random amount of time and then senses the line again. The nonpersistent approach **reduces the chance of collision (advantage)** because it is unlikely that two or more stations will wait the same amount of time and retry to send simultaneously.

This method **reduces the efficiency of the network (drawback)** because the medium remains idle when there may be stations with frames to send.

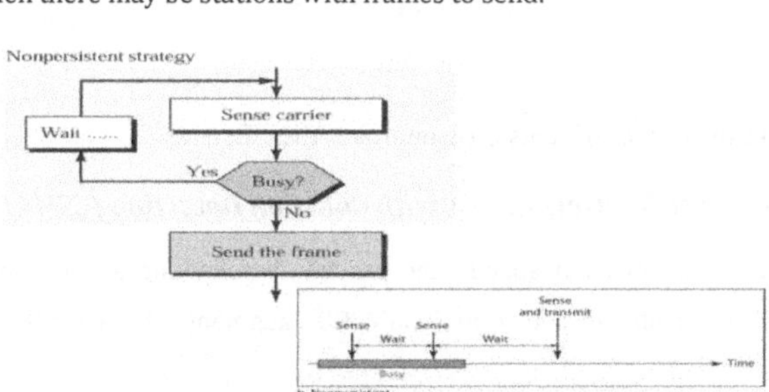

Advantage

- Reduces the chance of collision.

Disadvantage

- Two or more stations wait the same amount of time and retry again simultaneously. This reduces the efficiency of the network.

p-Persistent: In p-persistent method, the station senses the medium continuously if it finds a busy line. After the station finds the line idle it follows these steps:

1) With probability *p*, the station sends its frame.
2) With probability $q = 1 - p$, the station waits for the beginning of the next time slot and checks the line again.
    - If the line is idle, it goes to step 1.
    - If the line is busy, it acts as though a collision has occurred and uses the backoff procedure.

The p-persistent method is used if the channel has time slots with slot duration equal to or greater than the maximum propagation time. The p-persistent approach *reduces the chance of collision and improves efficiency*

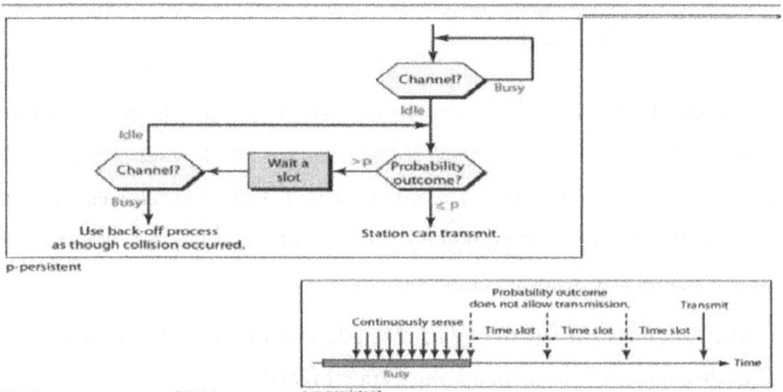

Advantage

- It reduces the chance of collision & improves the efficiency.

2.1.3. Carrier Sense Multiple Access with Collision Detection (CSMA/CD)

The CSMA method does not specify the procedure following a collision. Carrier sense multiple access with collision detection (CSMA/CD) augments the algorithm to handle the collision.

In this method, a station monitors the medium after it sends a frame to see if the transmission was successful. If so, the station is finished. If there is a collision, the frame is sent again.

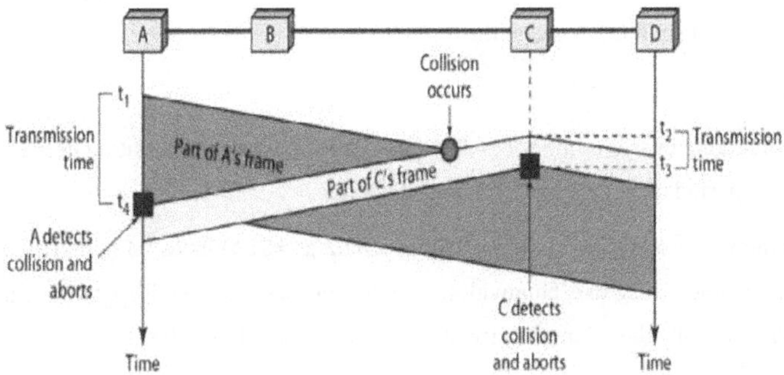

Collision and Abortion in CSMA/CD

At time t1, station A has executed its persistence procedure and starts sending the bits of its frame. At time *t2,* station C has not yet sensed the first bit sent by A. Station C executes its persistence procedure and starts sending the bits in its frame, which propagate both to the left and to the right.

The collision occurs sometime after time *t2,* Station C detects a collision at time *t3* when it receives the first bit of A's frame. Station C immediately aborts transmission. Station A detects collision at time *t4* when it receives the first bit of C's frame; it also immediately aborts transmission.

Minimum Frame Size

For *CSMA/CD* to work, we need a restriction on the frame size. Before sending the last bit of the frame, the sending station must detect a collision, if any, and abort the transmission.

This is because the station, once the entire frame is sent, does not keep a copy of the frame and does not monitor the line for collision detection. Therefore, the frame transmission time T_{fr} must be at least two times the maximum propagation time *Tp*.($T_{fr} = 2 \times Tp$)

To understand the reason, assume the two stations involved in a collision are the maximum distance apart, the signal from the first takes time *Tp* to reach the second, and the effect of the collision takes another time *Tp* to reach the first. So the requirement is that the first station must still be transmitting after *2Tp.*

Example

A network using *CSMA/CD* has a bandwidth of 10 Mbps. If the maximum propagation time (including the delays in the devices and ignoring the time needed to send a jamming signal) is 25.6 μs, what is the minimum size of the frame?

Solution

The frame transmission time is T_{fr} = 2 x Tp =51.2 μs. This means, a station needs to transmit a frame for a period of 51.2 μs to detect the collision.

The minimum size of the frame is 10 Mbps x 51.2 μs =512 bits or 64 bytes.(because frame transmission time = msg.size/bandwidth...so message size= bandwidth x frame transmission time). This is actually the minimum size of the frame for Standard Ethernet.

Procedure

CSMA/CD differs from ALOHA in the following ways:

1) Addition of persistence process
2) Frame transmission: In ALOHA, the entire frame is transmitted and then wait for an acknowledgment. In *CSMA/CD,* transmission and collision detection is a continuous process.
3) Sending a short jamming signal.

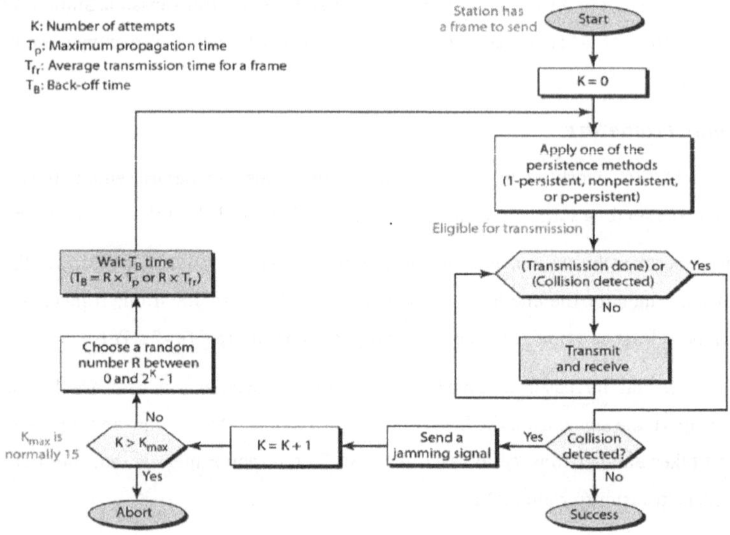

The sender needs to sense the channel before we start sending the frame by using one of the persistence processes (nonpersistent, 1-persistent, or p-persistent).

CSMA/CD does not send the entire frame and then look for a collision. The station transmits and receives continuously and simultaneously.

We use a loop to show that transmission is a continuous process. The station constantly monitors in order to detect one of two conditions: either transmission is finished or a collision is detected. Either event stops transmission. When we come out of the loop, if a collision has not been detected, it means that transmission is complete; the entire frame is transmitted. Otherwise, a collision has occurred.

A short jamming signal is to alert the other stations that have not yet sensed the collision.

Energy Level

A station that has a frame to send or is sending a frame needs to monitor the energy level to determine if the channel is idle, busy, or in collision mode. At the normal level, a station has successfully captured the channel and is sending its frame. At the abnormal level, there is a collision and the level of the energy is twice the normal level.

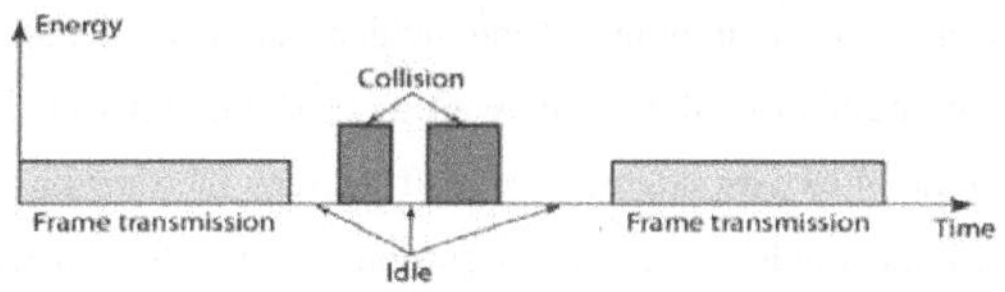

Throughput

The throughput of *CSMA/CD* is greater than that of pure or slotted ALOHA. For 1-persistent method the maximum throughput is around 50 percent when G =1. For nonpersistent method, the maximum throughput can go up to 90 percent when G is between 3 and 8.

2.1.4. Carrier Sense Multiple Access with Collision Avoidance (CSMA/CA)

In a wireless network, much of the sent energy is lost in transmission. The received signal has very little energy. Therefore, a collision may add only 5 to 10 percent additional energy. This is not useful for effective collision detection.

To avoid collisions on wireless networks because the energy cannot be detected Carrier sense multiple access with collision avoidance **(CSMA/CA)** was invente. Collisions are avoided through the use of CSMA/CA's three strategies: the interframe space, the contention window, and acknowledgments.

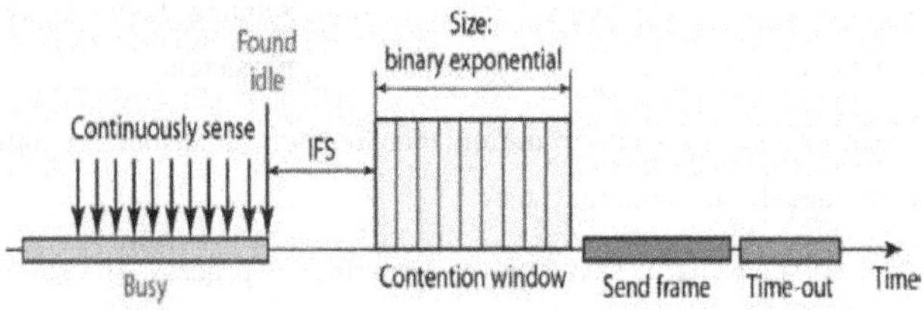

Inter Frame Space (IFS)

First, collisions are avoided by deferring transmission even if the channel is found idle. It waits for a period of time called the interframe space or IFS. Even though the channel may appear idle when it is sensed, a distant station may have already started transmitting.

The distant station's signal has not yet reached this station. The IFS time allows the front of the transmitted signal by the distant station to reach this station. If after the IFS time the channel is still idle, the station can send, but it still needs to wait a time equal to the contention time.

Contention Window

The contention window is an amount of time divided into slots. A station that is ready to send chooses a random number of slots as its wait time. The number of slots in the window changes according to the binary exponential back-off strategy. This means that it is set to one slot the first time and then doubles each time the station cannot detect an idle channel after the IFS time.

The station needs to sense the channel after each time slot. However, if the station finds the channel busy, it does not restart the process; it just stops the timer and restarts it when the channel is sensed as idle. This gives priority to the station with the longest waiting time.

Acknowledgment

The positive acknowledgment and the time-out timer can help guarantee that the receiver has received the frame.

Procedure

The channel needs to be sensed before and after the IFS. The channel also needs to be sensed during the contention time. For each time slot of the contention window, the channel is sensed. If it is found idle, the timer continues; if the channel is found busy, the timer is stopped and continues after the timer becomes idle again.

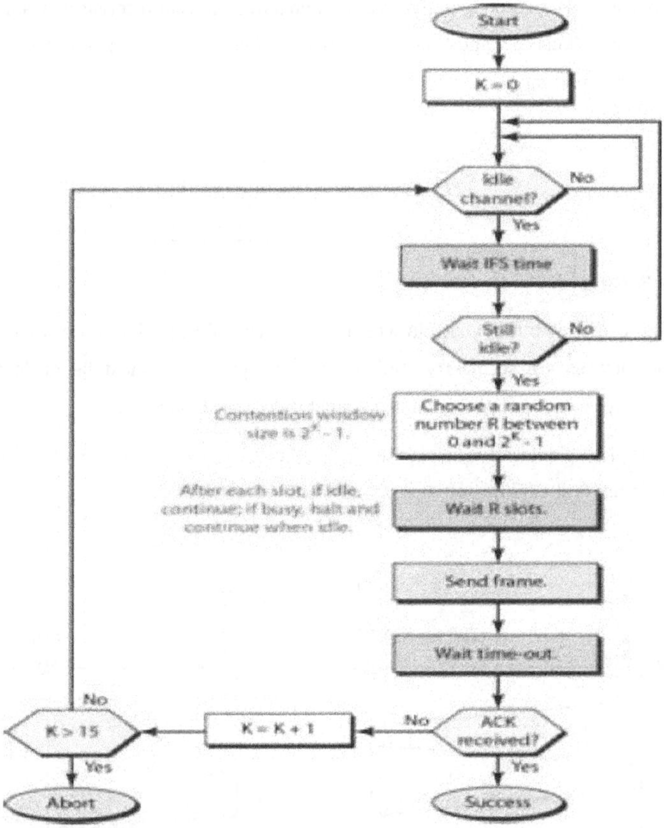

2.2. Controlled Access

In controlled access, the stations consult one another to find which station has the right to send. A station cannot send unless it has been authorized by other stations.

2.2.1. Reservation

In the reservation method, a station needs to make a reservation before sending data. Time is divided into intervals. In each interval, a reservation frame precedes the data frames sent in that interval.

If there are *N* stations in the system, there are exactly *N* reservation minislots in the reservation frame. Each minislot belongs to a station. When a station needs to send a data frame, it makes a reservation in its own minislot and can send their data frames after the reservation frame.

Figure shows a situation with five stations and a five-minislot reservation frame. In the first interval, only stations 1, 3, and 4 have made reservations. In the second interval, only station 1 has made a reservation.

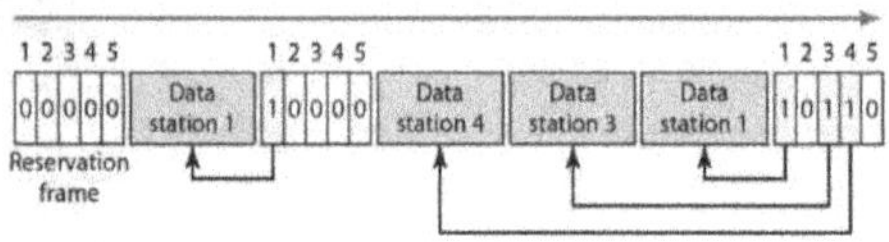

2.2.2. *Polling*

Polling works with topologies in which one device is designated as a primary station and the other devices are secondary stations. All data exchanges must be made through the primary device even when the ultimate destination is a secondary device.

Primary device determines which device is allowed to use the channel at a given time. The primary device is always the initiator of a session.

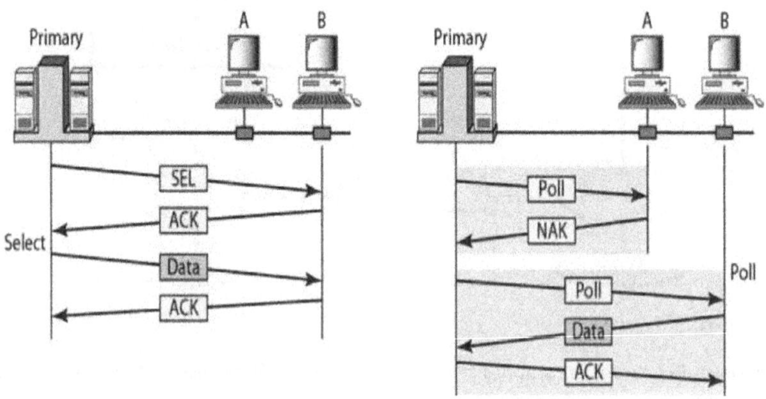

If the primary wants to receive data, it asks the secondaries if they have anything to send; this is called poll function. If the primary wants to send data, it tells the secondary to get ready to receive; this is called select function.

Select

The *select* function is used whenever the primary device has something to send. Before sending data, the primary creates and transmits a **select (SEL)** frame, one field of which includes the address of the intended secondary.

Poll

The *poll* function is used by the primary device to solicit transmissions from the secondary devices. When the primary is ready to receive data, it must ask (poll) each device in turn if it has anything to send. When the first secondary is approached, it responds either with a NAK frame if it has nothing to send or with data if it does. If the response is negative (a NAK frame), then the primary polls the next secondary in the same manner until it finds one station with data to send. When the response is positive (a data frame), the primary reads the frame and returns an acknowledgment (ACK frame), verifying its receipt.

2.2.3. Token Passing

In the token-passing method, the stations in a network are organized in a logical ring. In this method, a special packet called a token circulates through the ring. The possession of the token gives the station the right to access the channel and send its data.

When a station has some data to send, it waits until it receives the token from its predecessor. It then holds the token and sends its data. When the station has no more data to send, it releases the token, passing it to the next logical station in the ring. The station cannot send data until it receives the token again in the next round.

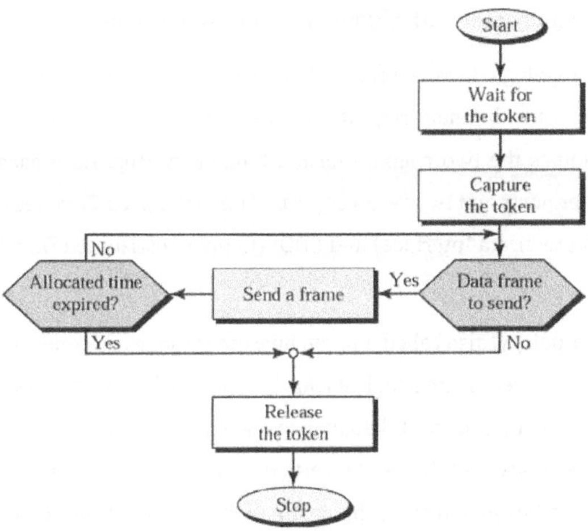

Token management is needed for this access method. Stations must be limited in the time they can have possession of the token. The token must be monitored to ensure it has not been lost or destroyed. For example, if a station that is holding the token fails, the token will disappear from the network

Another function of token management is to assign priorities to the stations and to the types of data being transmitted. And finally, token management is needed to make low-priority stations release the token to high priority stations.

Logical Ring

Figure below shows four different physical topologies that can create a logical ring.

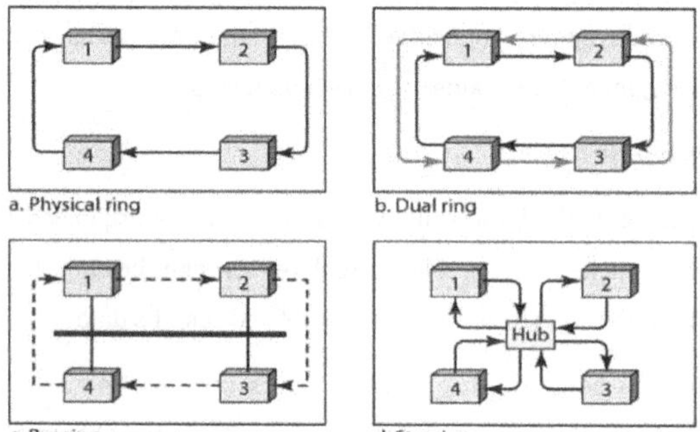

a. Physical ring b. Dual ring c. Bus ring d. Star ring

In the physical ring topology, when a station sends the token to its successor, the token cannot be seen by other stations; The problem with this topology is that if one of the links-the medium between two adjacent stations fails, the whole system fails.

The dual ring topology uses a second (auxiliary) ring which operates in the reverse direction compared with the main ring. If one of the links in the main ring fails, the system automatically combines the two rings to form a temporary ring. Here each station needs to have two transmitter ports and two receiver ports. The high-speed Token Ring networks called FDDI (Fiber Distributed Data Interface) and CDDI (Copper Distributed Data Interface) use this topology.

In the bus ring topology, also called a token bus, the stations are connected to a single cable called a bus. They, however, make a logical ring, because each station knows the address of its successor (and also predecessor for token management purposes). When a station has finished sending its data, it releases the token and inserts the address of its successor in the token. Only the station with the address matching the destination address of the token gets the token to access the shared media. The Token Bus LAN, Standardized by IEEE, uses this topology.

In a star ring topology, the physical topology is a star. There is a hub, however, that acts as the connector. The wiring inside the hub makes the ring; the stations are connected to this ring through the two wire connections. This topology makes the network less prone to failure because if a link goes down, it will be bypassed by the hub and the rest of the stations can operate. Also adding and removing stations from the ring is easier. This topology is still used in the Token Ring LAN designed by IBM.

2.3. Channelization

Channelization is a multiple-access method in which the available bandwidth of a link is shared in time, frequency, or through code, between different stations. Three channelization protocols: FDMA, TDMA, and CDMA.

2.3.1. Frequency-Division Multiple Access (FDMA)

In frequency-division multiple access (FDMA), the available bandwidth is divided into frequency bands. Each station is allocated a band to send its data. Each station also uses a bandpass filter to confine the transmitter frequencies. To prevent station interferences, the allocated bands are separated from one another by small *guard bands.*

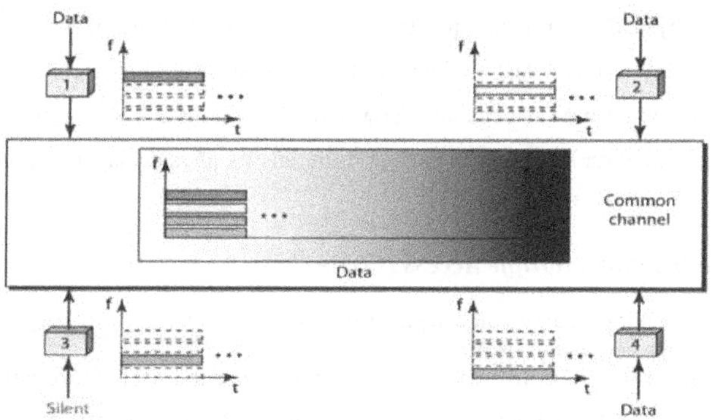

In FDMA, the available bandwidth of the common channel is divided into bands that are separated by guard bands. FDM is a physical layer technique that combines the loads from low-bandwidth channels and transmits them by using a high-bandwidth channel.

FDMA is an access method in the data link layer. The data link layer in each station tells its physical layer to make a bandpass signal from the data passed to it. The signal must be created in the allocated band.

2.3.2. Time-Division Multiple Access (TDMA)

In time-division multiple access (TDMA), the stations share the bandwidth of the channel in time. Each station is allocated a time slot during which it can send data. Each station transmits its data in is assigned time slot.

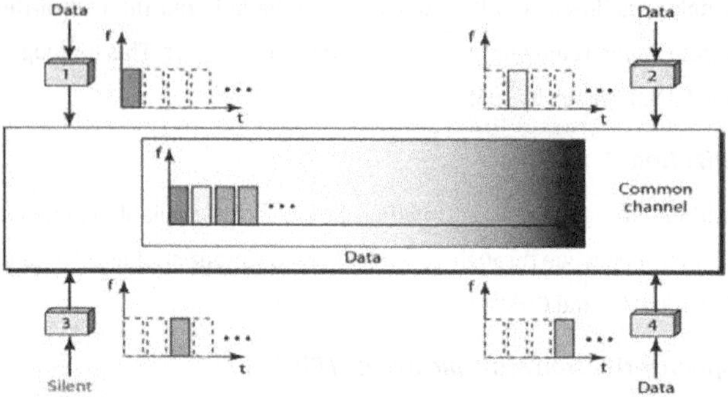

In TDMA, the bandwidth is one channel that is timeshared between different stations. The main problem with TDMA lies in achieving synchronization between the different stations. Each station needs to know the beginning of its slot and the location of its slot. To compensate for the delays, we can insert *guard*

TDM is a physical layer technique that combines the data from slower channels and transmits them by using a faster channel. The process uses a physical multiplexer that interleaves data units from each channel. TDMA, on the other hand, is an access method in the data link layer. The data link layer in each station tells its physical layer to use the allocated time slot.

2.3.3. Code-Division Multiple Access (CDMA)

In CDMA, one channel carries all transmissions simultaneously.

CDMA differs from FDMA because only one channel occupies the entire bandwidth of the link. It differs from TDMA because all stations can send data simultaneously; there is no timesharing.

Chips / codes

Each station is assigned with a chip.code. Let us assume we have four stations 1, 2, 3, and 4 connected to the same channel. The data from station 1,2,3,4 are d1,d2,d3,d4 respectively. The code assigned to the stations are c1,*c2, c3, c4*. Codes are called orthogonal sequences and have the following properties:

1) Each sequence is made of *N* elements, where *N* is the number of stations.
2) **Inner Product of Two Equal Sequences :** If we multiply two equal sequences, element by element, and add the results, we get *N*, where *N* is the number of elements in the each sequence. For example,

$$[+1\ +1 -1\ -1] \cdot [+1\ +1\ -1\ -1] = 1 + 1 + 1 + 1 = 4$$

3) If we multiply two different sequences, element by element, and add the results, we get 0. This is called inner product of two different sequences. For example,

$$[+1\ +1\ -1\ -1] \bullet [+1\ +1\ +1\ +1] = 1 + 1 - 1 - 1 = 0$$

Sequence Generation

To generate chip sequence, we use Walsh table. Walsh is a two dimensional table With an equal number of rows and columns. According to walsh if the table (W_N) or N sequences is known then table for 2N sequences (W_{2N}) can be created. In Walsh table, each row is a sequence of chips. W1 for one chip sequence has one row and one column. It can be +1 or -1.

$$W_1 = \begin{bmatrix} +1 \end{bmatrix} \qquad W_{2N} = \begin{bmatrix} W_N & W_N \\ W_N & \overline{W_N} \end{bmatrix}$$

a) Two Basic rules

$$W_1 = \begin{bmatrix} +1 \end{bmatrix} \qquad W_2 = \begin{bmatrix} +1 & +1 \\ +1 & -1 \end{bmatrix} \qquad W_4 = \begin{bmatrix} +1 & +1 & +1 & +1 \\ +1 & -1 & +1 & -1 \\ +1 & +1 & -1 & -1 \\ +1 & -1 & -1 & +1 \end{bmatrix}$$

b) Generation of W_1, W_2, W_4

Encoding

1) Data representation:

Data bit 0 -> -1 Data bit 1 -> 1 Silence -> 0

2) Station 1 multiplies its data by its code to get $\mathbf{d_1} \cdot \mathbf{C_1}$. Station 2 multiplies its data by its code to get $d_2 \cdot c_2$ and so on. The data that go on the channel are the sum of all these terms.

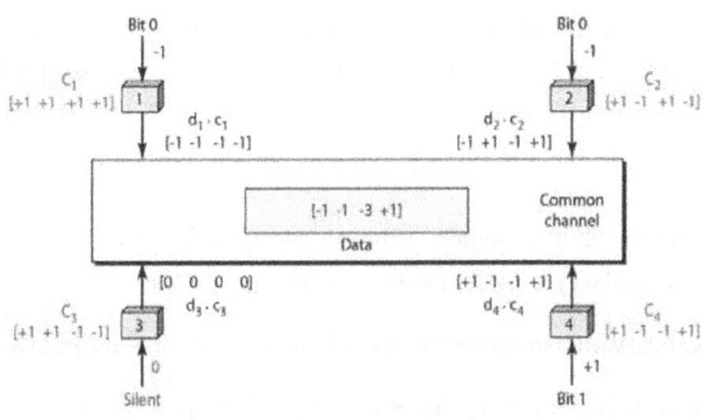

Decoding

Any station that wants to receive data from one of the other stations, multiplies the data on the channel by the code of the sender.

For example, Station 2 wants to hear what station 1 is saying. It multiplies the data on the channel by c1, the code of station 1.

data =*(d1* . C1 + d2 . C2 +*d3* . *C3* + *d4* . *c4)* . *C1* =*d 1*• *C1* . C1 + d2. C2 . C1 + *d3* . *C3* . Cl + *d4* . *C4* . CI

=4 X *d1*

Because (c1 . c1) is 4, but *(c2* . c1), *(c3* . c1), and *(c4* . c1) are all 0s, station 2 divides the result by 4 to get the data from station 1.

Example

Find the chips for a network with a. Two stations b. Four stations

Solution

We can use the rows of *W2* and *W4* .

1) For a two-station network, we have [+1 +1] and [+1 -1].
2) For a four-station network we have [+1 +1 +1 +1], [+1 -1 +1 -1], [+1 +1 -1 -1], and [+1-1-1 +1].

Example

Solution

The number of sequences needs to be 2^m. We need to choose m = 7 and N = 2^7 or 128. We can then use 90 of the sequences as the chips.

Example

Prove that a receiving station can get the data sent by a specific sender if it multiplies the entire data on the channel by the sender's chip code and then divides it bythe number of stations.

Solution

Let us prove this for the first station, using our previous four-station example. We can say that the data on the channel D = (d1 . c1 + d2 . c2 + d3 . c3 + d4 . c4).

The receiver which wants to get the data sent by station 1 multiplies these data by c1.

$$D \cdot c_1 = (d_1 \cdot c_1 + d_2 \cdot c_2 + d_3 \cdot c_3 + d_4 \cdot c_4) \cdot c_1$$

$$= d_1 \cdot c_1 \cdot c_1 + d_2 \cdot c_2 \cdot c_1 + d_3 \cdot c_3 \cdot c_1 + d_4 \cdot c_4 \cdot c_1$$
$$= d_1 \times N + d_2 \times 0 + d_3 \times 0 + d_4 \times 0$$
$$= d_1 \times N$$

When we divide the result by *N*, we get d1.

3. Wired LANs : Ethernet

The Computer Society of the IEEE started a project, called Project 802, to set standards to enable intercommunication among equipment from a variety of manufacturers. IEEE 802.3 called Ethernet is a way of specifying functions of the physical layer and the data link layer of major LAN protocols.

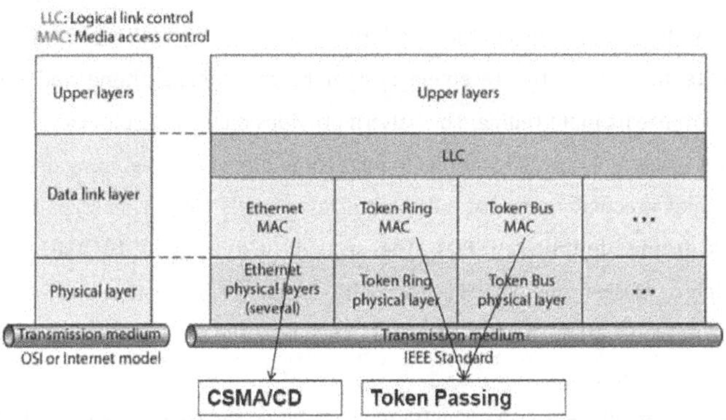

The original Ethernet was created in 1976 at Xerox's Palo Alto Research Center (PARC). Since then, it has gone through four generations: Standard Ethernet (lot Mbps), Fast Ethernet (100 Mbps), Gigabit Ethernet (l Gbps), and Ten-Gigabit Ethernet (l0 Gbps)

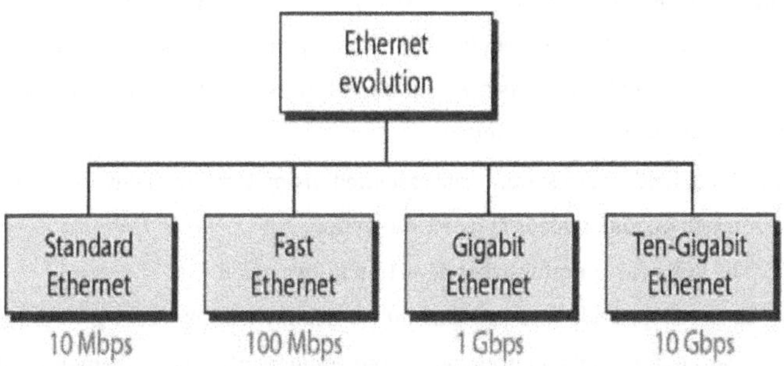

4. Standard Ethernet

4.1. MAC Sublayer

In Standard Ethernet, the MAC sublayer governs the operation of the access method. It also frames data received from the upper layer and passes them to the physical layer.

4.1.1. 802.3 Frame Format

The Ethernet Frame Contains 7 Fields

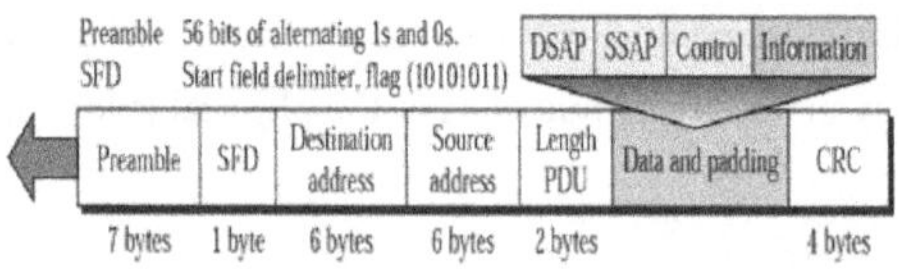

1) **Preamble**. The first field of the 802.3 frame contains 7 bytes (56 bits) of alternating 0s and 1s that alerts the receiving system to the coming frame and enables it to synchronize its input timing. The pattern provides only an alert and a timing pulse. The 56-bit pattern allows the stations to miss some bits at the beginning of the frame. The preamble is actually added at the physical layer and is not (formally) part of the frame.
2) **Start frame delimiter (SFD)**. The second field (1 byte: 10101011) signals the beginning of the frame. The SFD warns the station or stations that this is the last chance for synchronization. The last 2 bits is 11 and alerts the receiver that the next field is the destination address.
3) **Destination address (DA)**. The DA field is 6 bytes and contains the physical address of the destination station or stations to receive the packet.
4) **Source address (SA)**. The SA field is also 6 bytes and contains the physical address of the sender of the packet.
5) **Length or type**. This field is defined as a type field or length field. The original Ethernet used this field as the type field to define the upper-layer protocol using the MAC frame. The IEEE standard used it as the length field to define the number of bytes in the data field. Both uses are common today.
6) **Data**. This field carries data encapsulated from the upper-layer protocols. It is a minimum of 46 and a maximum of 1500 bytes.
7) **CRC.** The last field contains error detection information.

Ethernet does not provide any mechanism for acknowledging received frames, making it what is known as an unreliable medium. Acknowledgments must be implemented at the higher layers.

Frame Length

Ethernet has imposed restrictions on both the minimum and maximum lengths of a frame

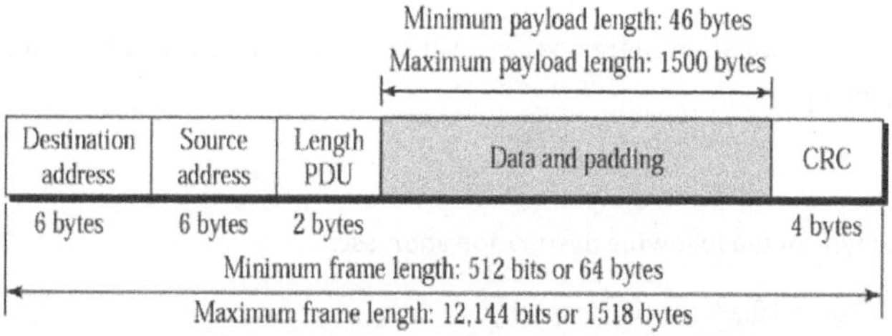

The minimum length restriction is required for the correct operation of *CSMA / CD.* An Ethernet frame needs to have a **minimum length of 512 bits** or 64 bytes. If we count 18 bytes of header and trailer (6 bytes of source address, 6 bytes of destination address, 2 bytes of length or type, and 4 bytes of CRC), then the minimum length of data from the upper layer is 64 - 18 = 46 bytes.

The standard defines the **maximum length of a frame as 1518 bytes.** If we subtract the 18 bytes of header and trailer, the maximum length of the payload is 1500 bytes.

The maximum length restriction has two reasons. First, memory was very expensive when Ethernet was designed: a maximum length restriction helped to reduce the size of the buffer. Second, the maximum length restriction prevents one station from monopolizing the shared medium, blocking other stations that have data to send.

4.1.2. Ethernet Addressing

Each station on an Ethernet network has its own network interface card (NIC) with a 6-byte physical address, normally written in hexadecimal notation, with a colon between the bytes.

06 : 01 : 02 : 01 : 2C : 4B

6 bytes = 12 hex digits = 48 bits

An example of Ethernet address in hexadecimal notation Unicast, Multicast, and Broadcast Addresses.

A source address is always a unicast address-the frame comes from only one station. The destination address, can be unicast, multicast, or broadcast.

If the least significant bit of the first byte in a destination address is 0, the address is unicast; otherwise, it is multicast.

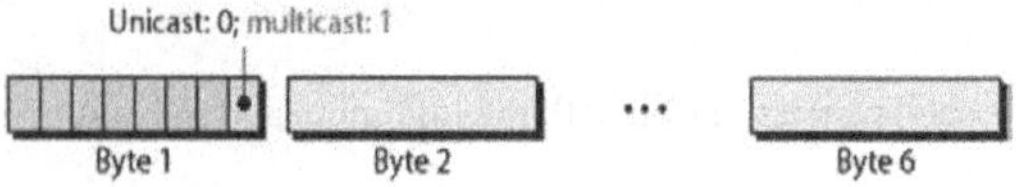

The broadcast destination address is a special case of the multicast address in which all bits are 1s.(FF:FF:FF:FF:FF:FF)

Example

Define the type of the following destination addresses:

a. 4A:30:10:21:10:1A
b. 47:20:1B:2E:08:EE
c. FF:FF:FF:FF:FF:FF

Solution

a. This is a unicast address because A in binary is 1010.
b. This is a multicast address because 7 in binary is 0111.
c. This is a broadcast address because all digits are F's.

Example

Show how the address 47:20:1B:2E:08:EE is sent out online.

Solution

The address is sent left-to-right, byte by byte; for each byte, it is sent right-to-left, bit by bit, as shown below:

47→20→1B→2E→08→EE

← 11100010 00000100 11011000 01110100 00010000 01110111

4.1.3. Access Method: CSMA/CD

Standard Ethernet uses 1-persistent CSMA/CD.

Slot Time

In an Ethernet network, the round-trip time required for a frame to travel from one end of a maximum-length network to the other plus the time needed to send the jam sequence is called the slot time.

Slot time = round trip time+ jam sequence time.

It is the time required for a station to send 512 bits depending on the data rate, for traditional 10Mbps Ethernet it is 51.2 microseconds.

Slot Time and Collision

Assume that the sender sends a minimum-size packet of 512 bits. Before the sender can send the entire packet out, the signal travels through the network and reaches the end of the network. If there is another signal at the end of the network (worst case), a collision occurs. The sender has a chance to abort the sending of the frame and to send a jam sequence to inform other stations of the collision.

The round-trip time plus the time required to send the jam sequence should be less than the time needed for the sender to send the minimum frame, 512 bits.

The sender needs to be aware of the collision before it has sent the entire frame.

If the station has sent out the first 512 bits and has not heard a collision, it is guaranteed that collision will never occur during the transmission of this frame. The reason is that the signal will reach the end of the network in less than one-half the slot time. If all stations follow the *CSMA/CD* protocol, they have already sensed the existence of the signal (carrier) on the line and have refrained from sending. If they sent a signal on the line before one-half of the slot time expired, a collision has occurred and the sender has sensed the collision. This means that after the sender sends the first 512 bits, it is guaranteed that collision will not occur during the transmission of this frame.

Slot Time and Maximum Network Length

$$\text{Max Length} = \text{propagation speed} * (\text{slot time}/2)$$

In most transmission media, the signal propagates at 2×10^8 m/s

$$\text{Max Length}=(2 \times 10^8) \times (512 \times 10^{-6}/2)=5120 \text{ m}$$

Considering the delay times in repeaters and interfaces and the time required to send the jamming signal the max. length of ethernet network is 2500m

4.1.4. Physical Layer Implementations

Encoding and Decoding

All standard implementations use digital signaling (baseband) at 10 Mbps. At the sender, data are converted to a digital signal using the Manchester scheme; at the receiver, the received signal is interpreted as Manchester and decoded into data.

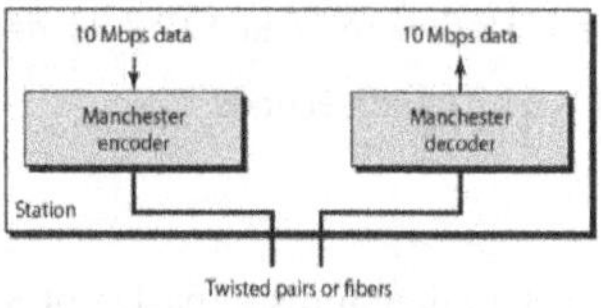

The Standard Ethernet defines several physical layer implementations

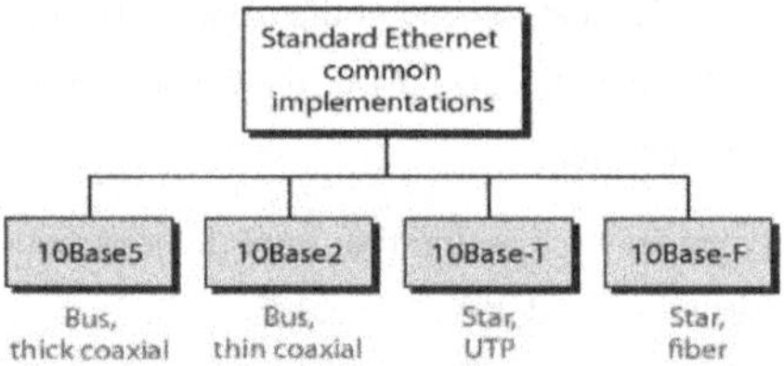

10Base5: Thick Ethernet

The first implementation is called **10BaseS, thick Ethernet, or Thicknet.**

l0Base5 was the first Ethernet specification to use a bus topology with an external **transceiver** (transmitter/receiver) connected via a tap to a thick coaxial cable.

10Base5 uses 1-persistent CSMA/CD on a coaxial cable at 10 Mbps

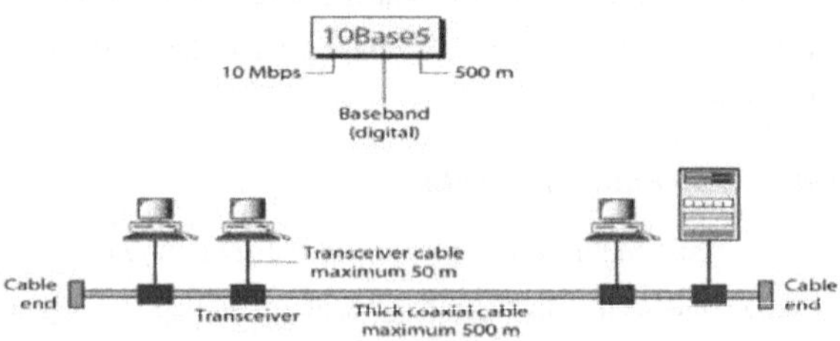

The transceiver is responsible for transmitting, receiving, and detecting collisions. The transceiver is connected to the station via a transceiver cable that provides separate paths for sending and receiving.

The maximum length of the coaxial cable must not exceed *500* m

10Base2: Thin Ethernet

The second implementation is called l0Base2, **thin** Ethernet, or Cheapernet. IOBase2 also uses a bus topology, but the cable is much thinner and more flexible. The transceiver is normally part of the network interface card (NIC), which is installed inside the station.

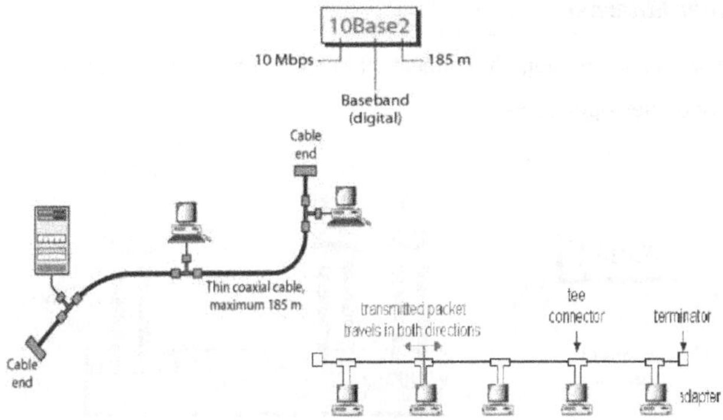

This implementation is more cost effective than 10BaseS because thin coaxial cable is less expensive than thick coaxial and the tee connections are much cheaper than taps.

Installation is simpler because the thin coaxial cable is very flexible. However, the length of each segment cannot exceed *185* m (close to 200 m) due to the high level of attenuation in thin coaxial cable.

lOBase-T: Twisted-Pair Ethernet

The third implementation is called l0Base-T or twisted-pair Ethernet.

10Base-T uses a physical star topology. The stations are connected to a hub via two pairs of twisted cable.

Two pairs of twisted cable create two paths (one for sending and one for receiving) between the station and the hub. Any collision here happens in the hub.

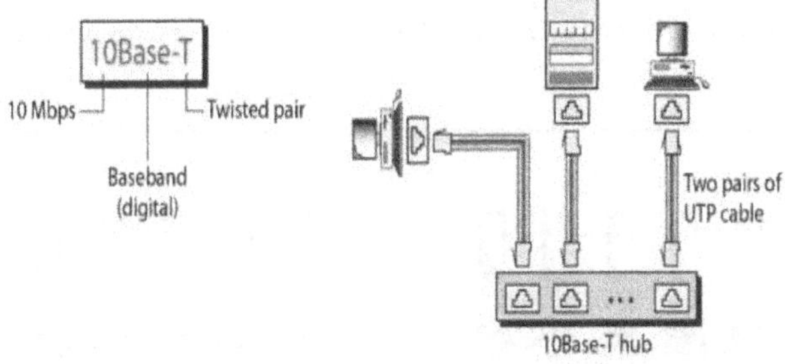

The maximum length of the twisted cable here is defined as 100 m, to minimize the effect of attenuation in the twisted cable.

10Base-F: Fiber Ethernet

10Base-F uses a star topology to connect stations to a hub. The stations are connected to the hub using two fiber-optic cables.

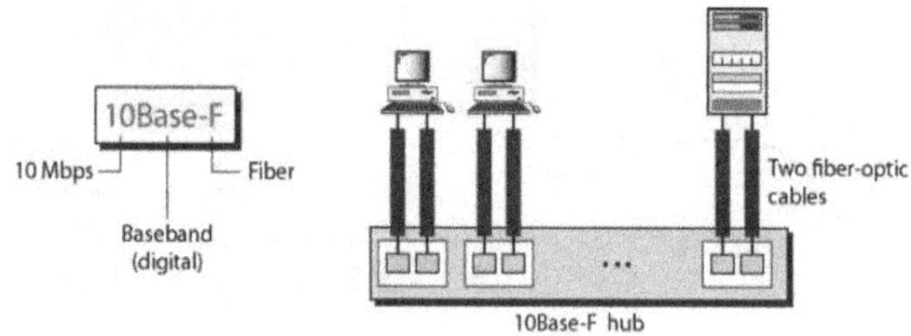

Summary of Standard Ethernet implementations

	10Base 5	10Base2	10Base-T	10Base-F
Media	Thick coaxial cable	Thin coaxial cable	Two UTP	2 Fiber
Maximum length	500 m	185 m	100 m	2000 m
Topology	Bus	Bus	Star	star

Changes in the Standard Ethernet

The 10-Mbps Standard Ethernet has gone through several changes before moving to the higher data rates.

1) Bridged Ethernet

The first evolution in the Ethernet was the division of a LAN by bridges.

Bridges have two effects on an Ethernet LAN: They raise the bandwidth and they separate collision domains.

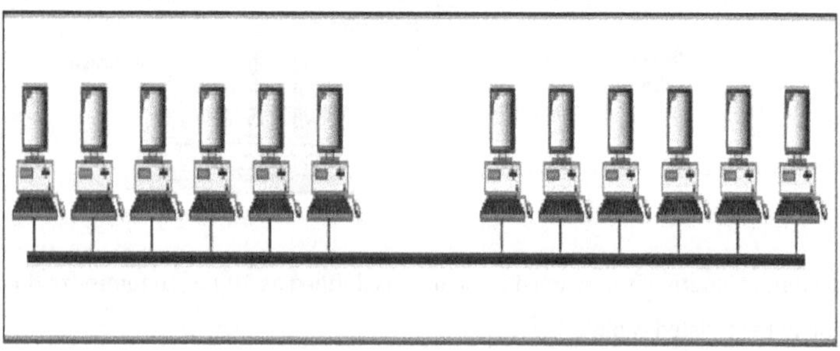

a. Without bridging

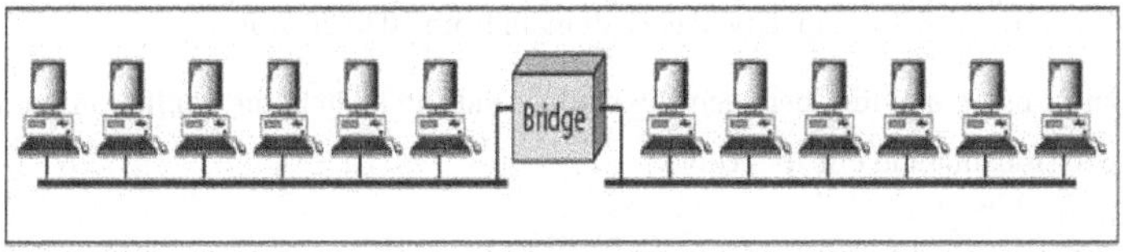

b. With bridging

a) Raising the Bandwidth

In an unbridged Ethernet network, the total capacity (10 Mbps) is shared among all stations with a frame to send;.bridge divides the network into two or more networks. Bandwidth-wise, each network is independent.

For example, in Figure a network with 12 stations is divided into two networks, each with 6 stations. Now each network has a capacity of 10 Mbps. The l0-Mbps capacity in each segment is now shared between 6 stations gaining 10 Mbps more.

If we further divide the network, we can gain more bandwidth for each segment.

b) Separating Collision Domains

Using bridges, collision domain **becomes** much smaller and the probability of collision is reduced.

2) Switched Ethernet

A layer 2 switch is an N-port bridge with additional sophistication that allows faster handling of the packets.

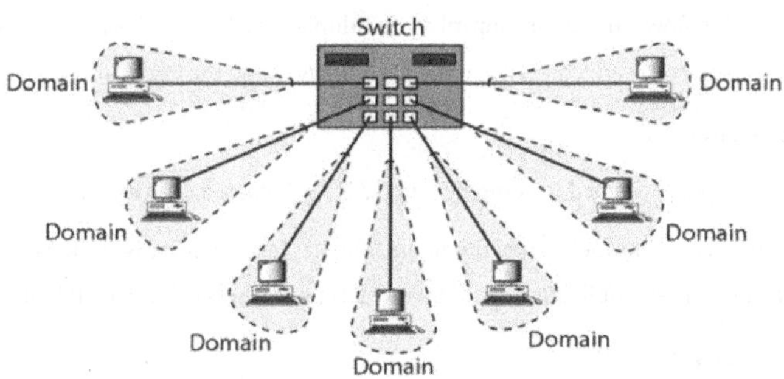

The bandwidth is shared only between the station and the switch (5 Mbps each). In addition, the collision domain is divided into *N* domains.

3) Full-Duplex Ethernet

Limitation of 10Base5 and 10Base2 is that communication is half-duplex.

Full-duplex doubles the capacity of each domain from 10 to 20 Mbps.

Instead of using one link between the station and the switch, the configuration uses two links: one to transmit and one to receive.

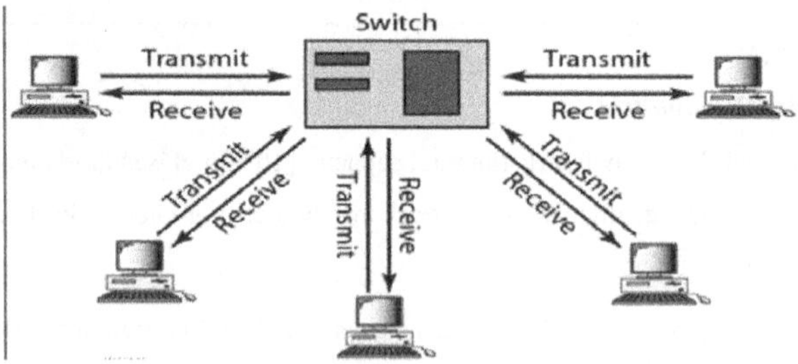

No Need for CSMA/CD

Each station is connected to the switch via two separate links.

As Each link is a point-to-point dedicated path between the station and the switch. There is no longer a need for carrier sensing; there is no longer a need for collision detection.

MAC Control Layer

Standard Ethernet was designed as a connectionless protocol at the MAC sublayer.

There is no explicit flow control or error control to inform the sender that the frame has arrived at the destination without error.

To provide for flow and error control in full-duplex switched Ethernet, a new sublayer, called the MAC control, is added between the LLC sublayer and the MAC sublayer.

4.2. Fast Ethernet

Fast Ethernet was designed to compete with LAN protocols such as FDDI.

IEEE created Fast Ethernet under the name 802.3u. Fast Ethernet is backward-compatible with Standard Ethernet, but it can transmit data 10 times faster at a rate of 100 Mbps.

Goals of Fast Ethernet

1) Upgrade the data rate to 100 Mbps.
2) Make it compatible with Standard Ethernet.
3) Keep the same 48-bit address.

4) Keep the same frame format.

5) Keep the same minimum and maximum frame lengths.

4.2.1. MAC Sublayer

A decision was made to drop the bus topologies and keep only the star topology. For the star topology, there are two choices: half duplex and full duplex.

Half-duplex approach:

1) The stations are connected via a hub.
2) The access method is CSMA/CD

Full-duplex approach:

1) The connection is made via a switch with buffers at each port.
2) No need for CSMA/CD

Autonegotiation

Autonegotiation allows two devices to negotiate the mode or data rate of operation. It was designed for the following purposes:

1) To allow incompatible devices to connect to one another. For example, a device with a maximum capacity of 10 Mbps can communicate with a device with a 100 Mbps capacity
2) To allow one device to have multiple capabilities.
3) To allow a station to check a hub's capabilities.

4.2.2. Physical Layer

Topology

If there are only two stations, they can be connected point-to-point. Three or more stations need to be connected in a star topology with a hub or a switch at the center.

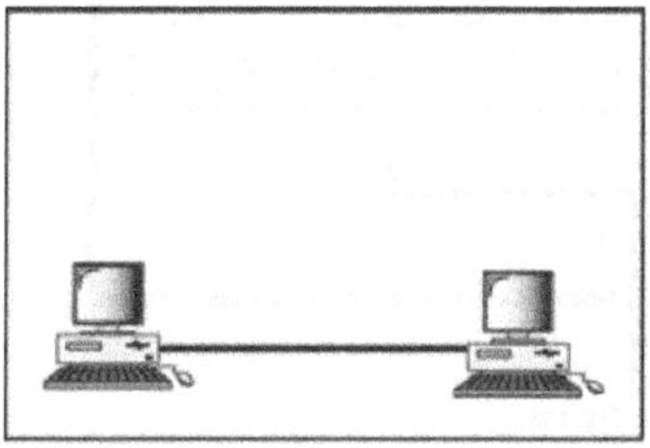

a. Point-to-point

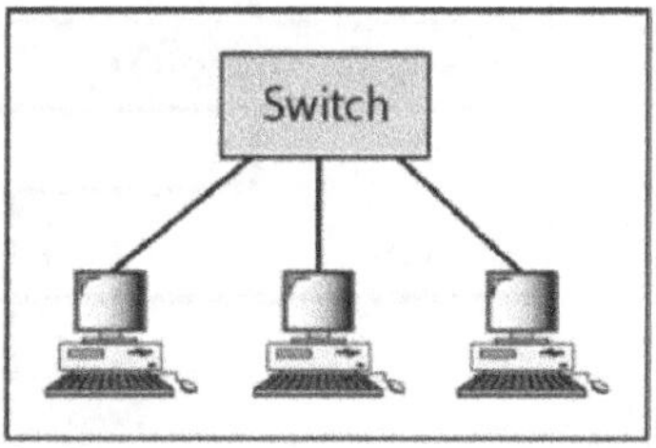

b. Star

Physical Layer Implementation

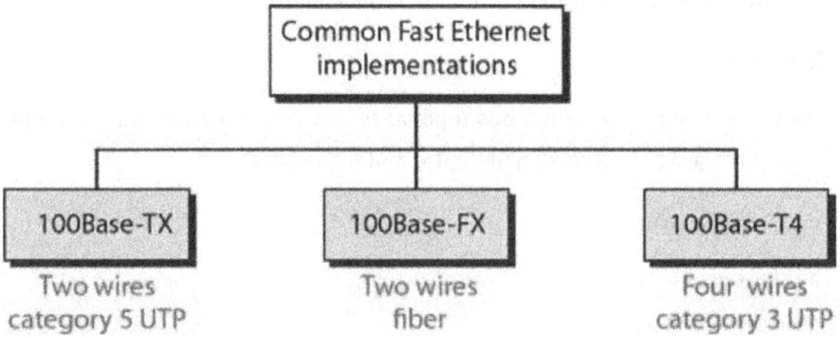

Encoding

Manchester encoding needs a 200-Mbaud bandwidth for a data rate of 100 Mbps In Fast Ethernet , three different encoding schemes were chosen depending on the implementation:

1) 100Base-TX.
2) 100Base-FX.
3) 100Base-T4.

Encoding: 100Base-TX

Uses two pairs of twisted-pair cable (either category 5 UTP or STP).

1) Provide data rate of 100 Mbps.
2) 4B/5B block coding is used to provide bit synchronization.

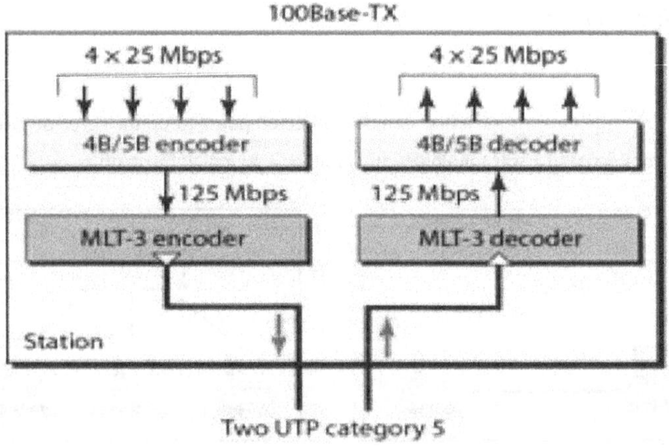

Encoding: 100Base-FX

1) Uses two pairs of fiber-optic cables.
2) Uses NRZ-I encoding scheme(bit synchronization problem.)
3) To overcome this problem, 4B/5B block coding is used.
4) Block coding increase the bit rate from 100 to 125 Mbps

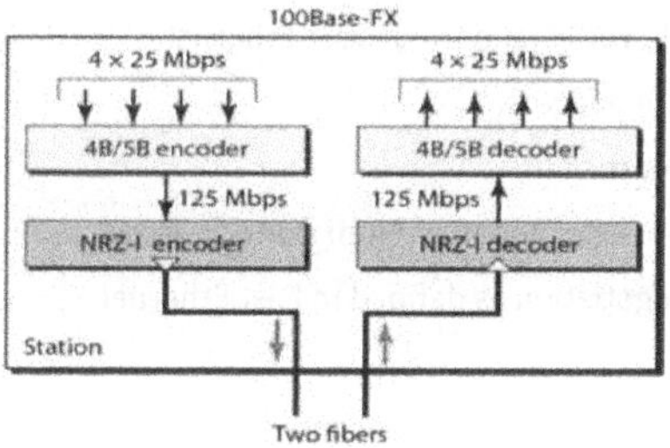

Encoding: 100Base-T4

1) Uses four pairs of category 3 or higher UTP.
2) Transmit 100 Mbps. -Encoding more complicated.
3) Category 3 cannot easily handle more than 25 Mbaud.
4) In this design.
   a) One pair switches between sending and receiving.
   b) 3 pairs handle only 75 Mbaud (25 each).
5) Uses 8B/6T encoding scheme to convert 100 Mbps to 75Mbaud.

Summary of Fast Ethernet implementations

	100Base -TX	10Base-FX	10Base-T4
Media	Cat 5 UTP or STP	Fiber	Cat 3 UTP or higher
Number of wires	2	2	4
Maximum length	100 m	400 m (2000 full duplex)	100 m
Topology	Star	Star	Star
Data rate	100 Mbps	100 Mbps	100 Mbps
Block encoding	4B/5B	4B/5B	8B/6T
Line encoding	MLT-3	NRZ-I	NRZ

4.3. Gigabit Ethernet(802.3z)

The need for an even higher data rate resulted in the design of the Gigabit Ethernet protocol (1000 Mbps). The IEEE committee calls the standard **802.3z**.

The goals of the Gigabit Ethernet design can be summarized as follows:

1) Upgrade the data rate to 1 Gbps.
2) Make it compatible with Standard or Fast Ethernet.
3) Use the same 48-bit address.
4) Use the same frame format.
5) Keep the same minimum and maximum frame lengths.
6) To support autonegotiation as defined in Fast Ethernet.

4.3.1. MAC Sublayer

Gigabit Ethernet has two distinctive approaches for medium access: half-duplex and full-duplex.

Full-Duplex Mode

In full-duplex mode, there is a central switch connected to all computers or other switch. Each switch has buffers for each input port in which data are stored until they are transmitted. There is no collision in this mode. So *CSMA / CD* is not used. Lack of collision implies that the maximum length of the cable is determined by the signal attenuation in the cable, not by the collision detection process.

Half-Duplex Mode

Gigabit Ethernet can also be used in half-duplex mode switch can be replaced by a hub, which acts as the common cable in which a collision might occur. The half-duplex approach uses *CSMA/CD* the maximum length of the network in this approach is totally dependent on the minimum frame size. Three methods have been defined: traditional, carrier extension, and frame bursting.

Traditional: In the traditional approach, the minimum length of the frame is 512 bits. However, because the length of a bit is 1/100 shorter in Gigabit Ethernet than in 10-Mbps Ethernet, the slot time for Gigabit Ethernet is 512 bits x 1/1000 μs, which is equal to 0.512 μs. This means that the maximum length of the network is 25 m.

Carrier Extension: The carrier extension approach defines the minimum length of a frame as 512 bytes (4096 bits). This method forces a station to add extension bits (padding) to any frame that is less than 4096 bits. In this way, the maximum length of the network can be increased 8 times to a length of 200 m. This allows a length of 100 m from the hub to the station.

Frame Bursting: Carrier extension is very inefficient if we have a series of short frames to send. To improve efficiency, frame bursting was proposed. Instead of adding an extension to each frame, multiple frames are sent. sTo make these multiple frames look like one frame, padding is added between the frames so that the channel is not idle.

4.3.2. Physical Layer

Topology

Gigabit Ethernet is designed to connect two or more stations. If there are only two stations, they can be connected point-to-point. Three or more stations need to be connected in a star topology with a hub or a switch at the center.

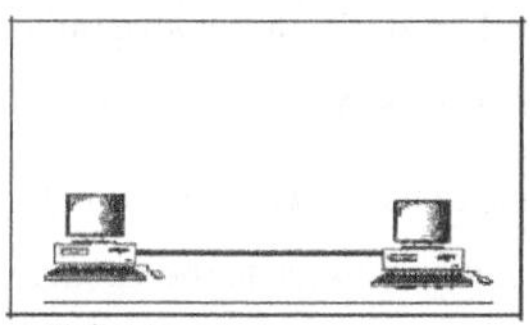

a. Point-to-point

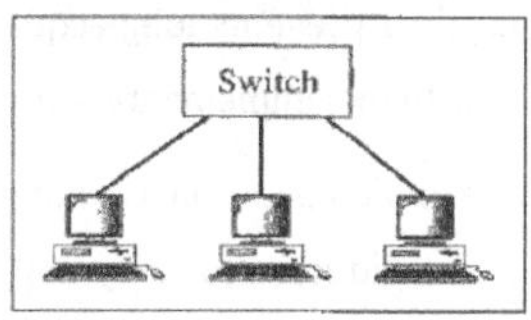

b. Star

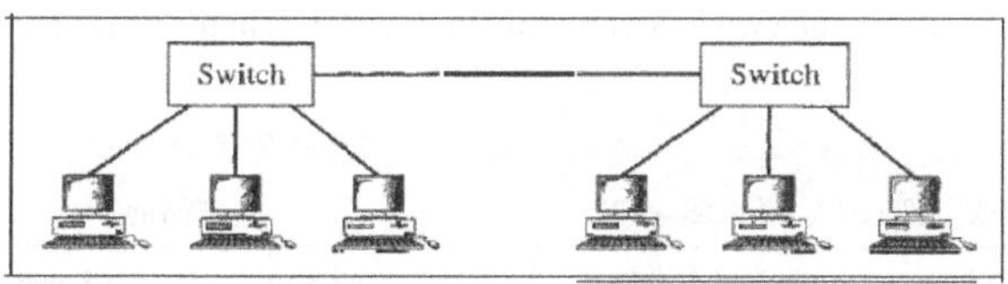

c. Two stars

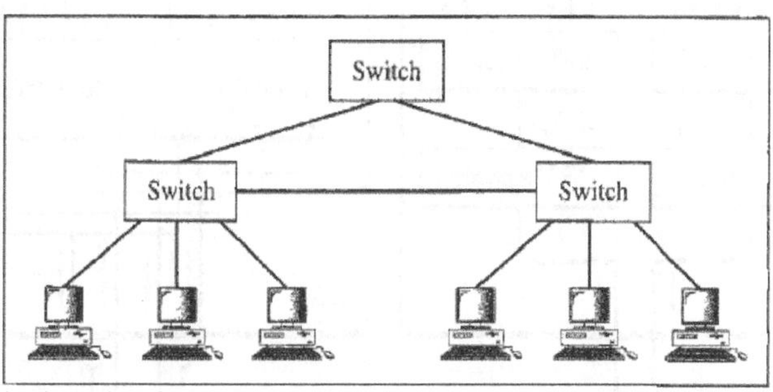

d. Hierarchy of stars

Physical Layer Implementation

Gigabit Ethernet can be categorized as either a two-wire or a four-wire implementation.

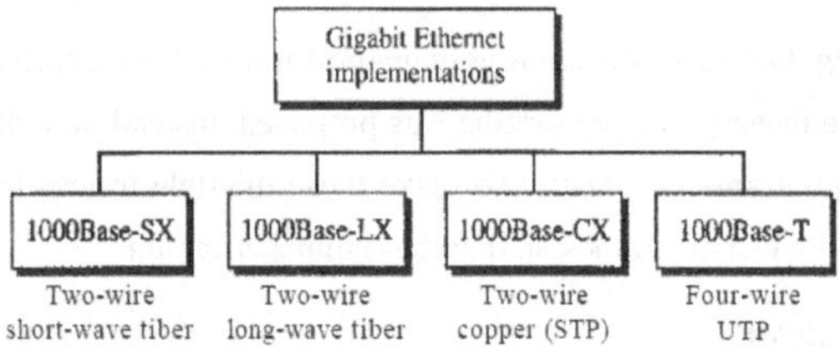

Encoding

Gigabit Ethernet cannot use the Manchester encoding scheme because it involves a very high bandwidth (2 GBaud). The two-wire implementations use an **NRZ scheme**, but NRZ does not self-synchronize properly. To synchronize bits 8B/10B block encoding, is used.

This block encoding prevents long sequences of 0s or 1s in the stream, but the resulting stream is 1.25 Gbps. In this implementation, one wire is used for sending and one for receiving.

In the four-wire implementation it is not possible to have 2 wires for input and 2 for output, because each wire would need to carry 500 Mbps, which exceeds the capacity for category 5 UTP. So 4D-PAM5 encoding is used to reduce the bandwidth. Thus, all four wires are involved in both input and output; each wire carries 250 Mbps, which is in the range for category 5 UTP cable

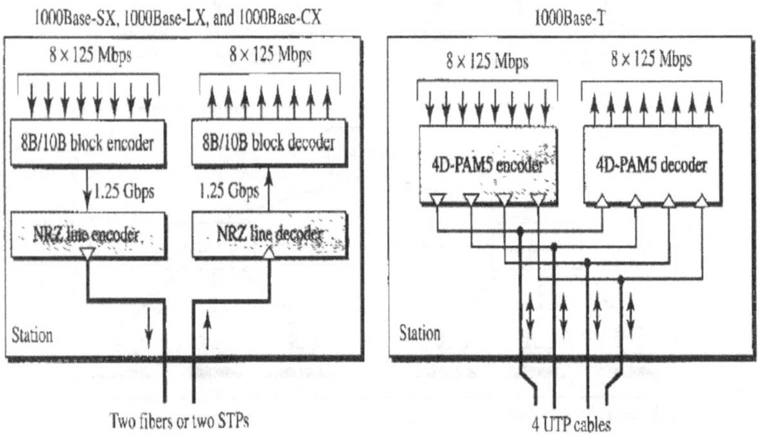

Summary of the Gigabit Ethernet Implementations

Characteristics	*1000Base-SX*	*1000Base-LX*	*1000Base-CX*	*1000Base-T*
Media	Fiber short-wave	Fiber long-wave	STP	Cat 5 UTP
Number of wires	2	2	2	4
Maximum length	550m	5000m	25m	100m
Block encoding	8B/10B	*8B/10B*	8B/10B	
Line encoding	NRZ	NRZ	NRZ	4D-PAM5

4.4. Ten-Gigabit Ethernet(802.3ae)

The IEEE committee created Ten-Gigabit Ethernet and called it Standard **802.3ae**.

The goals of the Ten-Gigabit Ethernet design can be summarized as follows:

1) Upgrade the data rate to 10 Gbps.
2) Make it compatible with Standard, Fast, and Gigabit Ethernet.
3) Use the same 48-bit address.
4) Use the same frame format.
5) *S.* Keep the same minimum and maximum frame lengths.
6) Allow the interconnection of existing LANs into a metropolitan area network (MAN) or a wide area network (WAN).
7) Make Ethernet compatible with technologies such as Frame Relay and ATM

4.4.1. MAC Sublayer

Ten-Gigabit Ethernet operates only in full duplex mode which means there is no need for contention; *CSMA/CD* is not used in Ten-Gigabit Ethernet.

4.4.2. Physical Layer

The physical layer in Ten-Gigabit Ethernet is designed for using fiber-optic cable over long distances. Three implementations are the most common: 10GBase-S, 10GBase-L, and 10GBase-E.

The below Table shows a Summary of the Ten-Gigabit Ethernet Implementations

Characteristics	*10GBase-S*	*10GBase-L*	*10GBase-E*
Media	Short-wave S50-nm multimode	Long-wave 1310-nm single mode	Extended 1550-mm single mode
Maximum length	300m	10km	40km

UNIT–7

Wireless LANs and Cellular Networks: Introduction, IEEE 802.11, Bluetooth, Connecting devices, Cellular Telephony.

1. IEEE 802.11

Architecture

The standard defines two kinds of services: the basic service set (BSS) and the extended service set (ESS).

Basic Service Set

IEEE 802.11 defines the basic service set (BSS) as the building block of a wireless LAN. A basic service set is made of stationary or mobile wireless stations and an optional central base station, known as the access point (AP). The figure shows two sets in this standard.

The BSS without an AP is a stand-alone network and cannot send data to other BSSs. It is called an ad hoc architecture. In this architecture, stations can form a network without the need of an AP; they can locate one another and agree to be part of a BSS. A BSS with an AP is sometimes referred to as an infrastructure network.

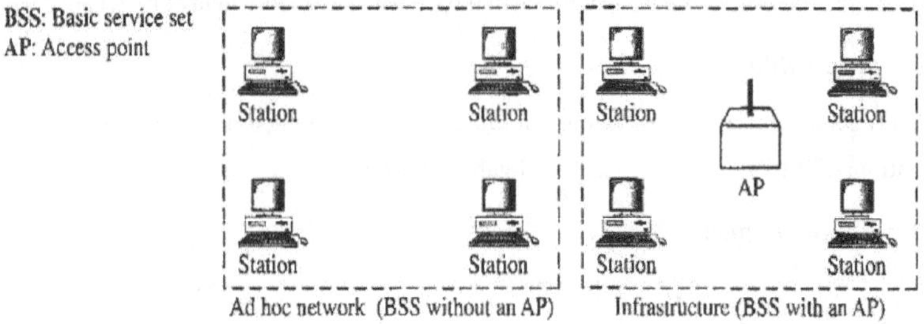

Extended Service Set

An extended service set (ESS) is made up of two or more BSSs with APs. In this case, the BSSs are connected through a distribution system, which is usually a wired LAN. The distribution system connects the APs in the BSSs. IEEE 802.11 does not restrict the distribution system; it can be any IEEE LAN such as an Ethernet. Note that the extended service set uses two types of stations: mobile and stationary. The mobile stations are normal stations inside a BSS. The stationary stations are AP stations that are part of a wired LAN. When BSSs are connected, the stations within reach of one another can communicate without the use of an AP. However, communication between two stations in two different BSSs usually occurs via two APs.

Station Types

IEEE 802.11 defines three types of stations based on their mobility in a wireless LAN: no-transition, BSS-transition, and ESS-transition mobility. A station with no-transition mobility is either stationary (not moving) or moving only inside a BSS. A station with BSS-transition mobility can move from one BSS to another, but the movement is confined inside one ESS. A station with ESS-transition mobility can move from one ESS to another. However, IEEE 802.11 does not guarantee that communication is continuous during the move.

MAC Sublayer

IEEE 802.11 defines two MAC sublayers: the distributed coordination function (DCF) and point coordination function (PCF). The figure shows the relationship between the two MAC sublayers, the LLC sublayer, and the physical layer.

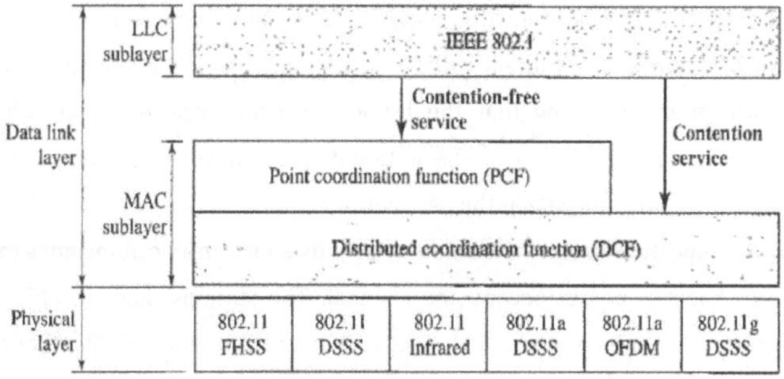

Distributed Coordination Function

One of the two protocols defined by IEEE at the MAC sublayer is called the distributed coordination function (DCF). DCF uses CSMA/CA as the access method. Wireless LANs cannot implement CSMA/CD for three reasons:

1) For collision detection a station must be able to send data and receive collision signals at the same time. This can mean costly stations and increased bandwidth requirements.
2) Collision may not be detected because of the hidden station problem.
3) The distance between stations can be great. Signal fading could prevent a station at one end from hearing a collision at the other end.

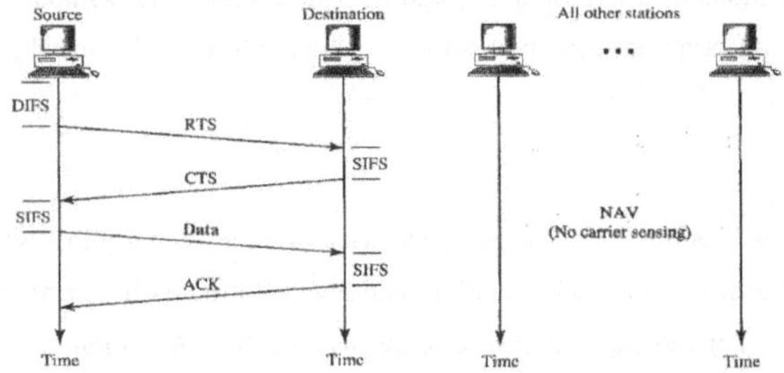

1) Before sending a frame, the source station senses the medium by checking the energy level at the carrier frequency. After the station is found to be idle, the station waits for a period of time called the distributed interframe space (DIFS); then the station sends a control frame called the request to send (RTS).
2) After receiving the RTS and waiting a period of time called the short interframe space (SIFS), the destination station sends a control frame, called the clear to send (CTS), to the source station. This control frame indicates that the destination station is ready to receive data.
3) The source station sends data after waiting an amount of time equal to SIFS.
4) The destination station, after waiting an amount of time equal to SIFS, sends an acknowledgment to show that the frame has been received. Acknowledgment is needed in this protocol because the station does not have any means to check for the successful arrival of its data at the destination
5) Network Allocation Vector When a station sends an RTS frame, it includes the duration of time that it needs to occupy the channel. The stations that are affected by this transmission create a timer called a network allocation vector (NAV) that shows how much time must pass before these stations are allowed to check the channel for idleness. Each time a station accesses the system and sends an RTS frame, other stations start their NAV. In other words, each station, before sensing the physical medium to see if it is idle, first checks its NAV to see if it has expired.

Point Coordination Function (PCF)

The point coordination function (PCF) is an optional access method that can be implemented in an infrastructure network (not in an ad hoc network). It is implemented on top of the DCF and is used mostly for time-sensitive transmission.

1) To give priority to PCF over DCF, another set of interframe spaces has been defined: PIFS and SIFS. The SIFS is the same as that in DCF, but the PIFS (PCF IFS) is shorter than

the DIFS. This means that if, at the same time, a station wants to use only DCF and an AP wants to use PCF, the AP has priority.

2) Due to the priority of PCF over DCF, stations that only use DCF may not gain access to the medium. To prevent this, a repetition interval has been designed to cover both contention-free (PCF) and contention-based (DCF) traffic. The repetition interval, which is repeated continuously, starts with a special control frame, called a beacon frame. When the stations hear the beacon frame, they start their NAV for the duration of the contention-free period of the repetition interval. The figure shows an example of a repetition interval.

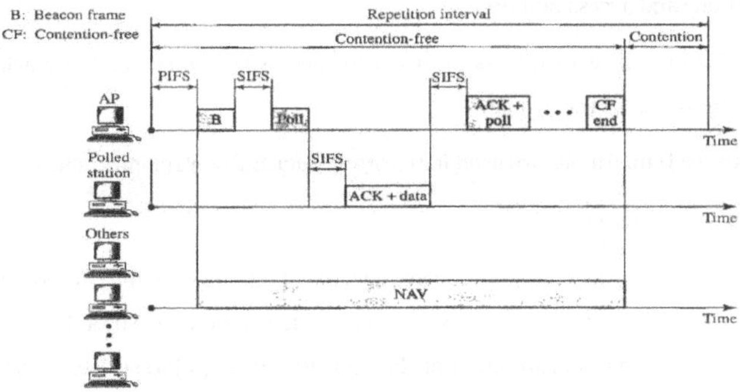

Frame Format

The MAC layer frame consists of nine fields, as shown.

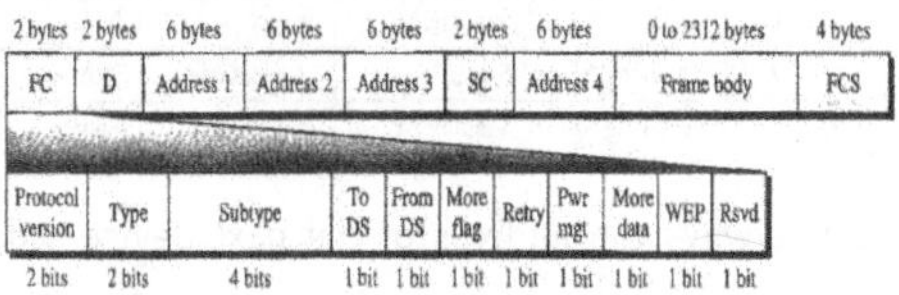

Frame control (FC): The FC field is 2 bytes long and defines the type of frame and some control information. The table describes the subfields.

D: In all frame types except one, this field defines the duration of the transmission that is used to set the value of NAV. In one control frame, this field defines the ID of the frame.

Addresses: There are four address fields, each 6 bytes long. The meaning of each address field depends on the value of the To DS and From DS subfields and will be discussed later.

Sequence Control: This field defines the sequence number of the frame to be used in flow control. Frame body. This field, which can be between 0 and 2312 bytes, contains information based on the type and the subtype defined in the FC field.

FCS: The FCS field is 4 bytes long and contains a CRC-32 error detection sequence.

Frame Types

A wireless LAN defined by IEEE 802.11 has three categories of frames: management frames, control frames, and data frames.

Management Frames: Management frames are used for the initial communication between stations and access points.

Control Frames: Control frames are used for accessing the channel and acknowledging frames. The figure shows the format.

Data Frames: Data frames are used for carrying data and control information

Addressing Mechanism

The IEEE 802.11 addressing mechanism specifies four cases, defined by the value of the two flags in the FC field, To DS and From DS. Each flag can be either 0 or 1, resulting in four different situations. The interpretation of the four addresses (address 1 to address 4) in the MAC frame depends on the value of these flags, as shown in the table.

To DS	From DS	Address 1	Address 2	Address 3	Address 4
0	0	Destination	Source	BSS ID	N/A
0	1	Destination	Sending AP	Source	N/A
1	0	Receiving AP	Source	Destination	N/A
1	1	Receiving AP	Sending AP	Destination	Source

Note that address 1 is always the address of the next device. Address 2 is always the address of the previous device. Address 3 is the address of the final destination station if it is not defined by address 1. Address 4 is the address of the original source station if it is not the same as address 2.

Case 1:00 In this case, To DS = 0 and From DS = 0. This means that the frame is not going to a distribution system (To DS = 0) and is not coming from a distribution system (From DS = 0). The frame is going from one station in a BSS to another without passing through the distribution system. The ACK frame should be sent to the original sender. The addresses are shown in figure.

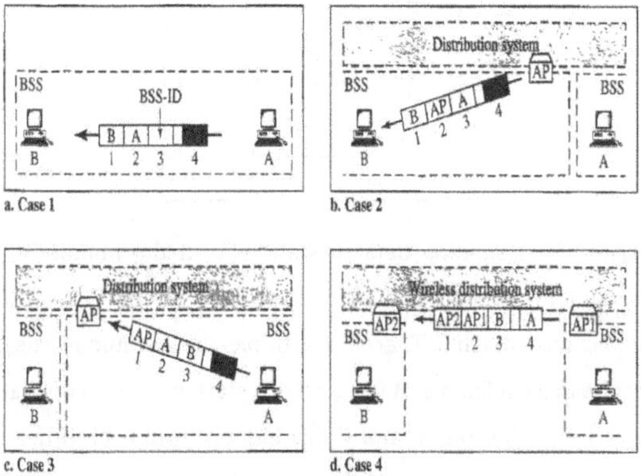

Case 2:01 In this case, To DS = 0 and From DS = 1. This means that the frame is coming from a distribution system (From DS = 1). The frame is coming from an AP and going to a station. The ACK should be sent to the AP. The addresses are as shown in Figure 14.9. Note that address 3 contains the original sender of the frame (in another BSS).

Case 3:10 In this case, To DS = 1 and From DS = 0. This means that the frame is going to a distribution system (To DS = 1). The frame is going from a station to an AP. The ACK is sent to the original station. The addresses are as shown in figure above. Note that address 3 contains the final destination of the frame (in another BSS).

Case 4:11 In this case, To DS = 1 and From DS = 1. This is the case in which the distribution system is also wireless. The frame is going from one AP to another AP in a wire-less distribution system. We do not need to define addresses if the distribution system is a wired LAN because the frame in these cases has the format of a wired LAN frame (Ethernet, for example). Here, we need four addresses to define the original sender, the final destination, and two intermediate APs.

Hidden and Exposed Station Problems

Hidden Station Problem The figure below shows an example of the hidden station problem. Station B has a transmission range shown by the left oval (sphere in space); every station in this range can hear any signal transmitted by station B. Station C has a transmission range shown by the right oval (sphere in space); every station located in this range can hear any signal transmitted by C. Station C is outside the transmission range of B; likewise, station B is outside the transmission range of C. Station A, however, is in the area covered by both B and C; it can hear any signal transmitted by B or C.

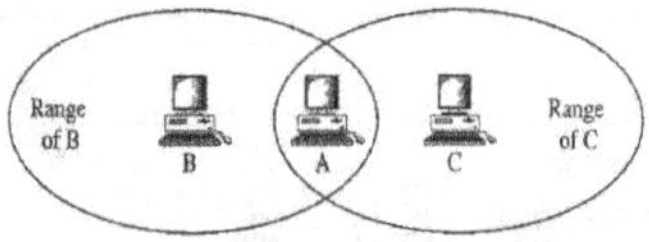

B and C are hidden from each other with respect to A.

Assume that station B is sending data to station A. In the middle of this transmission, station C also has data to send to station A. However, station C is out of B's range and transmissions from B cannot reach C. Therefore C thinks the medium is free. Station C sends its data to A, which results in a collision at A because this station is receiving data from both B and C. In this case, we say that stations B and C are hidden from each other with respect to A. Hidden stations can reduce the capacity of the network because of the possibility of collision. The solution to the hidden station problem is the use of the handshake frames (RTS and CTS) The figure shows that the RTS message from B reaches A, but not C. However, because both B and C are within the range of A, the CTS message, which contains the duration of data transmission from B to A reaches C. Station C knows that some hidden station is using the channel and refrains from transmitting until that duration is over.

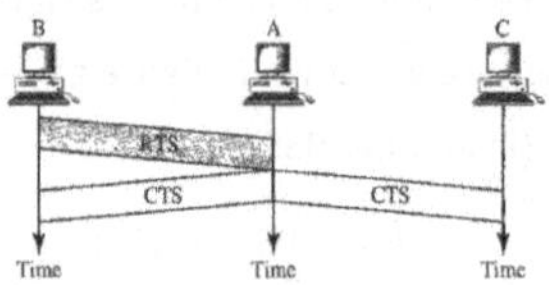

Exposed Station Problem Now consider a situation that is the inverse of the previous one: the exposed station problem. In this problem a station refrains from using a channel when it is, in fact, available. In the figure, station A is transmitting to station B. Station C has some data to send to station D, which can be sent without interfering with the transmission from A to B. However, station C is exposed to transmission from A; it hears what A is sending and thus refrains from sending. In other words, C is too conservative and wastes the capacity of the channel.

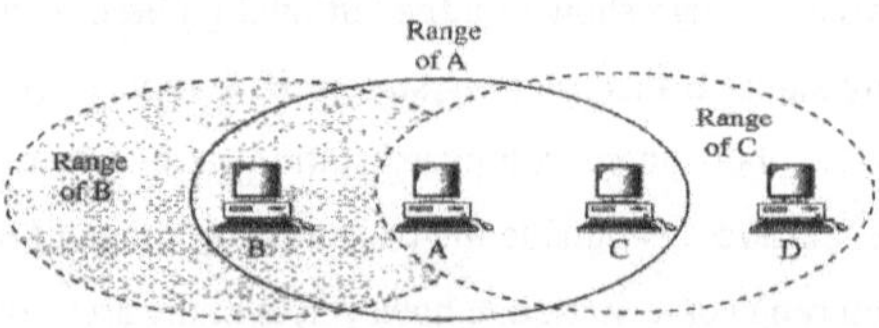

C is exposed to transmission from A to B.

The handshaking messages RTS and CTS cannot help in this case, despite what you might think. Station C hears the RTS from A, but does not hear the CTS from B. Station C, after hearing the RTS from A, can wait for a time so that the CTS from B reaches A; it then sends an RTS to D to show that it needs to communicate with D. Both stations B and A may hear this RTS, but station A is in the sending state, not the receiving state. Station B, however, responds with a CTS. The problem is here. If station A has started sending its data, station C cannot hear the CTS from station D because of the collision; it cannot send its data to D. It remains exposed until A finishes sending its data as the figure shows.

IEEE	*Technique*	*Band*	*Modulation*	*Rate (Mbps)*
802.11	FHSS	2.4 GHz	FSK	1 and 2
	DSSS	2.4 GHz	PSK	1 and 2
		Infrared	PPM	1 and 2
802.11a	OFDM	5.725 GHz	PSKorQAM	6 to 54
802.11b	DSSS	2.4 GHz	PSK	5.5 and 11
802.11g	OFDM	2.4 GHz	Different	22 and 54

2. Bluetooth

Bluetooth is a wireless LAN technology designed to connect devices of different functions such as telephones, notebooks, computers (desktop and laptop), cameras, printers, A Bluetooth LAN is an ad hoc network, which means that the network is formed spontaneously; the devices, sometimes called gadgets, find each other and make a network called a piconet.

Applications

1) Peripheral devices such as a wireless mouse or keyboard can communicate with the computer.
2) Monitoring devices can communicate with sensor devices in a small health care center.
3) Home security devices can use bluetooth to connect different sensors to the main security controller.
4) Conference attendees can synchronize their laptop computers at a conference.
5) Architecture Bluetooth defines two types of networks: piconet and scatternet.

Piconets

A Bluetooth network is called a piconet, or a small net. A piconet can have up to eight stations, one of which is called the primary;t the rest are called secondaries. Note that a piconet can have only one primary station. The communication between the primary and the secondary can be one-to-one or one-to-many.

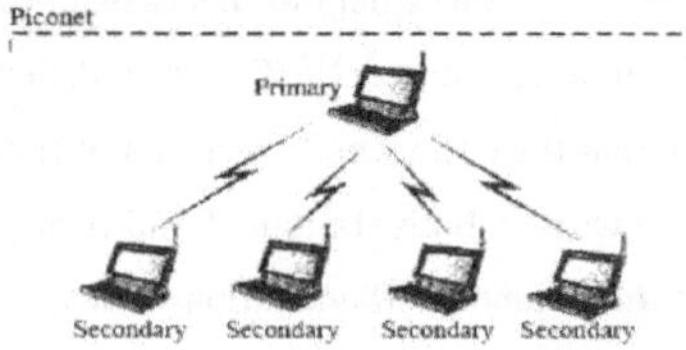

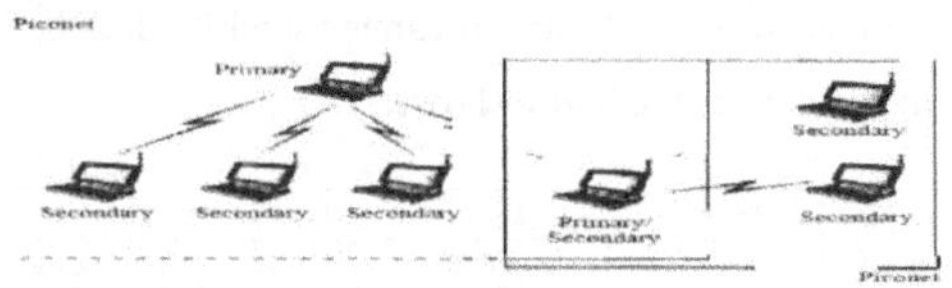

Although a piconet can have a maximum of seven secondaries, an additional eight secondaries can be in the parked state. A secondary in a parked state is synchronized with the primary, but cannot take part in communication until it is moved from the parked state. Because only eight stations can be active in a piconet, activating a station from the parked state means that an active station must go to the parked state.

Scatternet

Piconets can be combined to form what is called a scatternet. A secondary station in one piconet can be the primary in another piconet. This station can receive messages from the primary in the first piconet (as a secondary) and, acting as a primary, deliver them to secondaries in the second piconet. A station can be a member of two piconets

Bluetooth Layers

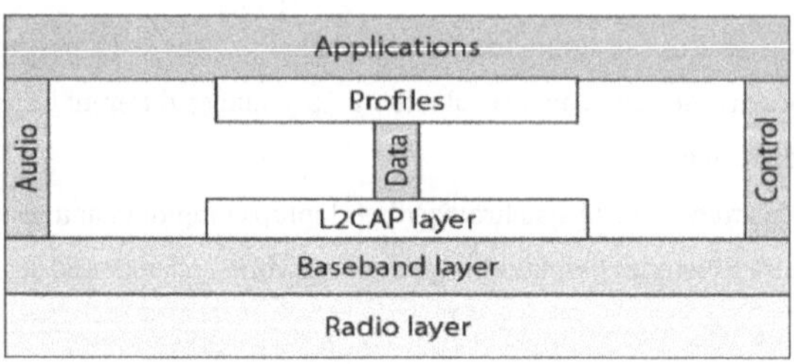

Bluetooth Devices

A Bluetooth device has a built-in short-range radio transmitter. The current data rate is 1 Mbps with a 2.4-GHz bandwidth. This means that there is a possibility of interference between the IEEE 802.11b wireless LANs and Bluetooth LANs.

Radio Layer: The radio layer is roughly equivalent to the physical layer of the Internet model. Bluetooth devices are low-power and have a range of 10 m.

Band: Bluetooth uses a 2.4-GHz ISM band divided into 79 channels of 1 MHz each.

FHSS: Bluetooth uses the frequency-hopping spread spectrum (FHSS) method in the physical layer to avoid interference from other devices or other networks. Bluetooth hops 1600 times per second, which means that each device changes its modulation frequency 1600 times per second. A device uses a frequency for only 625 Ils (1/1600 s) before it hops to another frequency; the dwell time is 625 Ils.

Modulation

Bluetooth uses GFSK (FSK with Gaussian bandwidth filtering; Bit 1 is represented by a frequency deviation above the carrier; bit zero represented by a frequency deviation below the carrier. The baseband layer is roughly equivalent to the MAC sublayer in LANs. The access method is TDMA . The primary and secondary communicate with each other using time slots. The length of a time slot is exactly the same as the dwell time, 625 Ils. This means that during the time that one frequency is used, a sender sends a frame to a secondary, or a secondary sends a frame to the primary. Note that the communication is only between the primary and a secondary; secondaries cannot communicate directly with one another.

TDMA

Bluetooth uses a form of TDMA that is called TDD-TDMA (timedivision duplex TDMA). TDD-TDMA is a kind of half-duplex communication in which the secondary and receiver send and receive data, but not at the same time (halfduplex); however, the communication for each direction uses different hops.

1) In slot 0, the primary sends a frame to secondary 1.
2) In slot 1, only secondary I sends a frame to the primary because the previous frame was addressed to secondary 1; other secondaries are silent.
3) In slot 2, the primary sends a frame to secondary 2.
4) In slot 3, only secondary 2 sends a frame to the primary because the previous frame was addressed to secondary 2; other secondaries are silent.
5) The cycle continues. We can say that this access method is similar to a poll/select operation with reservations. When the primary selects a secondary, it also polls it. The next time slot is reserved for the polled station to send its frame. If the polled secondary has no frame to send, the channel is silent.

Physical Links

Two types of links can be created between a primary and a secondary: SCO links and ACL links. A synchronous connection-oriented (SCO) link is used when avoiding latency (delay in data delivery) is more important than integrity (error-free delivery). In an SCO link, a physical link is created between the primary and a secondary by reserving specific slots at regular intervals. The basic unit of connection is two slots, one for each direction. If a packet is damaged, it is never retransmitted. SCO is used for real-time audio where avoiding delay is all-important. ACL An asynchronous connectionless link (ACL) is used when data integrity is more important than avoiding latency. In this type of link, if a payload encapsulated in the frame is corrupted, it is retransmitted.

Frame Format

Access code: This 72-bit field normally contains synchronization bits and the identifier of the primary to distinguish the frame of one piconet from another.

Header: This 54-bit field is a repeated I8-bit pattern.

1) Address: The 3-bit address subfield can define up to seven secondaries (l to 7). If the address is zero, it is used for broadcast communication from the primary to all secondaries.
2) Type: The 4-bit type subfield defines the type of data coming from the upper layers.
3) F: This I-bit subfield is for flow control. When set (I), it indicates that the device is unable to receive more frames (buffer is full).
4) A: This I-bit subfield is for acknowledgment. Bluetooth uses Stop-and-Wait ARQ; I bit is sufficient for acknowledgment.
5) S: This I-bit subfield holds a sequence number. Bluetooth uses Stop-and-Wait ARQ; I bit is sufficient for sequence numbering.
6) HEC: The 8-bit header error correction subfield is a checksum to detect errors in each 18-bit header section.
7) Payload: This subfield can be 0 to 2740 bits long. It contains data or control information corning from the upper layers

L2CAP

The Logical Link Control and Adaptation Protocol, or L2CAP (L2 here means LL), is roughly equivalent to the LLC sublayer in LANs. It is used for data exchange on an ACL link; SCO channels do not use L2CAP. The I6-bit length field defines the size of the data, in bytes, coming from the upper layers. Data can be up to 65,535 bytes. The channel ID (CID) defines a unique identifier for the virtual channel created at this level (see below). The L2CAP has specific duties: multiplexing, segmentation and reassembly, quality of service (QoS), and group management.

Multiplexing

The L2CAP can do multiplexing. At the sender site, it accepts data from one of the upper-layer protocols, frames them, and delivers them to the baseband layer. At the receiver site, it accepts a frame from the baseband layer, extracts the data, and delivers them to the appropriate protocol layer.

Segmentation and Reassembly

The maximum size of the payload field in the baseband layer is 2774 bits, or 343 bytes. This includes 4 bytes to define the packet and packet length. Therefore, the size of the packet that can arrive from an upper layer can only be 339 bytes. However, application layers sometimes need to send a data packet that can be up to 65,535 bytes (an Internet packet, for example). The L2CAP divides these large packets into segments and adds extra information to define the location of the segments in the original packet. The L2CAP segments the packet at the source and reassembles them at the destination.

QoS: Bluetooth allows the stations to define a quality-of-service level

Group Management: Another functionality of L2CAP is to allow devices to create a type of logical addressing between themselves. This is similar to multicasting

3. Connecting Devices

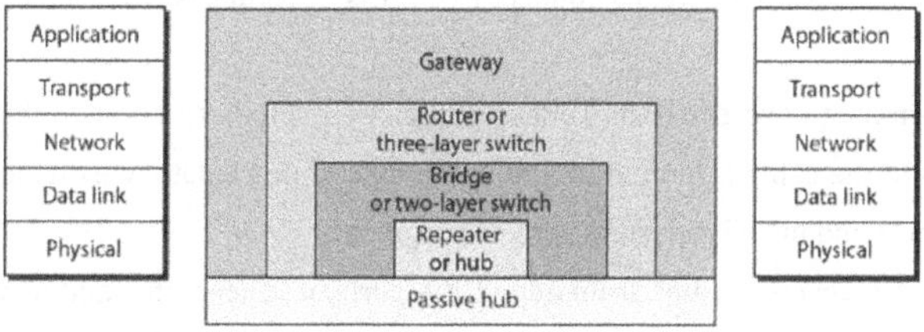

The five categories contain devices which can be defined as

1) Those which operate below the physical layer such as a passive hub.
2) Those which operate at the physical layer (a repeater or an active hub).
3) Those which operate at the physical and data link layers (a bridge or a two-layer switch).

4) Those which operate at the physical, data link, and network
5) Those which can operate at all five layers (a gateway).

Passive Hubs

A passive hub is just a connector. It connects the wires coming from different branches. In a star-topology Ethernet LAN, a passive hub is just a point where the signals coming from different stations collide; the hub is the collision point. This type of a hub is part of the media; its location in the Internet model is below the physical layer.

Repeaters

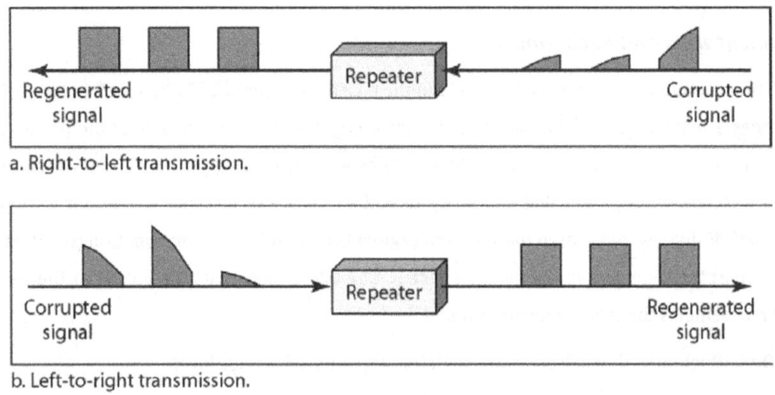

1) A repeater is a device that operates only in the physical layer.
2) A repeater receives a signal and, before it becomes too weak or corrupted, regenerates the original bit pattern. The repeater then sends the refreshed signal.
3) A repeater does not actually connect two LANs; it connects two segments of the same LAN.
4) A repeater can overcome the 10Base5 Ethernet length restriction. In this standard, the length of the cable is limited to 500 m. To extend this length, we divide the cable into segments and install repeaters between segments.
5) When it receives a frame from any of the ports, it regenerates and forwards it to the other port.
6) A repeater does not amplify the signal; it regenerates the signal. When it receives a weakened or corrupted signal, it creates a copy, bit for bit, at the original strength.
7) The location of a repeater on a link is vital. A repeater must be placed so that a signal reaches it before any noise changes the meaning of any of its bits.

Bridges

A bridge operates in both the physical and the data link layer. As a physical layer device, it regenerates the signal it receives. As a data link layer device, the bridge can check the physical (MAC) addresses (source and destination) contained in the frame.

Filtering

A bridge has filtering capability. It can check the destination address of a frame and decide if the frame should be forwarded or dropped. If the frame is to be forwarded, the decision must specify the port. A bridge has a table that maps addresses to ports.

Example

If a frame destined for station 712B13456142 arrives at port 1, the bridge consults its table to find the departing port. According to its table, frames for 7l2B13456142 leave through port 1; therefore, there is no need for forwarding, and the frame is dropped. On the other hand, if a frame for 712B13456141 arrives at port 2, the departing port is port 1and the frame is forwarded. In the first case, LAN 2 remains free of traffic; in the second case, both LANs have traffic. In our example, we show a two-port bridge; in reality a bridge usually has more ports. Note also that a bridge does not change the physical addresses contained in the frame

Transparent Bridges

A transparent bridge is a bridge in which the stations are completely unaware of the bridge's existence. If a bridge is added or deleted from the system, reconfiguration of the stations is unnecessary. According to the IEEE 802.1 d specification, a system equipped with transparent bridges must meet three criteria:

1) Frames must be forwarded from one station to another.
2) The forwarding table is automatically made by learning frame movements in the network.
3) Loops in the system must be prevented.

Forwarding: A transparent bridge must correctly forward the frames.

Learning: The earliest bridges had forwarding tables that were static. The systems administrator would manually enter each table entry during bridge setup. Although the process was simple, it was not practical. If a station was added or deleted, the table had to be modified manually. A better solution to the static table is a dynamic table that maps addresses to ports automatically. To make a table dynamic, we need a bridge that gradually learns from the frame movements. To do this, the bridge inspects both the destination and the source addresses. The destination address is used for the forwarding decision (table lookup); the source address is used for adding entries to the table and for updating purposes.

1) When station A sends a frame to station D, the bridge does not have an entry for either D or A. The frame goes out from all three ports; the frame floods the network. However, by looking at the source address, the bridge learns that station A must be located on the LAN connected to port .This means that frames destined for A, in the future, must be sent out through port 1. The bridge adds this entry to its table. The table has its first entry now.
2) When station E sends a frame to station A, the bridge has an entry for A, so it forwards the frame only to port 1. There is no flooding. In addition, it uses the source address of the frame, E, to add a second entry to the table.
3) When station B sends a frame to C, the bridge has no entry for C, so once again it floods the network and adds one more entry to the table. The process of learning continues as the bridge forwards frames.

Loop problem: Transparent bridges work fine as long as there are no redundant bridges in the system. Systems administrators, however, like to have redundant bridges (more than one bridge between a pair of LANs) to make the system more reliable. If a bridge fails, another bridge takes over until the failed one is repaired or replaced. Redundancy can create loops in the system, which is very undesirable..

1) Station A sends a frame to station D. The tables of both bridges are empty. Both forward the frame and update their tables based on the source address A.
2) Now there are two copies of the frame on LAN 2. The copy sent out by bridge 1 is received by bridge 2, which does not have any information about the destination address D; it floods the bridge. The copy sent out by bridge 2 is received by bridge 1 and is sent out for lack of information about D. Note that each frame is handled separately because bridges, as two nodes on a network sharing the medium, use an access method such as CSMA/CD. The tables of both bridges are updated, but still there is no information for destination D.
3) Now there are two copies of the frame on LAN 1. Step 2 is repeated, and both copies flood the network.
4) The process continues on and on. Note that bridges are also repeaters and regenerate frames. So in each iteration, there are newly generated fresh copies of the frames. To solve the looping problem, the IEEE specification requires that bridges use the spanning tree algorithm to create a loop less topology.

Spanning Tree

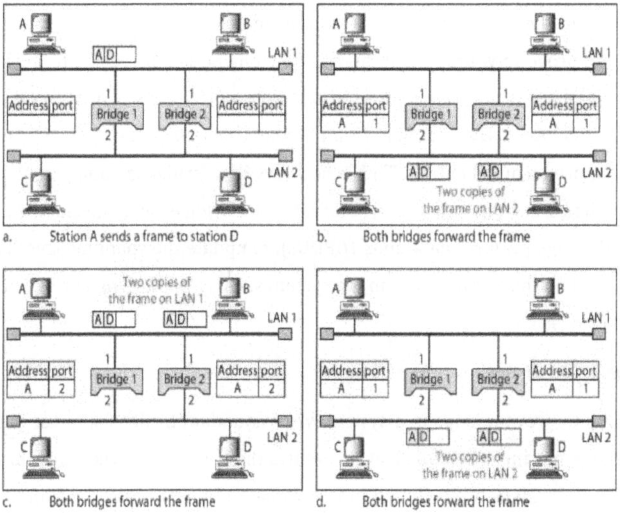

In graph theory, a spanning tree is a graph in which there is no loop. In a bridged LAN, this means creating a topology in which each LAN can be reached from any other LAN through one path only (no loop). We cannot change the physical topology of the system because of physical connections between cables and bridges, but we can create a logical topology that overlays the physical one.

1) Every bridge has a built-in ID (normally the serial number, which is unique). Each bridge broadcasts this ID so that all bridges know which one has the smallest ID. The bridge with the smallest ID is selected as the root bridge (root of the tree). We assume that bridge B1 has the smallest ID. It is, therefore, selected as the root bridge
2) The algorithm tries to find the shortest path (a path with the shortest cost) from the root bridge to every other bridge or LAN. The shortest path can be found by examining the total cost from the root bridge to the destination. Figure 15.9 shows the shortest paths.
3) The combination of the shortest paths creates the shortest tree
4) Based on the spanning tree, we mark the ports that are part of the spanning tree, the forwarding ports, which forward a frame that the bridge receives. We also mark those ports that are not part of the spanning tree, the blocking ports, which block the frames received by the bridge. Figure 15.10 shows the physical systems of LANs with

forwarding points (solid lines) and blocking ports (broken lines).

Note that there is only one single path from any LAN to any other LAN in the spanning tree system. This means there is only one single path from one LAN to any other LAN. No loops are created. You can prove to yourself that there is only one path from LAN 1 to LAN 2, LAN 3, or LAN 4. Similarly, there is only one path from LAN 2 to LAN 1, LAN 3, and LAN 4. The same is true for LAN 3 and LAN 4. Dynamic Algorithm We have described the spanning tree algorithm as though it required manual entries. This is not true. Each bridge is equipped with a software package that carries out this process dynamically. The bridges send special messages to one another, called bridge protocol data units (BPDUs), to update the spanning tree. The spanning tree is updated when there is a change in the system such as a failure of a bridge or an addition or deletion of bridges.

Source Routing Bridges

Another way to prevent loops in a system with redundant bridges is to use source routing bridges. In source routing, a sending station defines the bridges that the frame must visit. The addresses of these bridges are included in the frame. In other words, the frame contains not only the source and destination addresses, but also the addresses of all bridges to be visited

Bridges Connecting Different LANs

Theoretically a bridge should be able to connect LANs using different protocols at the data link layer, such as an Ethernet LAN to a wireless LAN. However, there are many issues to be considered:

1) Frame format. Each LAN type has its own frame format (compare an Ethernet frame with a wireless LAN frame).
2) Maximum data size. If an incoming frame's size is too large for the destination LAN, the data must be fragmented into several frames. The data then need to be reassembled at the destination. However, no protocol at the data link layer allows the fragmentation and reassembly of frames. We will see in Chapter 19 that this is allowed in the network layer. The bridge must therefore discard any frames too large for its system.
3) Data rate. Each LAN type has its own data rate. (Compare the 10-Mbps data rate of an Ethernet with the I-Mbps data rate of a wireless LAN.) The bridge must buffer the frame to compensate for this difference.
4) Bit order. Each LAN type has its own strategy in the sending of bits. Some send the most significant bit in a byte first; others send the least significant bit first.
5) Security. Some LANs, such as wireless LANs, implement security measures in the data

link layer. Other LANs, such as Ethernet, do not. Security often involves encryption When a bridge receives a frame from a wireless LAN, it needs to decrypt the message before forwarding it to an Ethernet LAN.

6) Multimedia support. Some LANs support multimedia and the quality of services needed for this type of communication; others do not.

Routers

A router is a three-layer device that routes packets based on their logical addresses (host-to-host addressing). A router normally connects LANs and WANs in the Internet and has a routing table that is used for making decisions about the route. The routing tables are normally dynamic and are updated using routing protocols

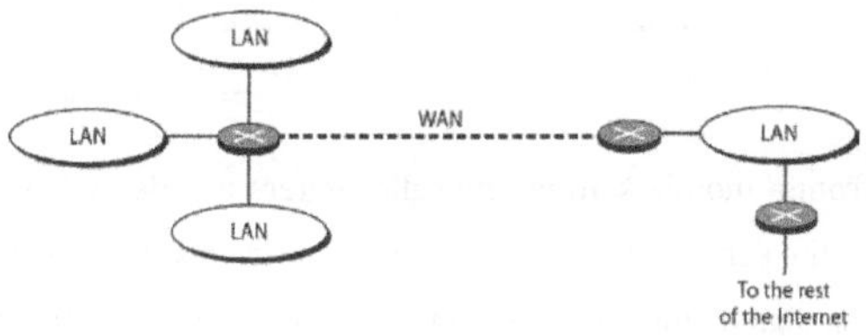

Gateway

A gateway is normally a computer that operates in all five layers of the Internet or seven layers of OSI model. A gateway takes an application message, reads it, and interprets it. This means that it can be used as a connecting device between two internetworks that use different models. For example, a network designed to use the OSI model can be connected to another network using the Internet model. The gateway connecting the two systems can take a frame as it arrives from the first system, move it up to the OSI application layer, and remove the message. Gateways can provide security.

4. Cellular Telephony

Cellular telephony is designed to provide communications between two moving units, called mobile stations (MSs), or between one mobile unit and one stationary unit, often called a land unit.

Frequency-Reuse Principle

In general, neighboring cells cannot use the same set of frequencies for communication because it may create interference for the users located near the cell boundaries. How-ever, the set of frequencies available is limited, and frequencies need to be reused. A frequency reuse pattern is a configuration of *N* cells, *N* being the **reuse factor,** in which each cell uses a unique set of frequencies. When the pattern is repeated, the frequencies can be reused. There are several different patterns. The numbers in the cells define the pattern. The cells with the same number in a pattern can use the same set of frequencies. We call these cells the *reusing cells.* As Figure shows, in a pattern with reuse factor 4, only one cell separates the cells using the same set of frequencies. In the pattern with reuse factor 7, two cells separate the reusing cells.

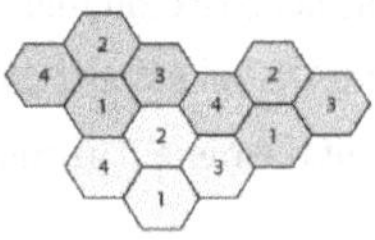
a. Reuse factor of 4

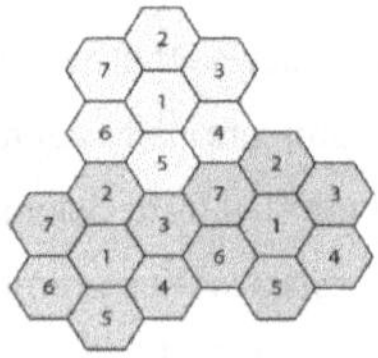
b. Reuse factor of 7

Transmitting

To place a call from a mobile station, the caller enters a code of 7 or 10 digits (a phone number) and presses the send button. The mobile station then scans the band, seeking a setup channel with a strong signal, and sends the data (phone number) to the closest base station using that channel. The base station relays the data to the MSC. The MSC sends the data on to the telephone central office. If the called party is available, a connection is made and the result is relayed back to the MSC. At this point, the MSC assigns an unused voice channel to the call, and a connection is established. The mobile station automatically adjusts its tuning to the new channel, and communication can begin.

Receiving

When a mobile phone is called, the telephone central office sends the number to the MSC. The MSC searches for the location of the mobile station by sending query sig-nals to each cell in a process called *paging.* Once the mobile station is found, the MSC transmits a ringing signal and, when the mobile station answers, assigns a voice channel to the call, allowing voice communication to begin.

Handoff

It may happen that, during a conversation, the mobile station moves from one cell to another. When it does, the signal may become weak. To solve this problem, the MSC monitors the level of the signal every few seconds. If the strength of the signal diminishes, the MSC seeks a new cell that can better accommodate the communication. The MSC then changes the channel carrying the call (hands the signal off from the old channel to a new one).

Hard Handoff Early systems used a hard handoff. In a hard handoff, a mobile station only communicates with one base station. When the MS moves from one cell to another, communication must first be broken with the previous base station before communication can be established with the new one. This may create a rough transition.

Soft Handoff New systems use a soft handoff. In this case, a mobile station can communicate with two base stations at the same time. This means that, during handoff, a mobile station may continue with the new base station before breaking off from the old one.

Roaming

One feature of cellular telephony is called roaming. Roaming means, in principle, that a user can have access to communication or can be reached where there is coverage. A service provider usually has limited coverage. Neighboring service providers can pro-vide extended coverage through a roaming contract. The situation is similar to snail mail between countries. The charge for delivery of a letter between two countries can be divided upon agreement by the two countries.

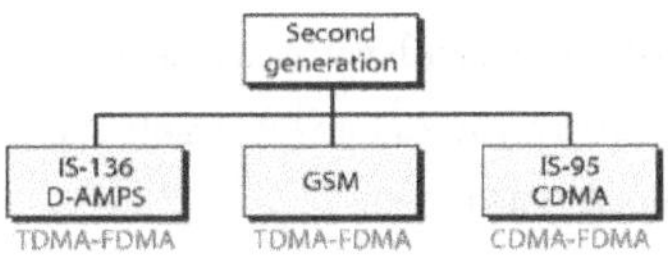

GSM

The Global System for Mobile Communication (GSM) is a European standard that was developed to provide a common second-generation technology for all Europe. The aim was to replace a number of incompatible first-generation technologies.

Bands GSM uses two bands for duplex communication. Each band is 25 MHz in width, shifted toward 900 MHz, as shown in Figure. Each band is divided into 124 channels of 200 kHz separated by guard bands.

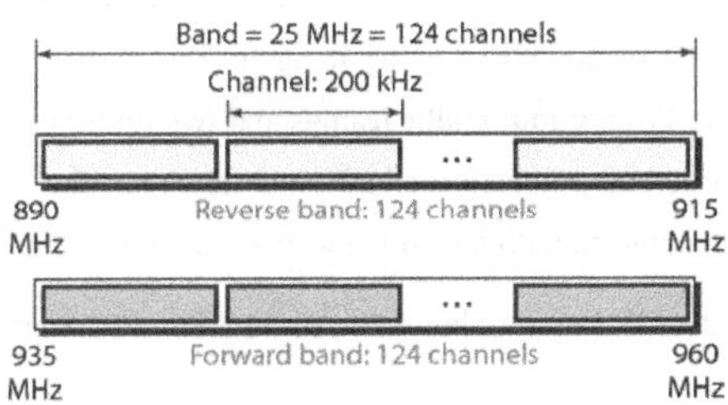

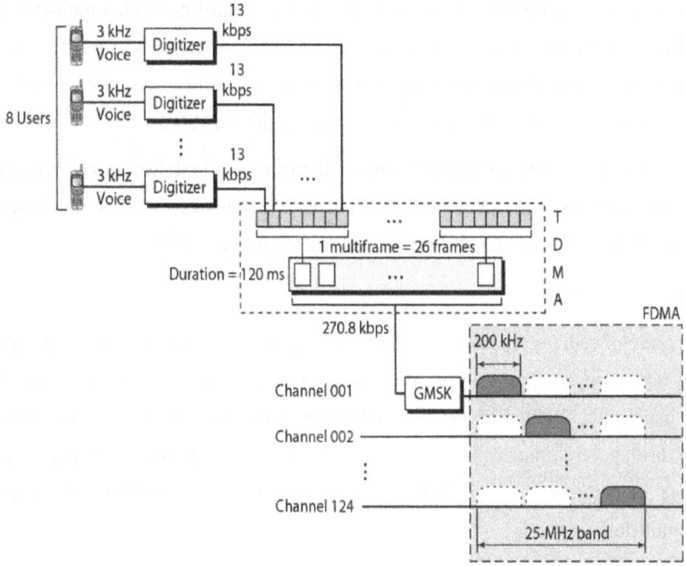

Transmission shows a GSM system. Each voice channel is digitized and compressed to a 13-kbps digital signal. Each slot carries 156.25 bits Eight slots share a frame (TDMA). Twenty-six frames also share a multiframe (TDMA).

We can calculate the bit rate of each channel as follows

Channel data rate = (1/120 ms) x 26 X 8 X 156.25=270.8 kbps

Each 270.8-kbps digital channel modulates a carrier using GMSK (a form of FSK used mainly in European systems); the result is a 200-kHz analog signal. Finally 124 analog channels of 200 kHz are combined using FDMA. The result is a 25-MHz band. Figure 16.9 shows the user data and overhead in a multiframe.

The reader may have noticed the large amount of overhead in TDMA. The user data are only 65 bits per slot. The system adds extra bits for error correction to make it 114 bits per slot. To this, control bits are added to bring it up to 156.25 bits per slot. Eight slots are encapsulated in a frame. Twenty-four traffic frames and two additional control frames make a multiframe. A multiframe has a duration of 120 ms. However, the architecture does define superframes and hyperframes that do not add any overhead; we will not discuss them here.

Reuse Factor Because of the complex error correction mechanism, GSM allows a reuse factor as low as 3.

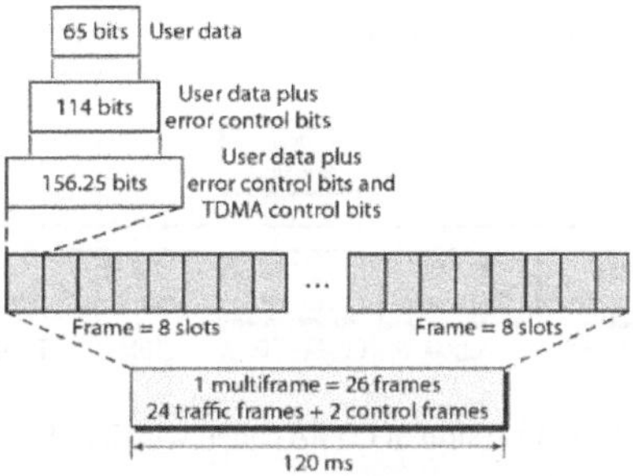

Third Generation

The third generation of cellular telephony refers to a combination of technologies that provide a variety of services. Ideally, when it matures, the third generation can provide both digital data and voice communication. Using a small portable device, a person should be able to talk to anyone else in the world with a voice quality similar to that of the existing fixed telephone network. A person can download and watch a movie, can download and listen to music, can surf the Internet or play games, can have a video conference, and can do much more. One of the interesting characteristics of a third generation system is that the portable device is always connected; you do not need to dial a number to connect to the Internet.

The third-generation concept started in 1992, when ITU issued a blueprint called the Internet Mobile Communication 2000 (IMT-2000).

The blueprint defines some criteria for third-generation technology as outlined below:

1) Voice quality comparable to that of the existing public telephone network.
2) Data rate of 144 kbps for access in a moving vehicle (car), 384 kbps for access as the user walks (pedestrians), and 2 Mbps for the stationary user (office or home).
3) Support for packet-switched and circuit-switched data services.
4) A band of 2 GHz.
5) Bandwidths of 2 MHz.
6) Interface to the Internet

IMT-2000 Radio Interface

Figure 16.12 shows the radio interfaces (wireless standards) adopted by 1MT-2000. All five are developed from second-generation technologies. The first two evolve from COMA technology. The third evolves from a combination of COMA and TOMA. The fourth evolves from TOMA, and the last evolves from both FOMA and TOMA.

IMT-2000 radio interfaces

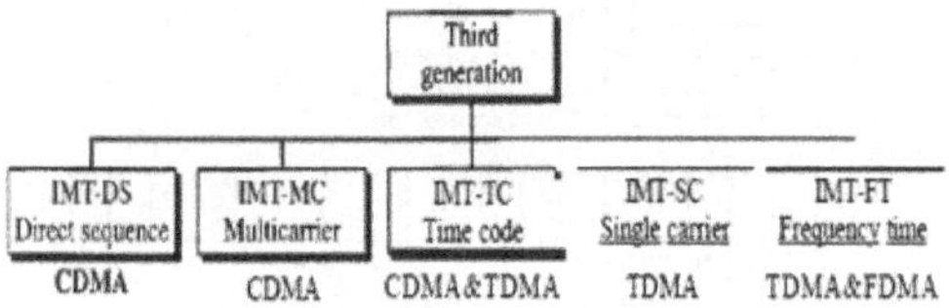

IMT-DS This approach uses a version of COMA called wideband COMA or W-COMA.

W-COMA uses a 5-MHz bandwidth. It was developed in Europe, and it is compatible with the COMA used in IS-95.

IMT-MC This approach was developed in North America and is known as COMA 2000. It is an evolution of COMA technology used in IS-95 channels. It combines the new wideband (I5-MHz) spread spectrum with the narrowband (l.25-MHz) COMA of IS-95. It is backward-compatible with IS-95. It allows communication on multiple 1.25-MHz channels (l, 3, 6, 9, 12 times), up to 15 MHz. The use of the wider channels allows it to reach the 2-Mbps data rate defined for the third generation.

IMT-TC This standard uses a combination of W-COMA and TDMA. The standard tries to reach the IMT-2000 goals by adding TOMA multiplexing to W-COMA.

IMT-SC This standard only uses TOMA.

IMT-FT This standard uses a combination of FDMA and TOMA.

UNIT-8

Network Layer: Introduction, Logical addressing, IPv4 addresses, IPv6 addresses, Internetworking basics, IPv4, IPv6, Comparison of IPv4 and IPv6 Headers.

1. IPv4 Addresses

An IPv4 address is a 32-bit address that uniquely and universally defines the connection of a device (for example, a computer or a router) to the Internet.

An IPv4 address is 32 bits long.

IPv4 addresses are unique. They are unique in the sense that each address defines one, and only one, connection to the Internet. Two devices on the Internet can never have the same address at the same time. We will see later that, by using some strategies, an address may be assigned to a device for a time period and then taken away and assigned to another device.

The IPv4 addresses are unique and universal.

Address Space

A protocol such as IPv4 that defines addresses has an address space. An address space is the total number of addresses used by the protocol. If a protocol uses *N* bits to define an address, the address space is *2N* because each bit can have two different values (0 or 1) and *N* bits can have *2N* values.

IPv4 uses 32-bit addresses, which means that the address space is 232 or 4,294,967,296 (more than 4 billion). This means that, theoretically, if there were no restrictions, more than 4 billion devices could be connected to the Internet. We will see shortly that the actual number is much less because of the restrictions imposed on the addresses.

The address space of IPv4 is 232 or 4,294,967,296.

Notations

There are two prevalent notations to show an IPv4 address: binary notation and dotted decimal notation.

Binary Notation

In binary notation, the IPv4 address is displayed as 32 bits. Each octet is often referred to as a byte. So it is common to hear an IPv4 address referred to as a 32-bit address or a 4-byte address. The following is an example of an IPv4 address in binary notation:

01110101 10010101 00011101 00000010

Dotted-Decimal Notation

To make the IPv4 address more compact and easier to read, Internet addresses are usually written in decimal form with a decimal point (dot) separating the bytes. The following is the dotted~decimal notation of the above address:

117.149.29.2

Figure 19.1 shows an IPv4 address in both binary and dotted-decimal notation. Note that because each byte (octet) is 8 bits, each number in dotted-decimal notation is a value ranging from 0 to 255.

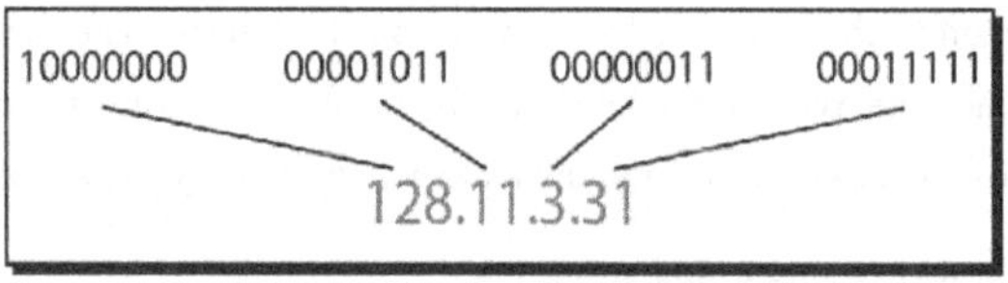

Figure 19.1: Format of IPv4

Classful Addressing

IPv4 addressing, at its inception, used the concept of classes. This architecture is called classful addressing. Although this scheme is becoming obsolete, we briefly discuss it here to show the rationale behind classless addressing. In classful addressing, the address space is divided into five classes: A, B, C, D, and E. Each class occupies some part of the address space.

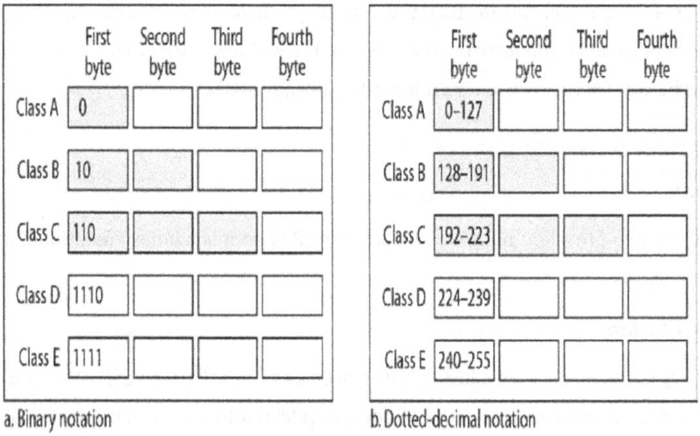

Figure 19.2: Structure of IPv4

Classes and Blocks

One problem with classful addressing is that each class is divided into a fixed number of blocks with each block having a fixed size as shown in Table 19.1.

Table 19.1 ***Number of blocks and block size in classful IPv4 addressing***

Class	*Number of Blocks*	*Block Size*	*Application*
A	128	16,777,216	Unicast
B	16,384	65,536	Unicast
C	2,097,152	256	Unicast
D	1	268,435,456	Multicast
E	1	268,435,456	Reserved

The last column of Table 19.2 shows the mask in the form *In* where *n* can be 8, 16, or 24 in classful addressing. This notation is also called slash notation or Classless Inter domain Routing (CIDR) notation. The notation is used in classless addressing, which we will discuss later. We introduce it here because it can also be applied to classful addressing. We will show later that classful addressing is a special case of classless addressing.

Table 19.2 ***Default masks for classful addressing***

Class	*Binary*	*Dotted-Decimal*	*CIDR*
A	11111111 00000000 00000000 00000000	255.0.0.0	/8
B	11111111 11111111 00000000 00000000	255.255.0.0	/16
C	11111111 11111111 11111111 00000000	255.255.255.0	/24

Subnetting

During the era of classful addressing, subnetting was introduced. If an organization was granted a large block in class A or B, it could divide the addresses into several contiguous groups and assign each group to smaller networks (called subnets) or, in rare cases, share part of the addresses with neighbors. Subnetting increases the number of Is in the mask, as we will see later when we discuss classless addressing.

Supernetting

The time came when most of the class A and class B addresses were depleted; however, there was still a huge demand for midsize blocks. The size of a class C block with a maximum number of 256 addresses did not satisfy the needs of most organizations. Even a midsize organization needed more addresses. One solution was supernetting. In supernetting, an organization can combine several class C blocks to create a larger range of addresses. In other words, several networks are combined to create a super network or a supemet. An organization can apply for a set of class C blocks instead of just one. For example, an organization that needs 1000 addresses can be granted four contiguous class C blocks. The organization can then use these addresses to create one supernetwork. Supernetting decreases the number of is in the mask. For example, if an organization is given four class C addresses, the mask changes from/24 to/22. We will see that classless addressing eliminated the need for supernetting.

Address Depletion

The flaws in classful addressing scheme combined with the fast growth of the Internet led to the near depletion of the available addresses. Yet the number of devices on the Internet is much less than the 232 address space. We have run out of class A and B addresses, and

a class C block is too small for most midsize organizations. One solution that has alleviated the problem is the idea of classless addressing. Classful addressing, which is almost obsolete, is replaced with classless addressing.

Classless Addressing

To overcome address depletion and give more organizations access to the Internet, classless addressing was designed and implemented. In this scheme, there are no classes, but the addresses are still granted in blocks.

Address Blocks

In classless addressing, when an entity, small or large, needs to be connected to the Internet, it is granted a block (range) of addresses. The size of the block (the number of addresses) varies based on the nature and size of the entity. For example, a household may be given only two addresses; a large organization may be given thousands of addresses. An ISP, as the Internet service provider, may be given thousands or hundreds of thousands based on the number of customers it may serve.

Restriction to simplify the handling of addresses, the Internet authorities impose three restrictions on classless address blocks:

1) The addresses in a block must be contiguous, one after another.
2) The number of addresses in a block must be a power of 2 (I, 2, 4, 8, ...).
3) The first address must be evenly divisible by the number of addresses.

Netid and Hostid

In classful addressing, an IP address in class A, B, or C is divided into netid and hostid. These parts are of varying lengths, depending on the class of the address. Figure 19.2 shows some netid and hostid bytes. The netid is in color, the hostid is in white. Note that the concept does not apply to classes D and E.

In class A, one byte defines the netid and three bytes define the hostid. In class B, two bytes define the netid and two bytes define the hostid. In class C, three bytes define the netid and one byte defines the hostid.

Mask

Although the length of the netid and hostid (in bits) is predetermined in classful addressing, we can also use a mask (also called the default mask), a 32-bit number made of contiguous Is followed by contiguous as. The masks for classes A, B, and C are shown in Table 19.2. The concept does not apply to classes D and E.

Address Allocation

The next issue in classless addressing is address allocation. How are the blocks allocated? The ultimate responsibility of address allocation is given to a global authority called the *Internet* Corporation *for Assigned Names and Addresses* (ICANN).

However, ICANN does not normally allocate addresses to individual organizations. It assigns a large block of addresses to an ISP. Each ISP, in turn, divides its assigned block into smaller subblocks and grants the sub locks to its customers. In other words, an ISP receives one large block to be distributed to its Internet users. This is called address aggregation: many blocks of addresses are aggregated in one block and granted to one ISP.

Example

An ISP is granted a block of addresses starting with 190.100.0.0/16 (65,536 addresses).

The ISP needs to distribute these addresses to three groups of customers as follows:

1) The first group has 64 customers; each needs 256 addresses.
2) The second group has 128 customers; each needs 128 addresses.
3) The third group has 128 customers; each needs 64 addresses.

Design the sub blocks and find out how many addresses are still available after these allocations.

Solution

1) Group 1

For this group, each customer needs 256 addresses. This means that 8 (log2256) bits are needed to define each host. The prefix length is then 32 - 8 =24. The addresses are:

1st Customer:

2nd Customer:

190.100.0.0/24

190.100.1.0/24

190.100.0.255/24

190.100.1.255/24

64th Customer: 190.100.63.0/24 190.100.63.255/24

Total =64 X 256 =16,384

2) Group 2

For this group, each customer needs 128 addresses. This means that 7 (10g2 128) bits are needed to define each host. The prefix length is then 32 - 7 =25. The addresses are

1st Customer: 190.100.64.0/25

2nd Customer: 190.100.64.128/25

190.100.64.127/25

190.100.64.255/25

128th Customer: 190.100.127.128/25 190.100.127.255/25

Total =128 X 128 = 16,384

3) Group 3

For this group, each customer needs 64 addresses. This means that 6 (logz 64) bits are needed to each host. The prefix length is then 32-6 =26. The addresses are:

Total =128 X 64 =8192

Number of granted addresses to the ISP: 65,536

Number of allocated addresses by the ISP: 40,960

Number of available addresses: 24,576

Network Address Translation (NAT)

The number of home users and small businesses that want to use the Internet is ever increasing. In the beginning, a user was connected to the Internet with a dial-up line, which means that she was connected for a specific period of time. An ISP with a block of addresses could dynamically assign an address to this user. An address was given to a user when it was needed. But the situation is different today.

Home users and small businesses can be connected by an ADSL line or cable modem. In addition, many are not happy with one address; many have created small networks with several hosts and need an IP address for each host. With the shortage of addresses, this is a serious problem. A quick solution to this problem is called network address translation (NAT).

NAT enables a user to have a large set of addresses internally and one address, or a small set of addresses, externally. The traffic inside can use the large set; the traffic outside, the small set.

To separate the addresses used inside the home or business and the ones used for the Internet, the Internet authorities have reserved three sets of addresses as private addresses, shown in Table 19.3.

Table 19.3 *Addresses for private networks*

Range			*Total*
10.0.0.0	to	10.255.255.255	2^{24}
172.16.0.0	to	172.31.255.255	2^{20}
192.168.0.0	to	192.168.255.255	2^{16}

Any organization can use an address out of this set without permission from the Internet authorities. Everyone knows that these reserved addresses are for private networks. They are unique inside the organization, but they are not unique globally. No router will forward a packet that has one of these addresses as the destination address. The site must have only one single connection to the global Internet through a router that runs the NAT software. Figure 19.3 shows a simple implementation of NAT.

As Figure 19.3 shows, the private network uses private addresses. The router that connects the network to the global address uses one private address and one global address. The private network is transparent to the rest of the Internet; the rest of the Internet sees only the NAT router with the address 200.24.5.8.

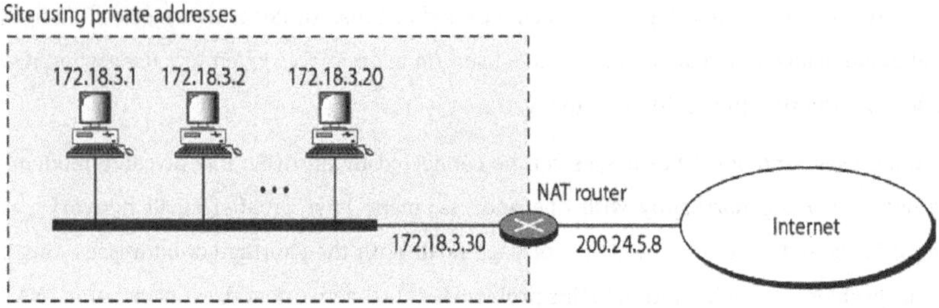

Figure 19.3: Implementation of NAT

Address Translation

All the outgoing packets go through the NAT router, which replaces the source address in the packet with the global NAT address. All incoming packets also pass through the NAT router, which replaces the destination address in the packet (the NAT router global address) with the appropriate private address. Figure 19.4 shows an example of address translation.

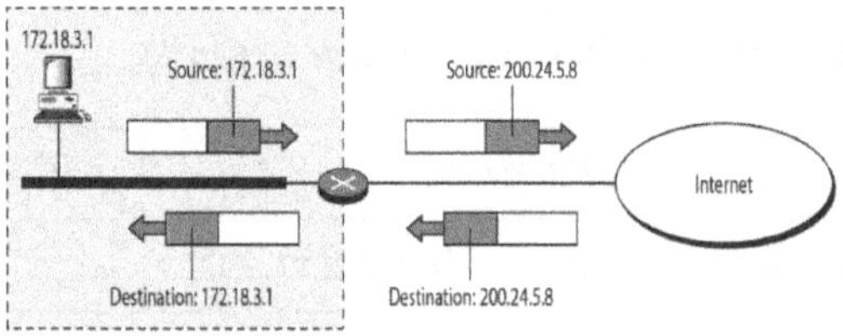

Figure 19.4: Example of Address Translation

Translation Table

The reader may have noticed that translating the source addresses for outgoing packets is straightforward. But how does the NAT router know the destination address for a packet coming from the Internet? There may be tens or hundreds of private IP addresses, each belonging to one specific host. The problem is solved if the NAT router has a translation table.

Using One IP Address In its simplest form, a translation table has only two columns: the private' address and the external address (destination address of the packet). When the router translates the source address of the outgoing packet, it also makes note of the destination address-where the packet is going. When the response comes back from the destination, the router uses the source address of the packet (as the external address) to find the private address of the packet. Figure 19.5 shows the idea. Note that the addresses that are changed (translated) are shown in color.

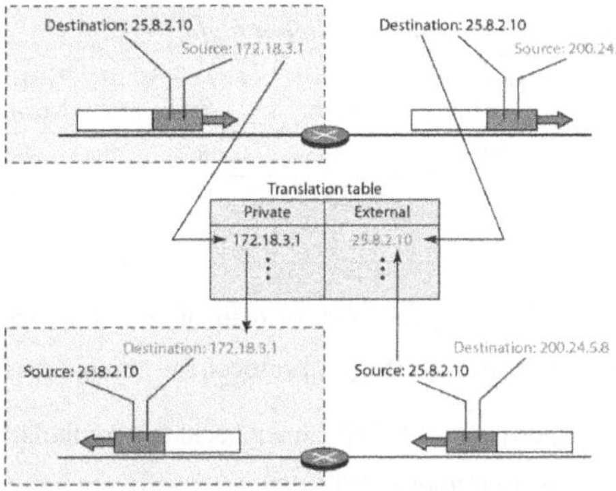

Figure 19.5: Address Translation

The NAT mechanism described requires that the private network start the communication. As we will see, NAT is used mostly by ISPs which assign one single address to a customer. The customer, however, may be a member of a private network that has many private addresses. In this case, communication with the Internet is always initiated from the customer site, using a client program such as HTTP, TELNET, or FTP to access the corresponding server program. For example, when e-mail that originates from a noncustomer site is received by the ISP e-mail server, the e-mail is stored in the mailbox of the customer until retrieved. A private network cannot run a server program for clients outside of its network if it is using NAT technology.

Using a Pool of IP Addresses Since the NAT router has only one global address, only one private network host can access the same external host. To remove this restriction, the NAT router uses a pool of global addresses. For example, instead of using only one global address (200.24.5.8), the NAT router can use four addresses (200.24.5.8, 200.24.5.9,200.24.5.10, and 200.24.5.11). In this case, four private network hosts can communicate with the same external host at the same time because each pair of addresses defines a connection. However, there are still some drawbacks. In this example, no more than four connections can be made to the same destination. Also, no private-network host can access two external server programs (e.g., HTTP and FfP) at the same time.

Using Both IP Addresses and Port Numbers To allow a many-to-many relationship between private-network hosts and external server programs, we need more information in the translation table. For example, suppose two hosts with addresses 172.18.3.1 and 172.18.3.2 inside a private network need to access the HTTP server on external host

Table 19.4 ***Five-column translation table***

Private Address	*Private Port*	*External Address*	*External Port*	*Transport Protocol*
172.18.3.1	1400	25.8.3.2	80	TCP
172.18.3.2	1401	25.8.3.2	80	TCP
...	...	...	...	...

If the translation table has five columns, instead of two, that include the source and destination port numbers of the transport layer protocol, the ambiguity is eliminated.

Note that when the response from HTTP comes back, the combination of source address (25.8.3.2) and destination port number (1400) defines the-private network host to which the response should be directed. Note also that for this translation to work, the temporary port numbers (1400 and 1401) must be unique.

NAT and ISP

An ISP that serves dial-up customers can use NAT technology to conserve addresses. For example, suppose an ISP is granted 1000 addresses, but has 100,000 customers. Each of the customers is assigned a private network address. The ISP translates each of the 100,000 source addresses in outgoing packets to one of the 1000 global addresses; it translates the global destination address in incoming packets to the corresponding private address. Figure 19.6 shows this concept.

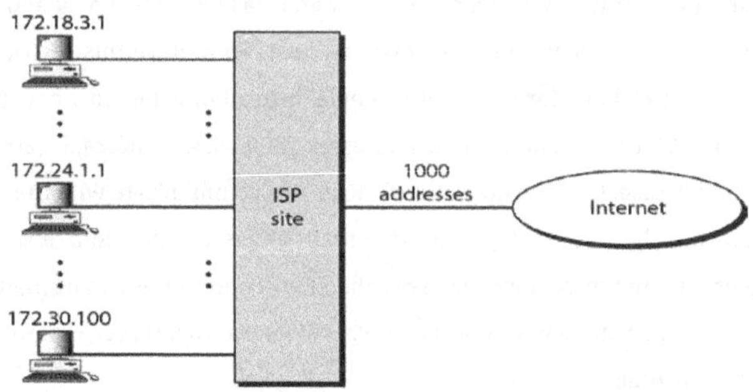

Figure 19.6: NAT and ISP

IPv6 Structure

An IPv6 address consists of 16 bytes (octets); it is 128 bits long.

An IPv6 address is 128 bits long.

Hexadecimal Colon Notation

To make addresses more readable, IPv6 specifies hexadecimal colon notation. In this otation, 128 bits is divided into eight sections, each 2 bytes in length. Two bytes in hexadecimal notation requires four hexadecimal digits. Therefore, the address consists of 32 hexadecimal digits, with every four digits separated by a colon, as shown in Figure 19.6.

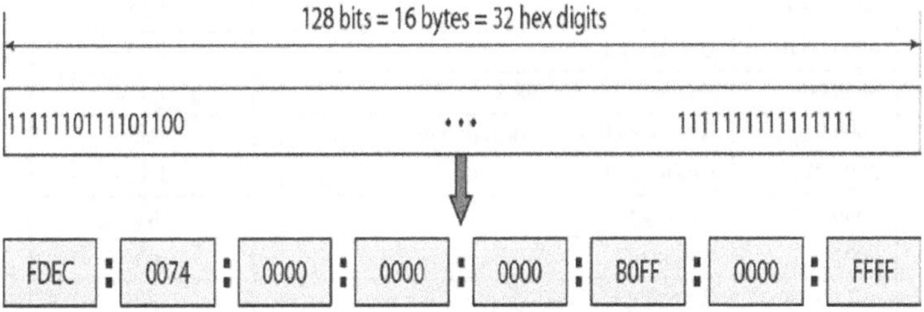

Figure 19.6: Format of IPv6

Abbreviation

Although the IP address, even in hexadecimal format, is very long, many of the digits are zeos.in this case, we can abbreviate the address. The leading zeros of a section (four digits between two colons) can be omitted. Only the leading zeros can be dropped, not the trailing zeros (see Figure 19.7).

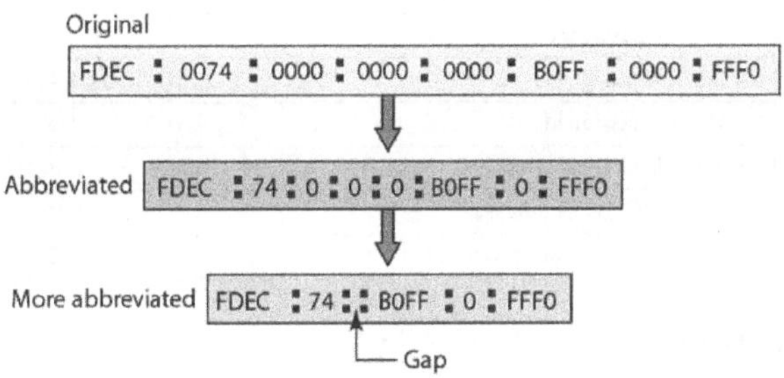

Figure 19.7: Structure of IPv6

Address Space

IPv6 has a much larger address space; 2128 addresses are available. The designers of IPv6 divided the address into several categories. A few leftmost bits, called the *type prefix,* in each address define its category. The type prefix is variable in length, but it is designed such that no code is identical to the first part of any other code. In this way, there is no ambiguity; when an address is given, the type prefix can easily be determined. Table 19.5 shows the prefix for each type of address. The third column shows the fraction of each type of address relative to the whole address space.

Table 19.5: Prefix for IPv6

Type Prefix	*Type*	*Fraction*
0000 0000	Reserved	1/256
0000 0001	Unassigned	1/256
0000 001	ISO network addresses	1/128
0000 010	IPX (Novell) network addresses	1/128
0000 011	Unassigned	1/128
0000 1	Unassigned	1/32
0001	Reserved	1/16
001	Reserved	1/8
010	Provider-based unicast addresses	1/8

Type Prefix	*Type*	*Fraction*
011	Unassigned	1/8
100	Geographic-based unicast addresses	1/8
101	Unassigned	1/8
110	Unassigned	1/8
1110	Unassigned	1/16
1111 0	Unassigned	1/32
1111 10	Unassigned	1/64
1111 110	Unassigned	1/128
1111 1110 0	Unassigned	1/512
1111 1110 10	Link local addresses	1/1024
1111 1110 11	Site local addresses	1/1024
1111 1111	Multicast addresses	1/256

Frame format of IPv4

IPv4 is a unreliable and connectionless datagram protocol-best effort delivery.

Unreliable: IP does not make an attempt to recover lost packets

Connectionless: Each packet ("datagram") is handled independently. IP is not aware that packets between hosts may be sent in a logical sequence

Best effort: IP does not make guarantees on the service (no throughput guarantee, no delay guarantee). Packets in IPv4 layer are known as Datagram which consists of two parts: a header and data (payload). The length of the header is 20 - 60 bytes and it contains essential information for routing and packet delivery.

Position of IPv4 in TCP/IP Protocol Suite

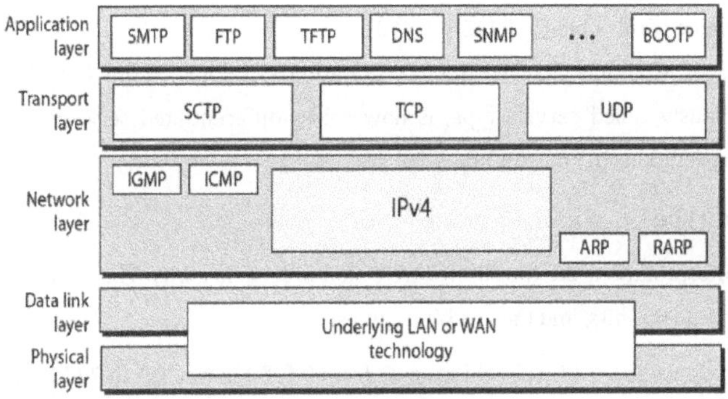

IPv4 Datagram Format

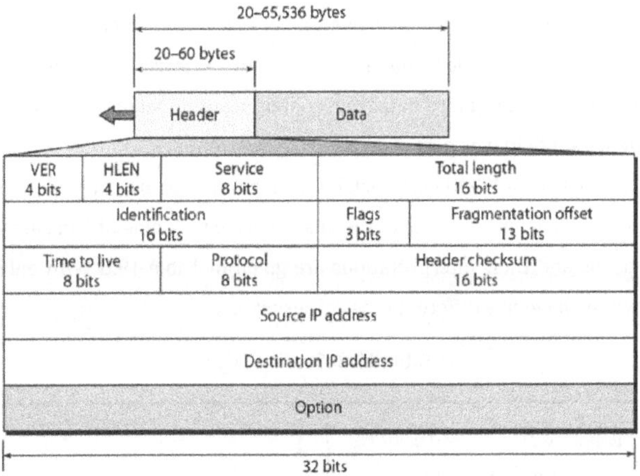

Version(VER). This 4-bit field defines the version of the IPv4 protocol. Currently the version is 4. However, version 6 (or IPng) may totally replace version 4 in the future. This field tells the IPv4 software running in the processing machine that the datagram has the format of version 4. All fields must be interpreted as specified in the fourth version of the protocol. If the machine is using some other version of IPv4, the datagram is discarded rather than interpreted incorrectly.

1) Header length (HLEN). This 4-bit field defines the total length of the datagram header in 4-byte words. This field is needed because the length of the header is variable (between 20 and 60 bytes). When there are no options, the header length is 20 bytes, and the value of this field is 5 (5 x 4 = 20). When the option field is at its maximum size, the value of this field is 15 (15 x 4 = 60).
2) Services. IETF has changed the interpretation and name of this 8-bit field. This field, previously called service type, is now called differentiated services. We show both interpretations in Figure 19.8.

1) Service Type

In this interpretation, the first 3 bits are called precedence bits. The next 4 bits are called type of service (TOS) bits, and the last bit is not used.

1) Precedence is a 3-bit subfield ranging from 0 (000 in binary) to 7 (111 in binary). The precedence defines the priority of the datagram in issues such as congestion. If a router is congested and needs to discard some datagrams, those datagrams with lowest precedence are discarded first. Some datagrams in the Internet are more important than others. For example, a datagram used for network management is much more urgent and important than a datagram containing optional information for a group. The precedence subfield was part of version 4, but never used.
2) TOS bits is a 4-bit subfield with each bit having a special meaning. Although a bit can be either 0 or 1, one and only one of the bits can have the value of 1 in each datagram. The bit patterns and their interpretations are given in Table 19.6 With only 1 bit set at a time, we can have five different types of services.

Table 19.8: Service Types

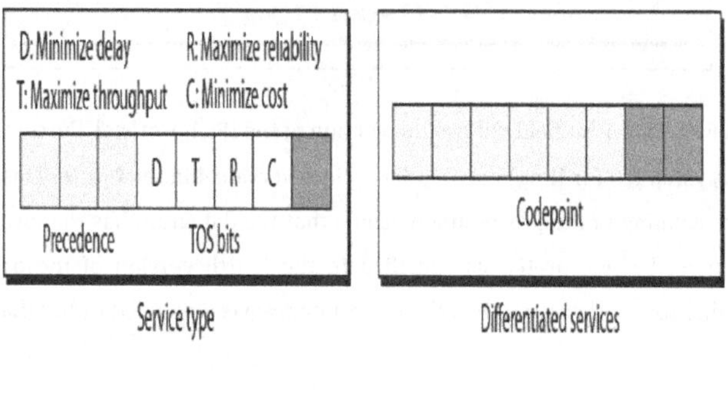

TOS Bits	*Description*
0000	Normal (default)
0001	Minimize cost
0010	Maximize reliability
0100	Maximize throughput
1000	Minimize delay

Differentiated Services

Protocol	*TOS Bits*	*Description*
ICMP	0000	Normal
BOOTP	0000	Normal
NNTP	0001	Minimize cost
IGP	0010	Maximize reliability
SNMP	0010	Maximize reliability
TELNET	1000	Minimize delay
FTP (data)	0100	Maximize throughput
FTP (control)	1000	Minimize delay
TFTP	1000	Minimize delay
SMTP (command)	1000	Minimize delay
SMTP (data)	0100	Maximize throughput
DNS (UDP query)	1000	Minimize delay
DNS (TCP query)	0000	Normal
DNS (zone)	0100	Maximize throughput

Differentiated Services

In this interpretation, the first 6 bits make up the codepoint subfield, and the last 2 bits are not used. The code point subfield can be used in two different ways.

1) When the 3 rightmost bits are 0s, the 3 leftmost bits are interpreted the same as the precedence bits in the service type interpretation. In other words, it is compatible with the old interpretation.
2) When the 3 rightmost bits are not all 0s, the 6 bits define 64 services based on the priority assignment by the Internet or local authorities. The first category contains 32 service types; the second and the third each contain 16.

The first category (numbers 0, 2,4, ... ,62) is assigned by the Internet authorities(IETF).

The second category (3, 7, 11, 15, , 63) can be used by local authorities (organizations).

The third category (1, 5, 9, ,61) is temporary and can be used for experimental purposes.

Note that the numbers are not contiguous. If they were,the first category would range from 0 to 31, the second from 32 to 47, and the third from 48 to 63. This would be incompatible with the TOS interpretation because XXXOOO (which includes 0, 8, 16, 24, 32, 40, 48, and 56) would fall into all three categories. Instead, in this assignment method all these services belong to category 1. Note that these assignments have not yet been finalized.

1) Total length. This is a In-bit field that defines the total length (header plus data) of the IPv4 datagram in bytes. To find the length of the data coming from the upper layer, subtract the header length from the total length. The header length can be found by multiplying the value in the HLEN field by 4.

Length of data =total length - header length

Since the field length is 16 bits, the total length of the IPv4 datagram is limited to 65,535 (216 -1) bytes, of which 20 to 60 bytes are the header and the rest is data from the upper layer. The total length field defines the total length of the datagram including the header. Though a size of 65,535 bytes might seem large, the size of the IPv4 datagram may increase in the near future as the underlying technologies allow even more throughput (greater bandwidth).

Ethernet protocol has a minimum and maximum restriction on the size of data that can be encapsulated in a frame (46 to 1500 bytes). If the size of an IPv4 datagram is less than 46 bytes, some padding will be added to meet this requirement. In this case, when a machine decapsulates the datagram, it needs to check the total length field to determine how much is really data and how much is padding (see Figure 19.9).

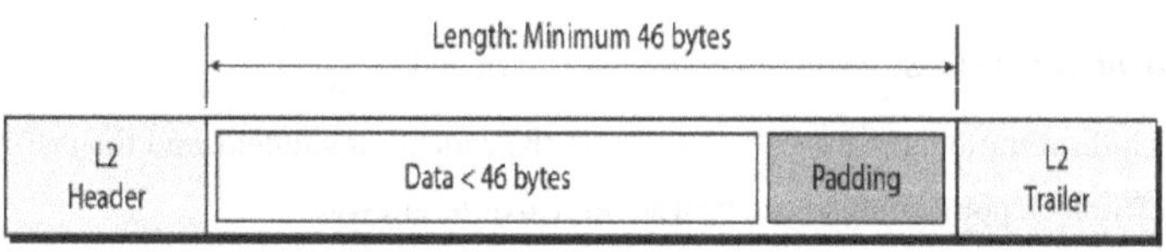

Figure 19.9: Datagram Format

1) Identification. This field is used in fragmentation (discussed in the next section).
2) Flags. This field is used in fragmentation (discussed in the next section).
3) Fragmentation offset. This field is used in fragmentation (discussed in the next section).
4) Time to live. A datagram has a limited lifetime in its travel through an internet. This field was originally designed to hold a timestamp, which was decremented by each visited router. The datagram was discarded when the value became zero. However, for this scheme, all the machines must have synchronized clocks and must know how long

it takes for a datagram to go from one machine to another. Today, this field is used mostly to control the maximum number of hops (routers) visited by the datagram. When a source host sends the datagram, it stores a number in this field. This value is approximately 2 times the maximum number of routes between any two hosts. Each router that processes the datagram decrements this number by 1.If this value, after being decremented, is zero, the router discards the datagram.

This field is needed because routing tables in the Internet can become corrupted. A datagram may travel between two or more routers for a long time without ever getting delivered to the destination host. This field limits the lifetime of a datagram. Another use of this field is to intentionally limit the journey of the packet. For example, if the source wants to confine the packet to the local network, it can store 1 in this field. When the packet arrives at the first router, this value is decremented to 0, and the datagram is discarded.

5) Protocol. This 8-bit field defines the higher-level protocol that uses the services of the IPv4 layer. An IPv4 datagram can encapsulate data from several higher-level protocols such as TCP, UDP, ICMP, and IGMP. This field specifies the final destination protocol to which the IPv4 datagram is delivered. In other words, since the IPv4 protocol carries data from different other protocols, the value of this field helps the receiving network layer know to which protocol the data belong (see Figure 19.10).

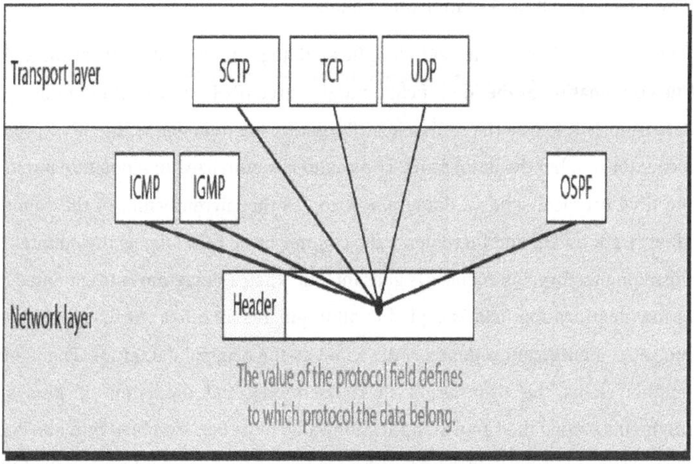

Figure 19.10: Protocol Type

Value	*Protocol*
1	ICMP
2	IGMP
6	TCP
17	UDP
89	OSPF

6) Checksum. The checksum concept and its calculation are discussed later in this chapter.
7) Source address. This 32-bit field defines the IPv4 address of the source. This field must remain unchanged during the time the IPv4 datagram travels from the source host to the destination host.
8) Destination address. This 32-bit field defines the IPv4 address of the destination. This field must remain unchanged during the time the IPv4 datagram travels from the source host to the destination host.

Fragmentation

Fields Related to Fragmentation

The fields that are related to fragmentation and reassembly of an IPv4 datagram are the identification, flags, and fragmentation offset fields.

1) Identification. This 16-bit field identifies a datagram originating from the source host. The combination of the identification and source IPv4 address must uniquely define a datagram as it leaves the source host. To guarantee uniqueness, the IPv4 protocol uses a counter to label the datagrams. The counter is initialized to a positive number. When the IPv4 protocol sends a datagram, it copies the current value of the counter to the identification field and increments the counter by'~ 1. As long as the counter is kept in the main memory, uniqueness is guaranteed. When a datagram is fragmented, the value in the identification field is copied to all fragments. In other words, all fragments have the same identification number, the same as the original datagram. The identification number helps the destination in reassembling the datagram. It knows that all fragments having the same identification value must be assembled into one datagram.
2) Flags. This is a 3-bit field. The first bit is reserved. The second bit is called the do not fragment bit. If its value is 1, the machine must not fragment the datagram. If it cannot pass the datagram through any available physical network, it discards the datagram

and sends an ICMP error message to the source host ,if its value is 0, the datagram can be fragmented if necessary. The third bit is called the more fragment bit. If its value is 1, it means the datagram is not the last fragment; there are more fragments after this one. If its value is 0, it means this is the last or only fragment

3) Fragmentation offset. This 13-bit field shows the relative position of this fragment with respect to the whole datagram. It is the offset of the data in the original datagram measured in units of 8 bytes. Figure 19.11 shows a datagram with a data size of 4000 bytes fragmented into three fragments.

The bytes in the original datagram are numbered 0 to 3999. The first fragment carries bytes 0 to 1399. The offset for this datagram is 0/8 =0. The second fragment carries bytes 1400 to 2799; the offset value for this fragment is 1400/8 = 175. Finally, the third fragment carries bytes 2800 to 3999. The offset value for this fragment is 2800/8 =350.

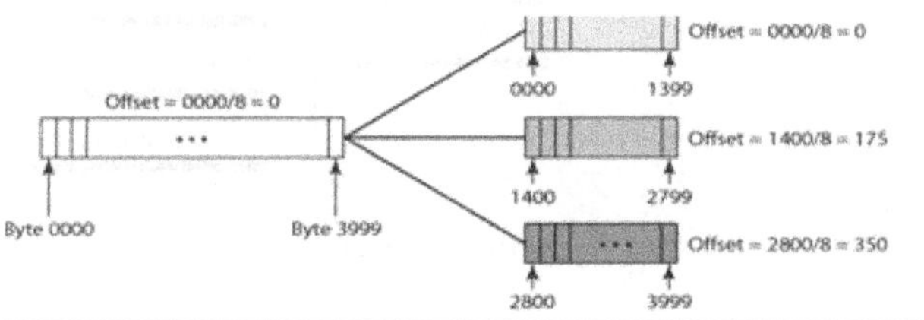

Figure 19.11: Fragmentation

Checksum

The implementation of the checksum in the IPv4 packet follows the same principles. First, the value of the checksum field is set to 0. Then the entire header is divided into 16-bit sections and added together. The result (sum) is complemented and inserted into the checksum field.

The checksum in the IPv4 packet covers only the header, not the data. There are two good reasons for this. First, all higher-level protocols that encapsulate data in the IPv4 datagram have a checksum field that covers the whole packet. Therefore, the checksum for the IPv4 datagram does not have to check the encapsulated data. Second, the header of the IPv4 packet changes with each visited router, but the data do not. So the checksum includes only the part that has changed. If the data were included, each router must recalculate the checksum for the whole packet, which means an increase in processing time.

Options

The header of the IPv4 datagram is made of two parts: a fixed part and a variable part. The fixed part is 20 bytes long and was discussed in the previous section. The variable part comprises the options that can be a maximum of 40 bytes. Options, as the name implies, are not required for a datagram. They can be used for network testing and debugging. Although options are not a required part of the IPv4 header, option processing is required of the IPv4 software. This means that all implementations must be able to handle options if they are present in the header. The detailed discussion of each option is beyond the scope of this book. We give the taxonomy of options in Figure 19.12 and briefly explain the purpose of each.

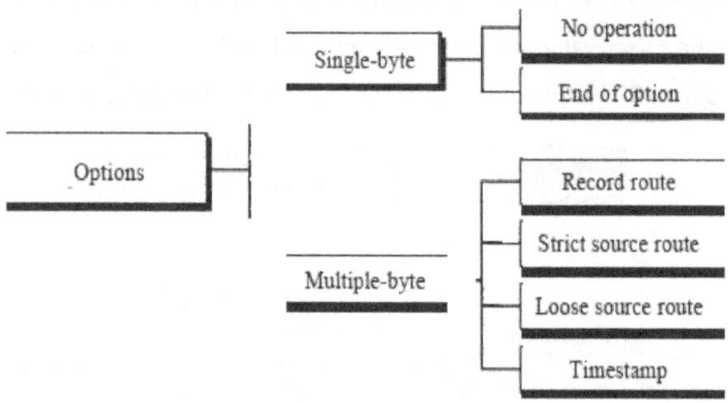

Figure 19.12: Options

No Operation

A no-operation option is a I-byte option used as a filler between options.

End of Option

An end-of-option option is a I-byte option used for padding at the end of the option field. It, however, can only be used as the last option.

Record Route

A record route option is used to record the Internet routers that handle the datagram. It can list up to nine router addresses. It can be used for debugging and management purposes.

Strict Source Route

A strict source route option is used by the source to predetermine a route for the datagram as it travels through the Internet. Dictation of a route by the source can be useful for several purposes. The sender can choose a route with a specific type of service, such as minimum delay or maximum throughput. Alternatively, it may choose a route that is safer or more reliable for the sender's purpose. For example, a sender can choose a route so that its datagram does not travel through a competitor's network.

If a datagram specifies a strict source route, all the routers defined in the option must be visited by the datagram. A router must not be visited if its IPv4 address is not listed in the datagram. If the datagram visits a router that is not on the list, the datagram is discarded and an error message is issued. If the datagram arrives at the destination and some of the entries were not visited, it will also be discarded and an error message issued.

Loose Source Route

A loose source route option is similar to the strict source route, but it is less rigid. Each router in the list must be visited, but the datagram can visit other routers as well.

Timestamp

A timestamp option is used to record the time of datagram processing by a router. The time is expressed in milliseconds from midnight, Universal time or Greenwich mean time. Knowing the time a datagram is processed can help users and managers track the behavior of the routers in the Internet. We can estimate the time it takes for a datagram to go from one router to another. We say *estimate* because, although all routers may use Universal time, their local clocks may not be synchronized.

IPv6 Frame Format

The network layer protocol in the TCPIIP protocol suite is currently IPv4 (Internetworking Protocol, version 4). IPv4 provides the host-to-host communication between systems in the Internet. Although IPv4 is well designed, data communication has evolved since the inception of IPv4 in the 1970s. IPv4 has some deficiencies (listed below) that make it unsuitable for the fast-growing Internet. Despite all short-term solutions, such as subnetting, classless addressing, and NAT, address depletion is still a long-term problem in the Internet.

The Internet must accommodate real-time audio and video transmission. This type of transmission requires minimum delay strategies and reservation of resources not provided in the IPv4 design.

The Internet must accommodate encryption and authentication of data for some applications. No encryption or authentication is provided by IPv4. To overcome these deficiencies, IPv6 (Internetworking Protocol, version 6), also known as IPng (Internetworking Protocol, next generation), was proposed and is now a standard. In IPv6, the Internet protocol was extensively modified to accommodate the unforeseen growth of the Internet. The format and the length of the IP address were changed along with the packet format.

Advantages

The next-generation IP, or IPv6, has some advantages over IPv4 that can be summarized as follows:

1) Larger address space. An IPv6 address is 128 bits long, as we discussed in Chapter19. Compared with the 32-bit address of IPv4, this is a huge (296) increase in the address space.
2) Better header format. IPv6 uses a new header format in which options are separated from the base header and inserted, when needed, between the base header and the upper-layer data. This simplifies and speeds up the routing process because most of the options do not need to be checked by routers.
3) New options. IPv6 has new options to allow for additional functionalities.
4) Allowance for extension. IPv6 is designed to allow the extension of the protocol if required by new technologies or applications.
5) Support for resource allocation. In IPv6, the type-of-service field has been removed, but a mechanism (calledjlow *label)* has been added to enable the source to request special handling of the packet. This mechanism can be used to support traffic such as real-time audio and video.
6) Support for more security. The encryption and authentication options in IPv6 provide confidentiality and integrity of the packet.

Packet Format

The IPv6 packet is shown in Figure 19.3. Each packet is composed of a mandatory base header followed by the payload. The payload consists of two parts: optional extension headers and data from an upper layer. The base header occupies 40 bytes, whereas the extension headers and data from the upper layer contain up to 65,535 bytes of information.

Base Header

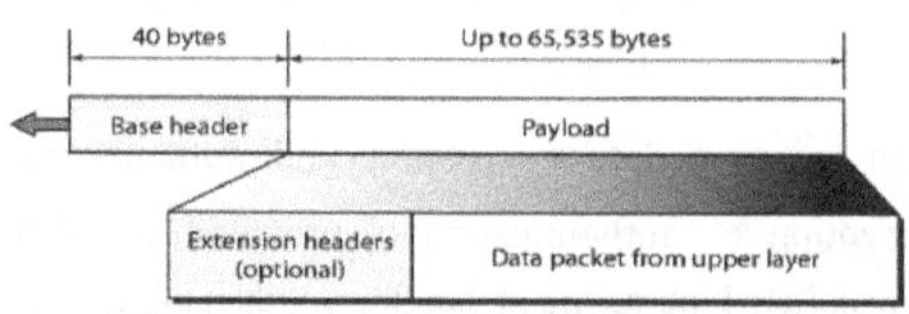

Format of Base Header

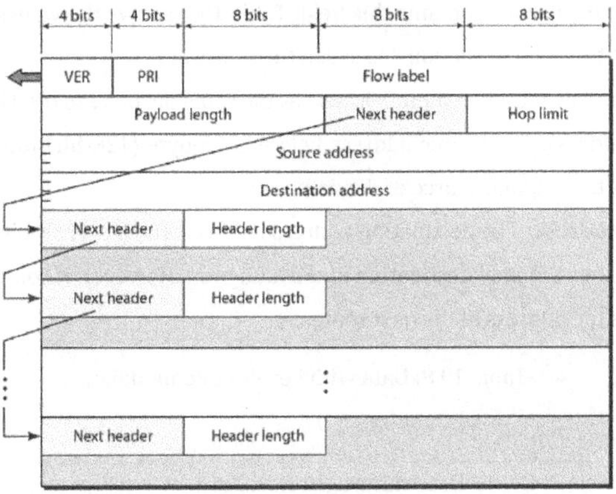

These fields are as follows:

1) Version. This 4-bit field defines the version number of the IP. For IPv6, the value is 6.
2) Priority. The 4-bit priority field defines the priority of the packet with respect to traffic congestion. We will discuss this field later.

Flow label. The flow label is a 3-byte (24-bit) field that is designed to provide special handling for a particular flow of data. We will discuss this field later.

Next Header Codes for IPv6

Table 19.7: Next Headers

Code	*Next Header*
0	Hop-by-hop option
2	ICMP
6	TCP
17	UDP
43	Source routing
44	Fragmentation
50	Encrypted security payload
51	Authentication
59	Null (no next header)
60	Destination option

1) Payload length. The 2-byte payload length field defines the length of the IP datagram excluding the base header.
2) Next header. The next header is an 8-bit field defining the header that follows the base header in the datagram. The next header is either one of the optional extension headers used by IP or the header of an encapsulated packet such as UDP or TCP. Each

extension header lso contains this field. Table 19.7 shows the values of next headers. Note that this field in version 4 is called the protocol.

3) Hop limit. This 8-bit hop limit field serves the same purpose as the TIL field in IPv4.
4) Source address. The source address field is a 16-byte (128-bit) Internet address that identifies the original source of the datagram.

Destination Address: The destination address field is a 16-byte (128-bit) Internet address that usually identifies the final destination of the datagram. However, if source routing is used, this field contains the address of the next router.

Table 19.8: Data with Levels of Redundancy

Priority	*Meaning*
8	Data with greatest redundancy
...	...
15	Data with least redundancy

Table 19.9: Priority

Priority	*Meaning*
0	No specific traffic
1	Background data
2	Unattended data traffic
3	Reserved
4	Attended bulk data traffic
5	Reserved
6	Interactive traffic
7	Control traffic

Priority

The priority field of the IPv6 packet defines the priority of each packet with respect to other packets from the same source. For example, if one of two consecutive datagrams must be discarded due to congestion, the datagram with the lower **packet priority** will be discarded. IPv6 divides traffic into two broad categories: congestion-controlled and non congestion-controlled.

Congestion-Controlled Traffic If a source adapts itself to traffic slowdown when there is congestion, the traffic is referred to as **congestion-controlled traffic.** For example, TCP, which uses the sliding window protocol, can easily respond to traffic. **In** congestion-controlled traffic, it is understood that packets may arrive delayed, lost, or out of order. Congestion-controlled data are assigned priorities from 0 to 7, as listed in Table 19.9. A priority of 0 is the lowest; a priority of 7 is the highest.

Noncongestion-Controlled Traffic This refers to a type of traffic that expects minimum delay. Discarding of packets is not desirable. Retransmission in most cases is impossible. In other words, the source does not adapt itself to congestion. Real-time audio and video are examples of this type of traffic. Priority numbers from 8 to 15 are assigned to noncongestion-controlled traffic.

Although there are not yet any particular standard assignments for this type of data, the priorities are usually based on how much the quality of received data is affected by the discarding of packets. Data containing less redundancy (such as low-fidelity audio or video) can be given a higher priority (15). Data containing more redundancy (such as high-fidelity audio or video) are given a lower priority (8). See Table 19.9

Comparison Between IPv4 and IPv6 Headers

1. The header length field is eliminated in IPv6 because the length of the header is fixed in this version.
2. The service type field is eliminated in IPv6. The priority and flow label fields together takeover the function of the service type field.
3. The total length field is eliminated in IPv6 and replaced by the payload length field.
4. The identification, flag, and offset fields are eliminated from the base header in IPv6. They are included in the fragmentation extension header.
5. The TTL field is called hop limit in IPv6.
6. The protocol field is replaced by the next header field.
7. The header checksum is eliminated because the checksum is provided by upper-layer protocols; it is therefore not needed at this level.
8. The option fields in IPv4 are implemented as extension headers in IPv6.

Extension Headers

The length of the base header is fixed at 40 bytes. However, to give greater functionality to the IP datagram, the base header can be followed by up to six extension headers. Many of these headers are options in IPv4. Six types of extension headers have been defined, as shown in Figure 19.14.

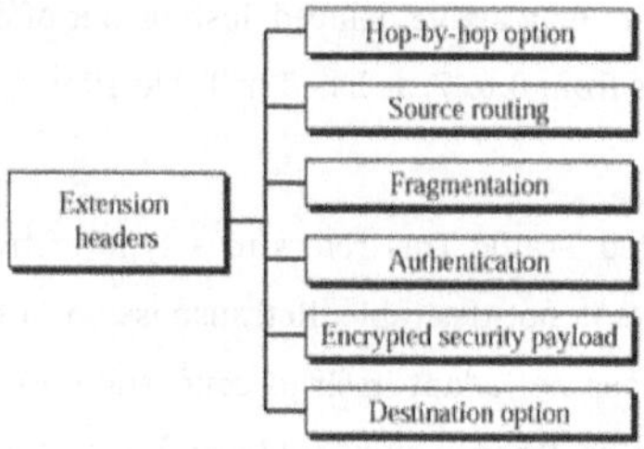

Figure 19.14: Six Types of Extension Headers

Hop-by-Hop Option

The hop-by-hop option is used when the source needs to pass information to all routers visited by the datagram. So far, only three options have been defined: Padl, PadN, and jumbo payload. The Padl option is 1 byte long and is designed for alignment purposes. PadN is similar in concept to Padi. The difference is that PadN is used when 2 or more bytes is needed for alignment. The jumbo payload option is used to define a payload longer than 65,535 bytes. Source Routing The source routing extension header combines the concepts of the strict source route and the loose source route options of IPv4.

Fragmentation

The concept of fragmentation is the same as that in IPv4. However, the place where fragmentation occurs differs. In IPv4, the source or a router is required to fragment if the size of the datagram is larger than the MTU of the network over which the datagram travels. In IPv6, only the original source can fragment. A source must use a path MTU discovery technique to find the smallest MTU supported by any network on the path. The source then fragments using this knowledge.

Authentication

The authentication extension header has a dual purpose: it validates the message sender and ensures the integrity of data.

Encrypted Security Payload

The encrypted security payload (ESP) is an extension that provides confidentiality and guards against eavesdropping. Destination Option The destination option is used when the source needs to pass information to the destination only. Intermediate routers are not permitted access to this information.

Comparison between IPv4 Options and IPv6 Extension Headers

Comparison

1) The no-operation and end-of-option options in IPv4 are replaced by Padl and PadN options in IPv6.
2) The record route option is not implemented in IPv6 because it was not used.
3) The timestamp option is not implemented because it was not used.
4) The source route option is called the source route extension header in IPv6.
5) The fragmentation fields in the base header section of IPv4 have moved to the fragmentation extension header in IPv6.
6) The authentication extension header is new in IPv6.
7) The encrypted security payload extension header is new in IPv6.

TRANSITION FROM IPv4 TO IPv6

Because of the huge number of systems on the Internet, the transition from IPv4 to IPv6 cannot happen suddenly. It takes a considerable amount of time before every system in the Internet can move from IPv4 to IPv6. The transition must be smooth to prevent any problems between IPv4 and IPv6 systems. Three strategies have been devised by the IETF to help the transition.

Dual Stack

It is recommended that all hosts, before migrating completely to version 6, have a **dual** stack of protocols. In other words, a station must run IPv4 and IPv6 simultaneously until all the Internet uses IPv6. See Figure 19.14 for the layout of a dual-stack configuration.

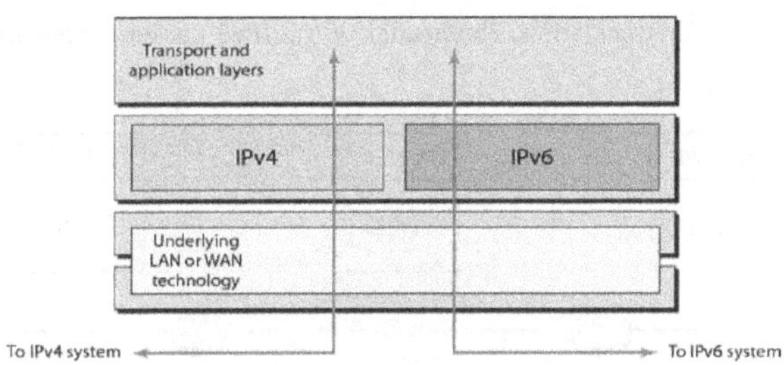

Figure 19.14: Dual-stack Configuration

To determine which version to use when sending a packet to a destination, the source host queries the DNS. If the DNS returns an IPv4 address, the source host sends an IPv4 packet. If the DNS returns an IPv6 address, the source host sends an IPv6 packet.

Tunneling

Thnneling is a strategy used when two computers using IPv6 want to communicate with each other and the packet must pass through a region that uses IPv4. To pass through this region, the packet must have an IPv4 address. So the IPv6 packet is encapsulated in an IPv4 packet when it enters the region, and it leaves its capsule when it exits the region. It seems as if the IPv6 packet goes through a tunnel at one end and emerges at the other end. To make it clear that the IPv4 packet is carrying an IPv6 packet as data, the protocol value is set to 41. Tunneling is shown in Figure 19.15.

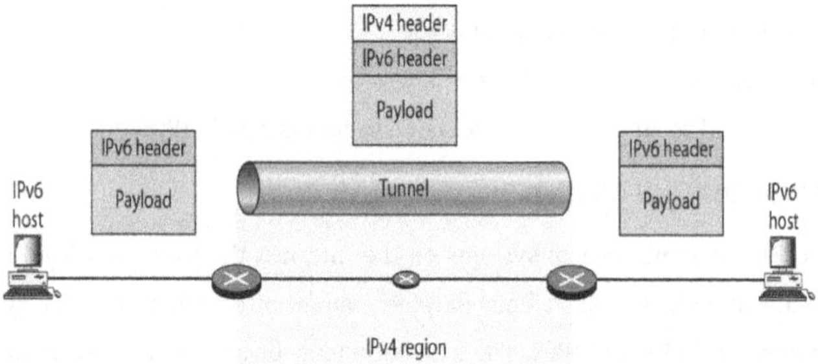

Figure 19.15: Tunneling

Header Translation

Header translation is necessary when the majority of the Internet has moved to IPv6 but some systems still use IPv4. The sender wants to use IPv6, but the receiver does not understand IPv6. Tunneling does not work in this situation because the packet must be in the IPv4 format to be understood by the receiver. In this case, the header format must be totally changed through header translation. The header of the IPv6 packet is converted to an IPv4 header (see Figure 19.16).

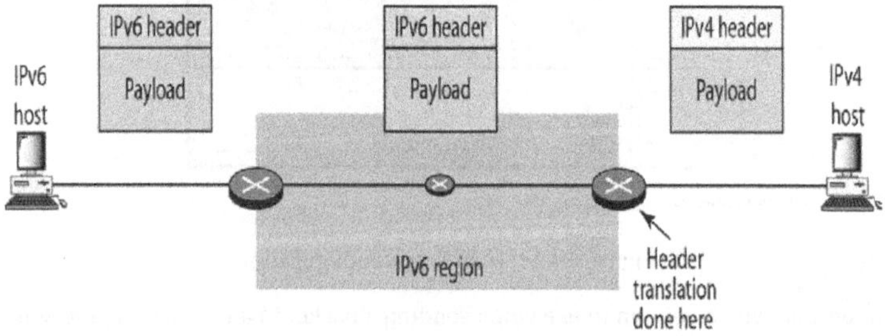

Figure 19.16: Header Translation

Header Translation Procedure

1) The IPv6 mapped address is changed to an IPv4 address by extracting the rightmost 32 bits.
2) The value of the IPv6 priority field is discarded.
3) The type of service field in IPv4 is set to zero.
4) The checksum for IPv4 is calculated and inserted in the corresponding field.
5) The IPv6 flow label is ignored.
6) Compatible extension headers are converted to options and inserted in the IPv4 header. Some may have to be dropped.
7) The length of IPv4 header is calculated and inserted into the corresponding field.
8) The total length of the IPv4 packet is calculated and inserted in the corresponding field.